KING ARTHUR

Hero and Legend

KING ARTHUR

Hero and Legend

RICHARD BARBER

St. Martin's Press · New York

First published in the United States of America in 1986

Printed in Great Britain
Library of Congress Cataloging-in-Publication Data
Barber, Richard W.
  King Arthur : hero and legend.
  Includes index.
  1. Arthur, King.   2. Arthurian romances—History
and criticism.   I. Title.
PN57.A6B33   1986   809'.93351   86–15634
ISBN 0–312–45427–9

Contents

A note on name forms

Because the names of heroes such as Tristan vary not only from language to language but often (in spelling) within the same medieval work, I have standardised, somewhat arbitrarily, to a generally recognised usage. Where more than one form is used in differing contexts for the same figure, cross-references are given in the index. To have retained original spelling throughout, quite apart from the difficulty of determining what it should be, would only have confused the reader.

Acknowledgements

It is difficult to make adequate acknowledgement for all the help that I have had in the making of this book, because it is the result of work over a period of nearly thirty years. All I can do is to list, in some sort of chronological order, the mentors and scholars who have helped to shape it. The germ of the idea for the book came from Gerald Murray at Marlborough College, a much-loved and inspiring teacher. John MacCallum Scott was bold enough to accept a schoolboy's venture into literary criticism for publication (and then to take me on as a member of his firm, Pall Mall Press). The original version appeared as *Arthur of Albion* in 1961; a little of it remains in the present book. It was reissued in 1971, and came to the attention of Anthony Cheetham, who encouraged me to revise it as a paperback, covering the whole range of Arthurian literature: this appeared in 1974 as *King Arthur in Legend and History*. The present version owes most, however, to the scholars with whom I have had the pleasure of working, as publisher and (more rarely) colleague, over the last ten years. I have drawn on a wide range of their research, which is, I hope, adequately acknowledged in the notes. I should like to single out those who have read the typescript in draft, notably Tony Hunt, whose valued and forthright criticisms have saved me from many a pitfall, and David Dumville, who read the first chapter. As will be all too clear from what follows, the opinions and errors in this book are entirely my own: I apologise to the reader for the latter, but hope that the former may contribute to the continuing debate about a heroic figure and his legend.

Chapter 1

The Elusive Hero

King Arthur is the greatest of British literary heroes, celebrated by poets and writers for over a thousand years. From the twelfth century to the twentieth, his exploits have been celebrated in prose and verse, and have inspired painters as well as poets. Yet as soon as we begin to ask the obvious question 'Who *was* this hero? Why did he become such a towering figure in our literature?', we are faced by one of the great enigmas of British history. It is this tension between the glory of the Arthurian vision and the obscurity of its beginnings that gives the legend much of its fascination. Any account of Arthur's literary career must begin by exploring the riddle of his existence: but the problems of doing this are formidable. We cannot even say with certainty in which century Arthur lived, for the records of his historical activity, genuine or otherwise, take us back to the fifth, sixth and seventh centuries AD, the obscure period when the institutions created by Roman rule in Britain were in decay and the new structure of society had not yet emerged, when the Welsh and English kingdoms which were to replace Roman government were in the process of formation.

First of all, however, we must clear away any preconceptions we have about Arthur; we must forget the regal and even imperial figure of the medieval romances and Victorian poets, and – most difficult of all – we must try to discount the aura which surrounds the mere name of Arthur. Then we can turn to the evidence, such as it is, and look at it dispassionately.

The history of the so-called 'dark ages' in Britain is extraordinarily obscure, for a number of reasons. Some of these reasons are clear; others are a matter of conjecture in themselves. We have no reliable contemporary account of what happened when, in the early fifth century, the Romans began to withdraw their troops from Britain to meet the onslaught of the barbarians

1

in Europe; we have no reliable contemporary account, either, of what happened when bands of the same barbarians first landed in Britain; and we have almost no historical narratives at all written by the defeated Britons. In broad outline, we can perceive the waning of the Roman pattern of military and civil authority from 410 to 450, and its replacement by a network of states ruled by local kings, who retained something of Roman institutions in a society which had otherwise reverted to its pre-Roman Celtic and tribal patterns.

These kingdoms warred among themselves, just as their ancient forebears had done; but the same challenge that perplexed the best generals of Rome itself faced them also. Since the late third century, if not before, raiders from what are now Germany, the Netherlands and Denmark had plagued the Channel coasts of England and France, and the Roman officer in charge of the seaward defence of eastern Britain had come to bear the title of *comes* 'of the Saxon shore', in other words the coast subject to Saxon attacks. As word of the withdrawal of the Roman garrison in about 406–7 reached these raiders, they increased their efforts; within at most half a century of the Romans' departure, they began to think in terms of settlement rather than plunder. Some of their comrades may have lived either temporarily or permanently in Britain as mercenaries employed by the Romans, and the history of the imperial conflict with the barbarians from the fourth century onwards is a kaleidoscope of shifting alliances, upstart local commanders with imperial ambitions and barbarian armies behind them, and a gradual blunting of the once sharp dividing line between *Romanitas* and the uncivilised tribes beyond the empire's frontiers. So the situation in Britain in the fifth century is not the result of a dramatic change in the island's fortunes, but stems from a gradual shift in the balance of power.

The first English kingdoms were established in the later fifth century in the east and south, but the great period of English expansion was in the early sixth century: by the mid-sixth century, the whole of the east and centre of England was under English rule, and the west Saxons had reached the Bristol Channel, cutting off Devon and Cornwall from their British compatriots to the north. By the end of the century, the British held only the west coast, and large bodies of them had crossed into Brittany and even to Galicia in northern Spain to escape the relentless invaders.

All this has to be reconstructed from the slenderest and most difficult of evidence. Even spectacular archaeological finds such as Sutton Hoo have to be placed in the timetable of the invasion by using much later and therefore potentially unreliable historical texts.

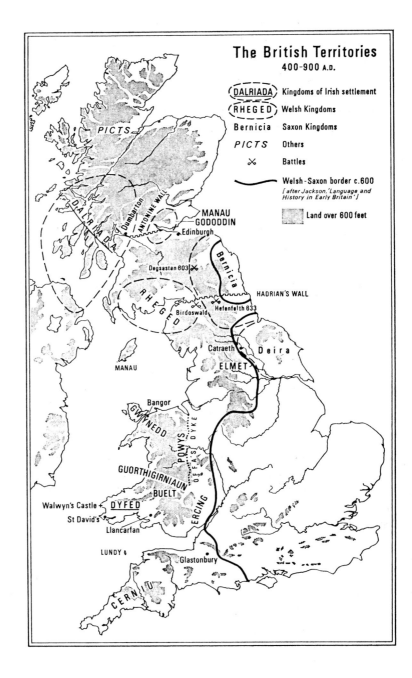

The British Territories

400-900 A.D.

DALRIADA Kingdoms of Irish settlement

RHEGED Welsh Kingdoms

Bernicia Saxon Kingdoms

PICTS Others

⚔ Battles

Welsh-Saxon border c.600
[after Jackson, 'Language and History in Early Britain']

Land over 600 feet

1 *The British territories, 400–900 AD.*

And when we come to Arthur, the problems are multiplied tenfold. The historical texts for the Saxons, as befits the victors in this great contest for Britain, celebrate their triumphs: the Britons were disinclined to record what was essentially a history of defeats, and in any case had little tradition of written history, both at the time of the invasions and in later centuries. The

3

written records of Welsh literature and history begin in the eleventh and twelfth centuries, and many texts from the eighth century or earlier are only known to us from manuscripts of the thirteenth or fourteenth century. The records of the British past were handed down through oral tradition, and only a very small part of this oral tradition* was ever committed to writing. Furthermore, the distinction we automatically make between history and literature was by no means so clearcut. Add to this all the misty problems of sources and dating, or of the authors' intentions in writing their works, and the interpretation of such texts as we have becomes a formidable exercise. This is immediately apparent when we turn to the first and most substantial account of Arthur's deeds in the Welsh records, an entry in the book entitled *Historia Brittonum, The History of the Britons,* often but wrongly ascribed to a certain Nennius or – in medieval times – to Gildas, a sixth-century writer who, had he really written it, would have been a first-rate authority for the events described. Unfortunately, *The History of the Britons* is far from being a sixth-century work, or even a history; a later editor thought that the author had 'piled together everything [he] could find', and what we can really discover from it concerns the culture and traditions of the Welsh people in the late eighth and early ninth century, which is the period at which it was put together. It is an attempt to explore the Welsh past, but its author is not writing in what we would consider a historical manner; there is no real chronology, and little attempt to examine the sources critically such as can be detected in his Anglo-Saxon predecessor Bede. The writer is more concerned with the ideology of the past and its implications for the present: he portrays the Welsh as a race of noble descent, capable of heroic deeds, treacherously driven out of their rightful lands by the Saxons. All of this has considerable relevance to the political ambitions of the Welsh at the end of the eighth and beginning of the ninth centuries, when there was a hope of a revival in their fortunes. We need to bear this in mind as we examine the *Historia Brittonum* text on Arthur, which reads as follows:

In those days the Saxons increased in numbers and grew stronger in Britain. But at Hengist's death, Octha his son went from the northern part of Britain to the kingdom of Kent and from him arose the kings of Kent.

Then in those days Arthur fought against them with the kings of the Britons, but he was a commander in the battles. The first battle was at the mouth of the river which is called Glein; the second, third, fourth and fifth on another river which is called Dubglas and is in the region of Linnuis; the sixth battle on the river Bassas. The seventh battle was in the forest of Celyddon, that is the battle of Coed Celyddon. The eighth battle was at Castellum

*This was not mere 'word of mouth', however, but a tradition handed down by the bards, whose training was designed to help them to memorise such things.

4

Guinnion, where Arthur carried the portrait of Saint Mary, ever Virgin, on his shoulders; and the pagans were routed on that day, and there was a great slaughter of them through the power of our Lord Jesus Christ and the strength of the holy Virgin Mary, his mother. The ninth battle was fought in the Urbs Legionis. The tenth battle was fought on the shore of the river called Tribruit. The eleventh battle was fought on the mountain called Agned. The twelfth battle was on Mons Badonis, where in one day nine hundred and sixty men were killed by one attack of Arthur's, and no-one but himself laid them low. And he appeared as victor in all the battles. And while they [the Saxons] were being overthrown in all the battles, they were seeking help from Germany; and they were being reinforced many times over without interruption. And they brought kings from Germany to rule over them in Britain, up to the time when Ida ruled who was son of Eoppa; he was the first king in Bernicia, that is in Berneich.[1]

This is the earliest version of the text; a century later, an English reviser produced a more polished narrative, using a manuscript which had had some additions made to it in Wales at a date between 875 and 925 AD. The principal alteration in the section on Arthur is at the beginning:

Then the warrior Arthur, with the soldiers and kings of Britain, used to fight against them [the Saxons]. And though there were many of more noble birth than he, he was twelve times leader in war and victor of the battles...[2]

At the end of the original version of the text, there is an account of the natural marvels of the British Isles, usually associated with particular heroes or traditions. Among these are two which refer to Arthur:

In the district which is called Buellt there is another marvel. There is a pile of stones there, and one stone with the footprint of a dog on it placed on top of the heap. When he hunted the boar Trwyd, Cafall – who was the dog of the warrior Arthur – imprinted the mark of his foot on it; and Arthur afterwards assembled a heap of stones under the stone on which was the footprint of his dog, and it is called Carn Gafall. And people come and carry away the stone in their hands for a period of a day and a night, and on the following day it is found on top of the heap.

In the district which is called Archenfield there is another marvel. There is a tomb there, next to a spring which is called Llygad Amr [*the fountain of Amr*]. And the name of the man who was buried in the tomb was called thus, Amr; he was the son of the warrior Arthur, and the latter killed him in that place and buried him. And people come to measure the tomb – it is now six feet, now nine, now twelve, now fifteen in length. At whatever size you will measure it on one occasion, you will not again find it of the same size. And I myself have tested it.[3]

2 The entry relating to Arthur's battles in one of the manuscripts of The History of the Britons *(British Library, MS Harleian 3859, f.187).*

[1] Translation by David Dumville from his edition of the *Historia Brittonum* (Woodbridge 1985–: in progress). See *The Arthurian Legends*, ed. Richard Barber (Woodbridge & Totowa N.J. 1979), 7–8.
[2] *The Arthurian Legends* (n. 1 above) p. 8.
[3] *Ibid.*

If we look at these four extracts together, we begin to get a clear idea of the nature of the *Historia Brittonum*; it is a record of a developing tradition, drawing on heroic poetry, on legends about place and names and on oral tales, a tradition which is by no means static but which is being elaborated all the time. Nor is it by any means at the head of this tradition; scholars have been able to show that we can uncover various layers of material, rather as an archaeological excavation can reveal the different periods of occupation of a site, each overlaid on the next.

So, underneath the synthesis of available material made by the author of *The History of the Britons*, is there a historical tradition at all? In other words, should we agree with those who have seen in Arthur a purely legendary figure, with no historical roots whatsoever, perhaps an ancient Celtic deity metamorphosed into human shape, much as the Celtic sea-god Llyr is the remote antecedent of king Lear? The answer is probably no. There is a dimly discernable historic record behind the *Historia Brittonum* account of Arthur, a record which may be confirmed by two very brief entries in a set of year by year entries or annals called *Annales Cambriae*, the Annals of Wales. These were compiled from the late eighth century onwards at St David's, in the extreme south-west of Wales, whereas the *Historia Brittonum*, as far as we can tell, has associations with north Wales. Furthermore, the Annals of Wales have additional information, so cannot derive from the *Historia*, but help to corroborate it. What the Annals say is as follows:

> Year 72: The battle of Badon in which Arthur bore the cross of our Lord Jesus Christ on his shoulders for three days and three nights, and the Britons were the victors.
> Year 93: Gueith [battle of] Camlann in which Arthur and Medraut perished; and there was plague in Britain and Ireland.[4]

The chronology of the Annals of Wales is an exceedingly difficult subject, even if there is a measure of agreement that year 1 equals AD 445, giving us AD 516 for the battle of Badon and AD 537 for the battle of Camlann. The question is, who worked out this chronology, and when? Professor Leslie Alcock has argued in *Arthur's Britain* that these entries were made at an early date in a table used for calculating the date of Easter for any given year;[5] but I would tend to agree with another scholar, the late Kathleen Hughes, who judged these dates to 'show signs of scholarly construction ultimately from scattered notes. These notes may have been made in the eighth and seventh centuries...'[6] In the absence of a really thorough study of the early chronology of this text, and in the light of what little we can glean about dated entries for this particular period of history, we have to accept

[4] *Ibid.* p. 7: there is no satisfactory complete edition of the *Annales Cambriae*, but for the text in BL MS Harley 3859 see *Y Cymmrodor* 9 (1888) 141–83.
[5] Leslie Alcock, *Arthur's Britain* (London 1971), 49.
[6] Kathleen Hughes, *Celtic Britain in the Early Middle Ages* (Woodbridge & Totowa N. J. 1980), 100.

that there is no evidence for the dating being other than guess-work. But the events themselves, and the concept of Arthur as leader of the resistance to the Saxon invaders at some time in the fifth or sixth centuries, *were* part of current historical tradition when *The History of the Britons* was written, and it is to this tradition that we must now turn.

Modern history relies on precise and written records. Given such a set of records, we can then call on other disciplines such as archaeology to supplement them. But without this framework, we cannot use archaeology as an aid to identifying specific places and events, or as a means of filling out details. Attempts to do just this are particularly tempting in the case of Arthur, precisely because the framework of records is missing. But the result is not history, but an archaeological myth of Arthur, a subject in itself, which has given us the Byzantine heavy cavalry charging down the slopes of mount Badon which found their way into the *Oxford History of England*,[7] and which has given us Cadbury Camp, a fascinating site, but one whose association with Arthur is so far purely wishful thinking.[8] Archaeologists can draw the contours of our metaphorical maps of time, the broad sweep of its landscape, and the details of roads and settlements; but only historical and epigraphical evidence can write the names on that map. In terms of modern history, we are looking for a person, not a population movement or a site or a cultural change, and – except by some extraordinary chance find – archaeology cannot help us to do this.

But it is also true that, in terms of modern history, the two texts we have cited are not what they seem. We have touched on some of the reasons for this; and we may well be puzzled by history which follows other rules than those we are used to, where dates count for little and persons and events for a great deal. Other societies than our own have taken a different view of history, while according it an equally respected place in their culture: the deeds of the past are seen either as an inspiration or as a warning to the men of the present, or as part of a vast divine scheme for man's spiritual salvation. Given these preoccupations, the emphasis becomes very different; the crucial question is *what* happened, and the events themselves become paramount. Today, by contrast, we tend to ask *when* and *how*, because we also want to know *why*, a question that does not arise under the view of history we have outlined. And in trying to come to grips with the sources for the historical Arthur, these conditions apply exactly: we want to know *when* and *how*, and all that the sources are prepared to tell us is *what*. And even that, to return to our analysis of the texts, is remarkably uncertain.

Most scholars who have studied this period are agreed that behind both the *Annals of Wales* and the *History of the Britons*

[7] R. G. Collingwood and J. N. L. Myres, *Roman Britain and the English Settlements* (Oxford 1937) p. 322.

[8] As claimed in, for example, *The Quest for Arthur's Britain* ed. Geoffrey Ashe (London 1968) 187–8.

there lies a set of historical notes (now lost), written in the Celtic territories of what is now the north of England. This chronicle was in turn a compilation from historical and what we might consider non-historical records. In the case of the entry for Arthur, if the *History of the Britons* reflects the content of the original accurately, it looks as if we are dealing with a poet's list of a hero's battles. I say 'a hero' rather than 'Arthur' advisedly; for we have similar battle-lists for five other Welsh kings or heroes, ranging from four to sixteen battles. Arthur's list actually consists of nine events, because the second to fifth battles, all on the Dubglas, look suspiciously like a later attempt to round the total up to the mystic number of twelve. Of these nine battles, four are to be found as sites of battles in the other surviving battle-lists; without going into a complex set of critical arguments, it is unlikely that these lists were drawn from Arthur's, but quite probable that the list in the *History of the Britons* drew on them, because the other lists survive in a much earlier form. It is noteworthy that the longest of these lists, that of Cadwallon's sixteen battles, has no overlaps with the other lists. It looks as if the compiler of the *History of the Britons* has indulged in some borrowing in order to provide one of his central heroic figures with the necessary heroic deeds.[9] In other words, faced with the question *what*, crucial to his turn of mind, he had no immediate information to hand, and turned to other sources.

There is, however, one battle that both here and in later Welsh literary tradition seems to be inescapably Arthur's victory: the battle of mount Badon. This is also the one item for which we have other evidence, in a nearly contemporary source, and if it is genuinely Arthur's, we can come somewhere near to placing Arthur in a modern historical framework. This battle had clearly become legendary by the eighth century; both *The History of the Britons* and *The Annals of Wales* give details of the conflict which are clearly embellishments on earlier stories. This may have been because it is one of the few specific events mentioned in that extraordinary book, *On the Ruin of Britain*, written by Gildas in the mid-sixth century. Here is what Gildas has to say:

> After a time, when the cruel plunderers [i.e. the Saxons] had gone home, God gave strength to the survivors. Wretched people fled to them from all directions, as eagerly as bees to the beehive when a storm threatens, and begged whole-heartedly, 'burdening heaven with their prayers', that they should not be altogether destroyed. Their leader was Ambrosius Aurelianus, a gentleman who, perhaps alone of the Romans, had survived the shock of this notable storm: certainly his parents, who had worn the purple, were slain in it. His descendants in our day have become greatly inferior to their grandfather's excellence. Under him our people regained their strength, and challenged the victors to battle. The Lord assented, and the battle went their way.

9 Richard Barber, *The Figure of Arthur* (London 1972) 97–103.

8

> From then on the victory went now to our countrymen, now to their enemies: so that in this people the Lord could make trial (as he tends to) of his latter-day Israel, to see whether it loves him or not. This lasted right up till the year of the siege of Badon Hill, pretty well the last defeat of the villains, and certainly not the least. That was the year of my birth; as I know, one month of the forty-fourth year since then has already passed.[10]

The site and date of the siege of Badon Hill are still, despite much learned argument, an unresolved mystery. The most recent work on the subject points to a date of about 500 AD; it is unlikely to have been earlier than 480 or later than 520. Other scholars have emphasised that Gildas's work is relatively sophisticated, particularly in its prose style, and must therefore belong to a time when the memory of Roman civilisation and Continental Christianity was fresh.[11] He seems to have written in the crucial decades when the tide was turning against the Britons, and one would give a great deal for a historical work by him. But *On the Ruin of Britain* is not history, but the indictment prepared by Gildas of a corrupt society; he is only concerned with events insofar as they support his case.

Our immediate problem, however, is this: Gildas does not mention Arthur as the commander at Badon, nor does he mention him elsewhere in the text, which is full of vivid character-demolitions of petty tyrants, with a rare favourable word thrown in. We have three possibilities for this situation: Gildas was ignorant of the commander's name, or he did not want to weaken his case by referring to a successful commander, or Arthur was not the commander in question. A fourth possibility does not bear directly on the question: it has been suggested that Arthur is referred to elsewhere in the text in an elaborate play on his name, but the argument seems farfetched and does not help us to resolve his role at Badon. The same air of a desperate search for solutions applies to the second alternative, that he knew the name and suppressed it, though we cannot prove or disprove the hypothesis.

This leaves the first and third alternatives, both equally impossible to prove or disprove. To revert for a moment to the suggestion that Gildas knew but did not mention Arthur's name, it would be possible to go on to argue that given what we know of Gildas' geographical knowledge, the connection between Badon and Cadbury Camp as the only likely base for such a commander could still be upheld. But the argument that Cadbury and Arthur are somehow connected depends on two facts: that the detail about Arthur in the *Historia Brittonum* as 'commander in battles' is correct, and that Cadbury is unique. Now Professor Alcock, in the Mortimer Wheeler lecture to the British Academy in 1983,[12] drew attention to northern parallels for the

[10] Gildas, *The Ruin of Britain*, ed. & tr. Michael Winterbottom (Chichester 1978), 28.
[11] Michael Lapidge, 'Gildas's Education', in *Gildas: New Approaches*, ed. Michael Lapidge and David Dumville (Woodbridge & Dover N. H. 1984), 47–50.
[12] Leslie Alcock, 'Cadbury – Camelot: A Fifteen Year Perspective', *Proceedings of the British Academy* lxviii 1982, 355–388.

refortification carried out at Cadbury, and showed that it is in fact merely one of a number of such sites. So this link in the chain no longer holds, and the Badon/Cadbury/Arthur connection rests only on a very hopeful reading of some extremely vague evidence.

But we can push the argument forward in one direction. Gildas's knowledge of Britain is apparently confined to the west of the island, and to immediately contemporary events. He paints a grim picture of a land where − unlike the rest of the Roman empire − the barbarian invaders had taken cities by storm and had killed or driven out the British population; and E. A. Thompson, in his recent study of the end of Roman Britain, argues that this picture is substantially correct, corroborated by the evidence of place-names and the ignorance of continental chroniclers as to affairs in Britain. The south-east and the remains of the Roman world beyond it are beyond Gildas's ken; and, even more alarming, he seems to have very little grasp of the whole Roman past of the island. The present consists of civil wars among the Britons and the calamity of each new Saxon thrust towards the west. Under these conditions, writes Professor Thompson

> Men's knowledge of their history, their own history, had evaporated. Of the four hundred years of the Roman occupation of Britain men knew now of little more than that kings across the sea had once ruled the island. Their governors had been harsh. There had been a Great Persecution of Christians and a ruler called Magnus Maximus. And that was practically all... The most frightening feature in the picture drawn by Gildas is not the destruction of city-life in Britain or the break-up of the Imperial system with its guarantee of peaceful life, but rather the destruction of knowledge itself. Knowledge of the outside world and knowledge of the past had been wiped out of men's minds.[13]

I believe that this assessment is critical to the analysis of the Arthurian sources with which we are concerned. Gildas, on this evidence, might well have been ignorant of the name of the commander at the victory at mount Badon. Now if he, writing only forty-four years after the event, did not know the commander's name, what reliance can we place on a source at least two centuries later which ascribes mount Badon to Arthur in a list of battles, some of which have been borrowed from elsewhere? The most obvious conclusion is that this is yet another borrowing, from one of the few authorities on the period whose work was (relatively speaking) well known. Furthermore, this view of British history as already obscure and half-forgotten in the next generation after the collapse of Roman institutions explains the unsatisfactory nature of the *Historia Brittonum*; it is not merely a work in a different tradition, as outlined above, but even if its

[13] E. A. Thompson, *Saint Germanus of Auxerre and the End of Roman Britain*, (Woodbridge 1984), 114–15.

author had wished to give us a 'modern' account of the previous centuries, he could not have done so because the materials never existed.

What did survive from these 'missing' centuries? We know that there was oral poetry containing historical traditions, but in the rapidly shifting political situation, this tradition was often disturbed and fragmented; oral traditions survive best in settled and peaceful societies, not in a world where whole kingdoms vanished before alien invaders. The clearest continuity in British oral traditions for this period is of course in the west, where, despite civil war, society was relatively stable and changes of dynasty less drastic. But some of the oral traditions of the Britons from lost lands to the north seem to have survived, even if nothing was known of the eastern past. So such traditions varied from the relatively complete to the fragmentary, and I would suggest that the figure of Arthur belongs to these fragments of the lost lore of an area overrun by the invaders at an early period. His name survived in historical tradition simply as a great hero about whom nothing was known; the deeds by which he had made his name had vanished in the mists of time and conquest. He was from the earliest times a 'hero without deeds', and we shall never know his true history.

There is however one possibility which we need to explore before we leave the problem of Arthur in history. If he was not the commander at Badon, it follows that he need not have been a fifth or sixth century figure at all, but someone who made his reputation at an earlier or later period, and was attributed to the wrong period in *The Annals of Wales* and *The History of the Britons* or some source common to both. The context of Arthur's historical deeds, if we allow him a historical existence at all, is the struggle between the Romano-Britons and their successors and the barbarians. This struggle, in its broadest sense, lasted from the fourth to the eighth century: we can preclude dates outside that period both because the nature of the political set-up in Britain was different and because we have much fuller historical sources in which Arthur would probably be recorded. So on the one hand he could be a late Roman commander from the Roman *gens* bearing the name Artorius. On the other hand, the oldest historical source to refer to an Arthur who was a warrior is in fact Adomnán's life of the Irish saint Columba, written in about 700. Here Arthur son of Aedán mac Gabráin, king of Dalriada, appears, a British prince who died in battle fighting an obscure tribe called the Miathi. There are other early occurrences of the name Arthur in Irish sources, also associated with the north of Britain, and with the Irish kingdom in Dyfed; but there are none in native Welsh tradition which can be clearly isolated from these Irish Arthurs. I have argued the case for

3 The earliest surviving written record that mentions the name Arthur: Adomnan's Life of Columba, *a manuscript of the seventh century (Stadtbibliothek, Schaffhausen: MS Gen.1, f.19). 'Arturius' is mentioned on the third line.*

Arthur son of Aedán mac Gabráin at length elsewhere;[14] when there is so little tangible material, any likely candidate needs to be investigated, but I would not claim that he is more than a possibility.

The starting point for the story of the development of the legend of Arthur is thus a bare minimum: a heroic figure from an obscure age of history about whom we know almost nothing. I would suggest that it is precisely this contrast between the lack of a known context and the evidently considerable fame which Arthur enjoyed from the beginning that makes him such an enticing figure to writers. The ninth-century author of the *History of the Britons* used him to create a heroic leader who, by his resistance to the Saxon invaders in the past, offered the hope that they might be defeated in the present. In the same way, Welsh poets used him for their own purposes from earliest times. But once again, the interpretation of what they tell us is fraught with difficulty. A thirteenth century satire, *Rhonabwy's Dream*, aptly sums up the problems:

> And then, lo and behold bards coming to chant song to Arthur, but no-one could understand that song, apart from Kadyreith ('Fine-Speech') himself, except that it was in praise of Arthur![15]

14 *The Figure of Arthur* (n. 9 above), passim.
15 Quoted by P. Sims-Williams, *Gildas: New Approaches* (n. 11 above), 183.

The first piece of literary evidence is also one of the most problematical. It is a poem describing the battle fought at Catterick in Yorkshire perhaps in the late sixth century, when a British force drawn from a people called the Gododdin was overwhelmed by the Angles. It is a praise-poem in honour of the fallen heroes of the Gododdin, and eighty warriors are commemorated in individual stanzas. In one of these stanzas, the warrior in question is said to have 'glutted black ravens on the rampart of the stronghold, even though he was no Arthur'.[16] Arthur was clearly regarded as a super-heroic figure, with whom a mere

4   The Gododdin, *a thirteenth century manuscript of a much earlier poem (Cardiff Public Library MS 1, f.37). Arthur is mentioned at the foot of the page.*

[16] Ed. I. Williams, *Canu Aneirin* (Cardiff 1938): see A. O. H. Jarman, 'The delineation of Arthur in early Welsh verse' in *An Arthurian Tapestry*, ed. Kenneth Varty (Glasgow 1981), 3–4.

slayer of the enemy could not compete. The original poem was written very shortly after the event, and on the face of it this is our earliest reference to Arthur. But like so much Welsh verse, the version we have was not written down for another three hundred to five hundred years, and scholars approach the reference with some caution. True, it is in the section of the poem whose language and spelling are that of the ninth century rather than of the thirteenth, but three hundred years is a long time-span. Furthermore, there is good evidence that Arthur's name was frequently substituted for that of earlier heroes; so there is reason to suspect an alteration to the original poem. There is a not dissimilar reference in an elegy for Cynddylan, a king of Powys who fell at the hands of the Mercians, perhaps about 660 AD; he and his sons are called 'whelps of Arthur, a mighty fortress'.[17] Here the gap between poem and manuscript is even greater: the latter was written in the seventeenth century, and Arthur's name is distorted But by and large both references are accepted as genuine; they merely add to the picture we have already painted, of a hero with a great reputation and no known deeds.

It is not until we reach the poems of the Black Book of Carmarthen and the Book of Taliesin, both manuscripts of the thirteenth century which contain verse written between the sixth and thirteenth centuries, that we begin to find tangible deeds ascribed to Arthur. The poems which mention him are all either contemporary with *The History of the Britons* or later, and there are ten of them in all. Five of these contain either passing references to Arthur or passages which have defied interpretation; of the other five, three bear some relation to *The History of the Britons*, but in a way that bears out our earlier conclusion that the latter is a record of what we would nowadays call literary rather than historical tradition. In a poem celebrating the deeds of Geraint, the sixth century ruler of Devon, there is a reference to Arthur as commander in battles:

> In Llongborth I saw Arthur -
> Brave men hewed with steel -
> Emperor, ruler of battle.

Another poem speaks of Llacheu, son of Arthur, 'wonderful in songs', and the writer says that he has been to the place where Llacheu was killed; in *The History of the Britons* Arthur's son is called Amr, but the writer also claims to have been to the place where Amr was killed and buried. A third poem is a dialogue between Arthur and the gatekeeper of a great fortress to which he is trying to gain admittance. The gatekeeper asks Arthur to name his followers, and he does so: the chief of them is Cai, and

[17] For these and the following references see Jarman, *ibid*. and K. H. Jackson, 'Arthur in Early Welsh Verse' in *Arthurian Literature in the Middle Ages*, ed. R. S. Loomis (Oxford 1959) 12–19.

there are other recognisable figures in the list, as well as many very obscure ones and others who never appear elsewhere in connection with Arthur. Among the latter is Manawydan son of Llŷr, who 'brought shattered shields from Tryfrwyd [the battle of Tribruit]'. All three references, therefore, point to a body of stories about Arthur current at some time before the thirteenth century, but stories which could be adapted and altered at will by any writer who took them up.

In the dialogue between Arthur and the gatekeeper, there is also a passage, apparently interpolated into the poem, about Arthur's fight with a hag in the hall of Awarnach. The context makes it seem likely that the name Arthur has been confused with the adjective *aruthr*, terrible, applied to Cai, because the exploit referred to is elsewhere attributed to the latter. However, a poem in *The Book of Taliesin* makes it clear that by this period Arthur had acquired some of the supernatural deeds which can be traced back to Celtic mythology. *The Spoils of Annwfn* is attributed to the poet Taliesin, court poet of the kings of Rheged in the sixth century. The attribution is false, because Taliesin quickly became a legendary figure himself, and a number of poems were written in his name. In *The Spoils of Annwfn*, Taliesin describes how he accompanied Arthur on an expedition to the Otherworld, in an attempt to seize the magic cauldron called The Head of Annwfn, of which he says that it will not boil the food of a coward. The expedition seems to have ended in disaster, for three loads of Arthur's ship Prydwen are said to have set out, and only seven men returned. Annwfn is variously described as Hell (using a specifically Christian term), as the Fairy Fortress, the Four-Cornered Fortress and the Fortress of Glass. This last name leads us back to *The History of the Britons* again, for we are also told in the poem that on Annwfn's wall stand three-score hundred men, and that it was difficult to talk with their sentinel. Now in the early part of *The History of the Britons*, a group of warriors from Spain who arrive to conquer Ireland, and who are the ancestors of the present inhabitants of that island, come to a glass tower in the middle of the sea, with men on it, but are unable to speak to them. They return to attack it, and only one out of thirty ships survives. Once again, we can relate *The History of the Britons* to a literary source about Arthur, but in this case it seems clear that Arthur's appearance in *The Spoils of Annwfn* postdates the account of his twelve battles, and is the first pointer on the road which was to lead to the world of Arthurian romance, with its blend of reality and the supernatural legacy of Celtic myth.

Another poem in *The Black Book of Carmarthen* concerns the graves of great heroes, listing about two hundred characters, chiefly from legend and folklore. One stanza reads as follows:

A grave for March, a grave for Gwythur,
A grave for Gwgawn of the Red Sword,
The world's wonder a grave for Arthur.[18]

The last line has been translated by another distinguished scholar as

Concealed till Doomsday the grave of Arthur.[19]

The implication is clearly that there is something mysterious either about Arthur's death or about his burial, though when the poet mentions the battle of Camlann in a later stanza, he does not link it to Arthur's death. By the early twelfth century, before Geoffrey of Monmouth created his immortal portrait of Arthur in *The History of the Kings of Britain*, there was current a belief that Arthur had not died, but would return again. William of Malmesbury, the greatest of the Anglo-Norman historians, records in his *Deeds of the Kings of Britain* that 'the tomb of Arthur is nowhere to be found, whence ancient fables pretend that he is yet to come';[20] and there was an episode recorded by a canon from Laon, when a party of his fellow-canons went to Cornwall in 1113 on a fund-raising venture.[21] They met a Cornishman who asserted that Arthur was not yet dead; the canons contradicted him, and there was almost a riot as a result. Nor does Geoffrey of Monmouth state explicitly that Arthur was killed at Camlann, merely saying ambiguously that he was taken to Avalon that his wounds might be dealt with. Yet again, we come back to *The History of the Britons*, which uses Arthur as an example to encourage the Welsh to believe that they might drive out the apparently invincible English. By the twelfth century, it seems, this had been transmuted by simpler minds into the idea that Arthur himself would be the leader in such a campaign.

If an examination of the evidence for Arthur as a historical figure and of the early stories about him leads to the inevitable conclusion that there are no easy answers, I hope that I have at least suggested why there are such gaps in our knowledge of the historical period in question. And I hope that I have also shown how crucial the milieu of ninth and tenth century Wales, the period of the *History of the Britons*, *The Annals of Wales* and the first poems to mention Arthur, is to our understanding of the development of the legend. These sources are more closely related than they at first appear, and Arthur as leader of battles and the list of his twelve victories belong to the world of literature rather than the world of history.

[18] Thomas Jones, 'The Black Book of Carmarthen "Stanzas of the Graves" ', *Proceedings of the British Academy* liii 1968, 127.
[19] R. S. Loomis, 'The Legend of Arthur's Survival' in *Arthurian Literature in the Middle Ages* (n. 17 above), 64.
[20] William of Malmesbury, *De gestis regum Anglorum*, ed. W. Stubbs (London, Rolls Series 1887–9) i.11.
[21] Hermann of Tournai, quoted in E. K. Chambers, *Arthur of Britain* (2nd edn, Cambridge & New York 1964), 249.

Chapter 2

Arthur the Emperor

Because we know so little about the historical reality behind the figure of Arthur, he is a literary figure from the very beginning. It is quite likely that all the apparently historical material in *The History of the Britons* and *The Annals of Wales* has its origins in literary works; and the concept of history and literature as separate disciplines had in any case no meaning for the Welsh in the period with which we are concerned. Nor was the distinction much more clearly marked in Latin writers: *historia*, after all, has as its prime meaning 'a story' without the modern implication that it should be a *true* story, and its Welsh equivalent 'ystorya' certainly embraces all oral records of the past, including myth and tradition.[1]

But even here we are faced with a major enigma: why was Arthur singled out to become the centre of an exceptional group of heroes, and why did his court become the most famous in all literature? As with the problem of his historical existence, there can be no clear-cut answers, because so much of the evidence is missing. If what we have so far suggested is correct, Arthur began as a 'hero without deeds' and was assigned the historical role of the last defender of Britain before the Welsh were pushed back into the western hills. Even in this role, his actual deeds were vague, beyond the fact that he was a 'leader in battles', *dux bellorum*. The one characteristic that the later version of *The History of the Britons* records, that 'there were many of more noble birth than he' was quickly forgotten, and Arthur's later role is a flat contradiction of this: he becomes the noblest of all noble kings.

The process by which Arthur's glittering court was created began in Welsh literature at some time between the ninth and eleventh centuries. We have a glimpse of Arthur as leader of a war band in *The Spoils of Annwfn*, and in the Black Book of

[1] Rachel Bromwich, *Trioedd Ynys Prydein: The Welsh Triads* (2nd edn, Cardiff 1979), lxxii.

Carmarthen the dialogue between Arthur and the gatekeeper is a roll-call of heroes who are his followers. In the *Triads of the Island of Britain*, the triad or group of three headings, a device 'used as a means of cataloguing a variety of technical information'[2] is applied to the tales told by the bards. The tales themselves are for the most part lost: all we have are the enigmatic titles for the bards' performances:

> Three Chieftains of Arthur's Court:
> Gobrwy son of Echel Mighty-Thigh,
> Cadrieith ('Fine-Speech') son of Porthawr Gadw,
> and Fleudur Fflam ('Flame').[3]

Just under a hundred of these aids to memory survive, mostly in very late manuscripts; in the later versions, 'llys Arthur' (Arthur's court) has become the usual meeting-place of heroes, replacing the vaguer 'ynys Prydein', island of Britain. But the triad just quoted is an early one, and we have one surviving work by an unknown writer working within the bardic tradition which shows how, by the end of the eleventh century, Arthur had acquired a remarkable group of heroes as his followers. This is *Culhwch and Olwen*, one of eleven Welsh prose stories known collectively since they were first translated into English in the nineteenth century as *The Mabinogion*.[4] These tales range from reworkings of ancient story material with strong mythological overtones to almost direct translations of the French romances about Arthurian heroes. *Culhwch and Olwen* comes somewhere between the two: the central figures do not bear the names of ancient Celtic gods, but the plot of the romance is woven together from a series of popular tales found independently in many languages. The basic tale is simple: Culhwch, Arthur's kinsman, one day catches sight of Olwen, daughter of the giant Ysbaddaden, whom he is fated to love. His father advises him to seek Arthur's help in winning her, and the whole resources of Arthur's court are employed to accomplish the tasks which Ysbaddaden sets his daughter's suitor. These are about forty in all, and the achieving of just over a dozen is actually described. Around the basic tale of 'hero wins giant's daughter', the author weaves a further series of motifs familiar in folklore. The main episode is the hunting of the magical boar Trwyth, a tale which was associated with Arthur when the marvels section of *The History of the Britons* was written; this is the last task to be accomplished before Ysbaddaden is combed and shaved for his daughter's wedding, and slain in revenge for past cruelties. Another episode concerns the search for a magic cauldron in which the wedding feast must be cooked, which brings us back to *The Spoils of Annwfn* where Arthur led his warriors in search of a similar vessel.

2 *Ibid.* lxiii.
3 *Ibid.*, 16 (Triad 9).
4 A misnomer: see *The Mabinogion* tr. Gwyn Jones and Thomas Jones (London & New York 1949), ix–x.

18

If the author of *Culhwch and Olwen* is working over familiar material, what he produces has a considerable claim to the title of the first masterpiece of Arthurian literature. He treats the magical and mysterious with exactly the right blend of awe, fantasy and dry humour: a flight of tremendous fancy can end in a wry aside, for he commands all the rhetoric of the bards and a dry wit into the bargain. If there is a flaw in his work, it is a tendency to extremes: when Culhwch asks a boon of Arthur, he invokes the names of all Arthur's warriors and all 'the gentle gold-torqued maidens of this Island', and the catalogue runs to hundreds of names.[5] Yet he can dispose of the achieving of one of the tasks so laconically that it is difficult to follow what is happening. But he never fails to hold our attention: the catalogue of warriors is full of marvellous asides, miniature character sketches of individual heroes: '... Sgilti Lightfoot, when the whim to run his lord's errand was in him, he never sought a road so long as he knew whither he was bound; but so long as there were trees along the tops of the trees would he go, and so long as there was a mountain on the tops of the reeds would he go, and throughout his life never a reed bent beneath his feet, much less did one break, so exceeding light of foot was he .... Uchdryd Cross-beard (who would throw the bristling red beard he had on him across fifty rafters which were in Arthur's hall) ... Clust son of Clustfeinad (were he to be buried seven fathom in the earth, he would hear an ant fifty miles off when it stirred from its couch of a morning) ...'

The author of *Culhwch and Olwen* handles the episodes with the giant and his followers with a deft touch, at once acknowledging the fearsome nature of the giant and suspending our disbelief by his wry humour. When Culhwch and his companions approach Ysbaddaden's fort they come to the house of a shepherd, of same stature as the giant, whose wife is Culhwch's aunt, but as huge as her husband:

> She ran with joy to meet them. Cei snatched a log out of the woodpile, and she came to meet them, to try to throw her arms about their necks. Cei thrust a stake between her two hands. She squeezed the stake so that it became a twisted withe. Quoth Cei, 'Woman, had it been I thou didst squeeze in this wise, there were no need for another to love me ever. An ill love, that !'[6]

We also encounter for the first time one of the great themes of Arthurian romance: the contrast between the ordered, formal world of the court and the wild mysterious world outside the walls of the fortress. Culhwch only gains entry to Arthur's court in breach of the rules. 'Knife has gone into meat, and drink into horn, and a thronging in Arthur's hall. Save the son of a king of a rightful dominion, or a craftsman who brings his craft, none may

[5] *Ibid.*, 100–107.
[6] *Ibid.*, 110.

enter,'[7] Glewlwyd Mighty-Grasp the porter tells him; but he is so struck by the stranger's appearance that he goes to Arthur, who orders that Culhwch shall be admitted, despite Cei's grumbling: 'If my counsel were acted upon, the laws of court would not be broken for his sake.'[8] Similar rules apply at the court of Ysbaddaden, and the interview in which he sets out the tasks which Culhwch must accomplish is a kind of ritual recital, a marshalling of magic held in only by its orderly naming:

> …'Though thou get that, there is that thou wilt not get. I must needs wash my head and shave my beard. The tusk of Ysgithyrwyn Chief Boar I must have, wherewith to shave myself. I shall be none the better for that unless it be plucked from his head while alive.'
>
> 'It is easy for me to get that, though thou think it is not easy.'
>
> 'Though thou get that, there is that thou wilt not get. There is no one in the world can pluck it from his head save Odgar son of Aedd king of Ireland.'
>
> 'It is easy for me to get that, though thou think it is not easy.'
>
> 'Though thou get that, there is that thou wilt not get. I will not entrust the keeping of the tusk to any save Cadw of Prydein. The threescore cantrefs of Prydein are under him. He will not come out of his kingdom of his own free will, nor can he be compelled.'
>
> 'It is easy for me to get that, though thou think it is not easy.'
>
> 'Though thou get that, there is that thou wilt not get. I must needs dress my beard for me to be shaved. It will never settle unless the blood of the Black Witch be obtained, daughter of the White Witch, from the head of the Valley of Grief in the uplands of Hell.'
>
> 'It is easy for me to get that, though thou think it is not easy.'[9]

Against this ritual and order the author of *Culhwch* sets the quest of the oldest animals, where time itself seems to dissolve as the seekers move from the ouzel of Cilgwri, who has seen a smith's anvil worn to nothing, by way of the eagle of Gwernabwy – 'when first I came hither I had a stone, and from its top I picked at the stars each evening; now it is not a hand-breadth in height' – to the Salmon of Llyn Llyw, ancient when the eagle of Gwernabwy was young.[10] And there is the great set-piece of the hunting of the boar Trwyth, 'a king, and for his wickedness God transformed him into a swine.'[11] Arthur 'and the hosts of the world' pursue him across a precisely–plotted landscape, from Ireland across Wales down to Severn by a route that can almost be followed on today's map. Trwyth and his seven young pigs wreak havoc on Arthur's men, until at last two of the treasures are plucked from between his ears, and Trwyth reaches Cornwall. 'Whatever mischief was come by before that was play to what was to come by then in seeking the comb. But from mischief to mischief the comb was won from him. And then he was forced out of Cornwall and driven straight forward into the sea. From

7 *Ibid.*, 97–8.
8 *Ibid.*, 99.
9 *Ibid.*, 116.
10 *Ibid.*, 125.
11 *Ibid.*, 131.

that time forth never a one has known where he went, and [the hounds] Aned and Aethlem with him'.[12] Even Arthur's hosts have met their match.

What a modern reader misses in *Culhwch and Olwen* is any sense of development of plot or character: there are mighty heroes and mighty deeds, but what happens is foreordained, and the character of each hero is set in a single sentence. Culhwch is described lovingly and at length as he sets out for Arthur's court, but it is a picture, not a portrait: in Gwyn Jones's words, 'everything is externalized'.[13] The picturesque and the marvellous are enticing enough, but there is more to the greatest Arthurian romances than that.

In *Culhwch and Olwen*, Arthur is portrayed in an entirely favourable light, a peerless prince. Elsewhere in Welsh tradition we find a very different view. A number of biographies of Welsh saints were written in Latin in the eleventh and twelfth centuries, and these though usually of little literary or historical significance, contain several references to Arthur, including two or three episodes in which he takes an active part. If nothing else, this is evidence of his popularity as a hero at about this time. These lives 'were the product ... of the collision of the Celtic and Anglo-Norman churches and cultures. They were in part the products of Anglo-Norman clerics who were curious about the traditions they had inherited with the area they had entered, and in part of the Welsh who wished to defend the honour and rights of the Welsh saints against the influx of foreign saints.'[14] The lives in which Arthur appears seem to belong to the latter group, and the patterns of the saints' lives are very similar to those of traditional Celtic heroes.

The first two stories are to be found in the *Life of St Cadoc*, written by one Lifris of Llancarfan about 1075[15]. Arthur is here halfway between the leader of Welsh tradition and the ruler of later legend, though he is not very favourably regarded by the author. If he and his companions are called *heroes strenui*, valiant heroes, it is only on account of their physical prowess, and Arthur is portrayed as no more than a petty tyrant. He first appears playing dice on a hilltop with Kay and Bedivere, and attempts to ravish a girl eloping with her lover, instead of rescuing them from their pursuers, until dissuaded by his companions; he then successfully defends the fugitives. He later reappears in a quarrel over blood-money for three men of his who have been killed; his obstinate refusal to accept anything except cattle of a certain colour is thwarted by a miracle worked by St Cadoc.

If Arthur is a tyrant, a little pagan magic is also used to help the saint's reputation, and the principle that the greater the rank of the sinner, the greater the glory of the saint, lies behind the

[12] *Ibid.*, 134.
[13] Gwyn Jones, *Kings Beasts and Heroes* (London & New York 1972), 134.
[14] Elissa Henken, *Traditions of the Welsh Saints* (Woodbridge & Dover N.H. 1986), [introduction]

episode. This is equally true of the *Life of St Carannog*[16]: Carannog comes to Arthur's realm in search of a marvellous altar which God had given him, which he had set adrift in order to see where he should go and preach. Arthur promises to help him if he will render harmless a serpent which is devastating Arthur's lands, and which Arthur has failed to kill. The saint succeeds by prayer where Arthur had failed with force: Arthur then produces the altar, and confesses that he had tried to use it as a table, but anything placed on it was at once thrown off. In the *Life of St Padarn* Arthur covets the saint's tunic and is swallowed up by the earth as far as the chin: he is only released when he praises God and St Padarn, and seeks pardon, and he accepts St Padarn as his patron before he departs.[17]

The *Life of St Gildas*, by another Llancarfan monk, Caradoc, was written about 1130. Here Arthur is portrayed, not as a local tyrant, but as 'king of the whole of Britain', who cannot brook any opposition to his rule. Gildas's brothers defy him: the eldest, Hueil, is killed in battle, to Gildas's great sorrow; but Gildas and Arthur are later reconciled. In addition to this, there is another incident, apparently imported from secular tradition, which is an early form of an episode in the story of Lancelot and Guinevere:

Gildas ... arrived at Glastonbury ... where king Melwas ruled the Summer Country. He was received by the abbot of Glastonbury, and taught the brothers and some of the laity, sowing the seed of the divine doctrines. Here he wrote the histories of the kings of the Britons. Glastonbury is the Town of Glass, first named thus in the British tongue. It was besieged by the ruler Arthur with a countless multitude because of Guennuvar his wife who had been violated and carried off by the aforesaid wicked king [i.e. Melwas], bringing her there because it was an impenetrable place, defended by reeds, rivers and marsh. The rebellious king [i.e. Arthur] had searched for the queen for a whole year, and had at last heard that she was there. At this news he raised the armies of all Cornwall and Devon, and the enemies prepared for war. Seeing this, the abbot of Glastonbury and his clergy and Gildas the Wise went out between the battle lines and peaceably counselled Melwas their king to return the lady he had carried off. So she was returned, as she should have been, in peace and goodwill.[18]

The influence of Gildas' own work is evident here. Arthur, although he was not one of the tyrants against whom Gildas ranted in vain, is grouped among the wicked princelings of the period. It is difficult to see what the author intended by 'rebellious king', particularly when he uses this epithet in the first incident, where it is clearly Gildas's brothers who are in revolt.

But these are only stray episodes and odd fragments of a much greater body of stories. The existence of a much more extensive

[15] Chambers (ch. 1, n. 21 above), 243–4. A second *Life* contains the latter episode only: Paul Grosjean, 'Vie de Saint Cadoc par Caradoc de Llancarfan', *Analecta Bollandiana* LX, 1942, 62–64.
[16] Chambers, 246–7.
[17] Chambers, 248.
[18] Chambers, 263–4: my translation.

legend is borne out by twelfth-century writers. Hermann of Tournai, in addition to the dispute over Arthur's return already quoted, says that the canons of Laon tell us that while in Devon they were shown 'the chair and oven of that king Arthur famous in the stories of the Britons', and were told 'that that same region had once been Arthur's.' William of Malmesbury, in the original version of his *Gesta Regum Anglorum (Deeds of the Kings of the English)*, 1125, says: 'This is that Arthur of whom the British tales rave today, who plainly deserves not lying fables, but true stories ... for he long sustained his sinking country, and roused the broken courage of its citizens for war: afterwards, in the siege of mount Badon, spurred on by the image of the mother of our Lord, which he habitually bore as his arms, he slew nine hundred of the enemy by his own hand in an incredible slaughter.'[19] William of Malmesbury is clearly contrasting the historical account he has found in *The History of the Britons* with much more romantic fictions he has encountered: if only he had deemed them worthy of record! He knows of the legend that Arthur will return, for in discussing the recently discovered tomb of Gawain on the Pembrokeshire coast, he says that Gawain was Arthur's nephew, and adds: 'But the grave of Arthur is nowhere to be seen, whence the ancient tales fable that he is to come again.' [20] Once again, we can identify William's source, *The Stanzas of the Graves*: perhaps there was not much more that he knew which has not survived. As with the historical Arthur, we are reduced to clutching at straws. The monk Ailred of Rievaulx, in his *Speculum Caritatis (Mirror of Charity)*, tells how a novice at the monastery (in north-east Yorkshire) was never moved by pious stories, although he had wept over tales which the common folk recited 'about some Arthur [Arcturus] or other' before he had entered the monastery.[21] This is unlikely to refer to Geoffrey's *History of the Kings of Britain* a Latin work accepted by the historians of the time as accurate, which Ailred, writing in about 1140, could scarcely call 'fables'. It sounds more like the work of some wandering story-teller.

We have so far been following all the threads of the stories about Arthur, whether in poems or histories, at the same time; with good reason, for we have seen how the distinction between the two hardly exists in the period with which we have been concerned. But in the twelfth century, that time of intellectual ferment when so many of the foundations of modern thought were laid, a clearer distinction was made between the respective arts of the historian and of the poet. It is by no means the almost absolute distinction we might make today, but from this time onwards Arthur's image in history is a very different matter from his image in literature.

[19] See ch. 1, n. 20.
[20] William of Malmesbury, (ch. 1, n. 20), ii, 342.
[21] Ailred of Rievaulx, *The Mirror of Charity*, tr. Geoffrey Webb & Adrian Walker (London 1962)

Arthur's place in medieval history was determined by the work of one man. Geoffrey of Monmouth's *History of the Kings of Britain*, which appeared in about 1135, caused something of a literary sensation: one of the leading historians of the Anglo-Norman realm, Henry of Huntingdon, at once wrote to a friend summarising it when he found a copy at the Norman abbey of Bec in 1139, saying that he was amazed to discover such a book, since he had been unable to obtain any real information on the kings of Britain before Julius Caesar, whose reigns were fully described in Geofrey's work, as were the deeds of the British kings after the Romans' departure. Arthur's reign was the climax of the whole work, 'the great book of Geoffrey Arthur', as Henry of Huntingdon calls it.

We know relatively little about the life and career of Geoffrey of Monmouth alias Geoffrey Arthur.[22] He is known to have been at Oxford in the period 1129–1151, and to have held the title 'Master', a rare one at the time, which implies that he was a learned man and a teacher. He may well have been a canon of the secular college of St George's, established in the church of Oxford Castle in 1074, and merged with Oseney priory in 1149: he was certainly friendly with the provost of the college, Walter of Oxford, archdeacon of the city. If he was a canon, he was also linked through St George's to Robert of Chesney, bishop of Lincoln from 1148 onwards. Both men were involved in his literary career, Robert of Chesney as the dedicatee of his *Life of Merlin*, Walter as the owner of 'an ancient book in the British tongue' from which, so Geoffrey said, he derived *The History of the Kings of Britain*. The overall impression is of a group of learned and distinguished men, working in a scholarly atmosphere: but their school was by no means an organised university, consisting merely of the students who chose to work with a given teacher or master. Walter was renowned as a speaker, but nothing written by him survives: Geoffrey used his pen to gain advancement in the church. His earliest surviving literary effort is the *Prophetia Merlini (Prophecies of Merlin)*, which was later incorporated in the *History of the Kings of Britain* as Book VII, and was completed about 1132–5. He tells us at the beginning of the book that he began the *History* first, intending to deal with the sayings of Merlin later. But stories about Merlin began to circulate from other sources, and he was urged by his friend Alexander, Bishop of Lincoln, and others, to complete this book first. This he did, and the *Prophecies* appeared independently before his major work. The *History of the Kings of Britain* seems to have been started about 1130 and finished about 1138, shortly before Henry of Huntingdon was astonished to discover a copy at Bec.[23] From the dedications we learn that Geoffrey was seeking the patronage of some important figure to secure him an

[22] See M. Dominica Legge, 'Master Geoffrey Arthur' in *Arthurian Tapestry* (ch. 1, n. 16), 22–27 and Geoffrey of Monmouth, *Historia Regum Britannie*, ed. N. Wright (Woodbridge & Dover N. H. 1985) I: *The Bern MS*, ix ff.
[23] Wright, *ibid.*, xvi.

ecclesiastical appointment. It was not until after he had written the last of his three known works, the Latin poem on the life of Merlin, in 1148, and dedicated it to Robert of Chesney, recently appointed Bishop of Lincoln, that he gained his object. He was ordained priest on 11 February 1152, and before the end of the same month consecrated bishop of St Asaph in Flintshire, probably through Robert's influence. The post was almost certainly a sinecure since Norman influence in the area was so uncertain that he may never even have visited his diocese. The legend according to which he was buried in the cathedral is without foundation. He died three years after his appointment.

Geoffrey's main interest was not the Church; he entered it merely because it was the most convenient career for a literary man. We have no evidence in his writings of a religious vocation, but in the times and circumstances this is by no means unusual. The greatest of the translators of the *History*, Maistre Wace, was given a canonry at Bayeux in similar fashion as a royal reward for a commissioned work. Far more important than Geoffrey's clerical standing is his Celtic descent. He describes himself as 'an abashed Briton', but we cannot tell whether he was a Breton (Monmouth had a Breton lord from 1075 onwards) or a Cornishman, or less probably, a Welshman. Both the Bretons and Cornish appear favourably in his works while the Welsh are seen as degenerate descendants of the ancient British.

The *History of the Kings of Britain* owes something to all these different elements: to scholarship, imaginative literature, the Celtic world. But it is most remarkable for its sheer novelty: no-one had ever written quite this kind of literary history with a romantic flavour before. Geoffrey was writing at a time when many changes were taking place, both in politics and in the intellectual world, a time as exciting in its way as the centuries of Renaissance and Reformation which are usually held to mark the beginning of the modern world. Yet many of our 'modern' ideas have their origins in an earlier renaissance, that of the twelfth century. In effect, Geoffrey invented a whole new world, where the learning of the schools mixed with ancient lore and legend and was welded into a masterpiece by literary imagination.

It would be fascinating to know exactly *why* Geoffrey wrote the *History of the Kings of Britain*, but even he himself might not have given us a clear answer. The main reason seems to have been national pride:[24] he was intent on giving the Welsh the kind of national history which had just been provided for the English by two distinguished writers, William of Malmesbury and Henry of Huntingdon. But, as befitted a successor of the Welsh bards, the work he produced is much more complex than theirs, if only because he had to create so much of it himself, lacking the raw material. He found his inspiration in everything from political

[24] Wright, *ibid.*, xix.

25

5   The opening page of a twelfth-century copy of Geoffrey of Monmouth's
History of the Kings of Britain. *The text starts at the point where there is an
initial of a charging knight. (Bürgerbibliothek, Bern, MS 568, f.18.)*

satire to a subtle view of the philosophy of history and even satire on his fellow-historians;[25] the learning of the schools provides much of the structure, while his quest for favour with prominent men shapes both the dedication – which appears in three different forms corresponding to changes in the unstable politics of Stephen's reign – and episodes within the *History* itself. There is a vein of propaganda, pleading for peace and reconciliation[26] in time of civil war: Geoffrey fills his narrative with examples of the disastrous consequences of civil strife and internecine wars, and he undoubtedly intended such passages as a warning to his contemporaries, just as the *Historia Brittonum* had tried to inspire the Welsh to new efforts against the Saxons by its examples of bygone heroes. Arthurian literature was to prove an ideal medium for such contemporary warrings on many subsequent occasions.

When Henry of Huntingdon first read Geoffrey's book, he wrote to Warin 'Brito'[27]: 'You asked me ... why I began to tell the story of our country from the time of Julius [Caesar] and omitted the flourishing reigns from Brutus to Julius. I reply that although I very often searched, I could find neither spoken or written words about those times.' Now, he went on, he had found Geoffrey's book. What did Geoffrey know that the greatest contemporary historian did not? What were Geoffrey's sources? What was the 'very ancient book in the British tongue' which he claims to have used? How historically reliable is his narrative? All four questions can best be answered by concentrating on the mysterious 'very ancient book'. In the prologue Geoffrey states clearly that he used such a book, which related the histories of all the British kings, from Brutus to Cadwallader, and that it was given to him by Walter, archdeacon of Oxford 'a man learned in the art of oratory and in exotic histories'.[28] However, if this book ever existed, it is now completely lost; we have nothing even remotely corresponding to it. The invocation of a lost source to give authority to a fictitious work is by no means unusual in medieval literature; for example, the romances about Troy were based on an imaginary work by one Dares, which had a considerable history attached to its discovery. And Geoffrey's *History* is romantic rather than factual history; we need not therefore accuse him of actual fraud. Let us say that here is an early example of a literary formula which has since been widely used, and that Geoffrey himself did not expect any great historical weight to be given to the result. It is fair to say that it was not Geoffrey, but his readers who decided that *The History of the Kings of Britain* was fact rather than fiction.

But this does not mean to say that he used no other source than his own imagination. He was clearly widely read, and his association with Walter, if it did not yield the 'ancient book'

[25] V. I. J. Flint, 'The *Historia Regum Britanniae* of Geoffrey of Monmouth: parody and its purpose. A suggestion', *Speculum* 54 (1979), 447–68.
[26] W. F. Schirmer, *Die frühen Darstellungen des Arthurstoffes* (Köln 1958), 25–8.
[27] The word may mean either 'Breton' or 'Briton'.
[28] Again, the translation is uncertain: 'in exoticis historiis' could mean 'strange stories', particularly in view of Walter's skill in oratory.

itself, evidently gave him access to unusual material, 'exotic histories'. Geoffrey's native language was probably Norman-French; as a teacher he was well read in Latin. As far as other languages went, he was familiar with spoken English and Welsh, but apparently did not read either language easily.[29] He seems to have neither read nor spoken Breton; but this does not preclude his having come from Brittany, as non-Breton Norman-French settlers were common in Brittany by his day. On the other hand, he certainly lived at Monmouth, and 'the *cyfarwydd* or story-teller was a familiar and valued figure in medieval Welsh society, and [he] could hardly have known the Welsh language without becoming acquainted with his art.'[30]

Part of Geoffrey's success lay in the fact that although he has in places concocted entire histories out of almost nothing, he restrained himself enough to give the result a convincing air of reality that made these stories accepted as accurate in outline, if not in detail, until the eighteenth century. Just as Arthur, as Geoffrey depicts him, is unhistorical, so is much of the rest. Brutus of Troy, the supposed founder of the British race and kingdom, Lud, from whom London was said to have got its name, King Lear, of Shakespearian fame, Caesar's three attempts to conquer Britain and final success only through treachery on the part of a British noble – all these are the products of Geoffrey's brilliant imagination working on a name or an odd reminiscence. Against this, we find only occasional touches of history: Caractacus appears, though Boadicea is conspicuously absent. For the period after the Roman withdrawal, Geoffrey draws on Gildas, whose phrases he often borrows,[31] and he includes such historical details as he can find: the appeal of the Britons to Aetius is historical fact. Geoffrey also draws on the *History of the Britons*, and uses it up to the beginning of Arthur's career. Other details show that he knew a number of Welsh legends. For example, the name of Arthur's father, Uther, may be due to a misunderstanding of 'Arthur mab uthr', Arthur the terrible, as Arthur son of Uther. Arthur's weapons are derived from various such Welsh stories: Caliburnus, his sword, better known as Excalibur, is derived from Caledfwlch in the Welsh, his lance Ron the same as Rhongomyniad, both found as his weapons in *Culhwch and Olwen*. Pridwen is a ship in the poem *The Spoils of Annwfn*, but appears as a shield in Geoffrey's account.

Geoffrey's account of Arthur's career is the climax of the *History* and occupies about one third of the whole book. This is the basis for all subsequent accounts of Arthur's career, and a brief summary is essential if we are to understand later developments. It is foreshadowed in Merlin's marvellous prophecies which immediately precede it; and it is with Merlin's supernatural

[29] T. D. Crawford, 'On the linguistic competence of Geoffrey of Monmouth', *Medium Aevum* LI, 1982, 152–162.
[30] *Ibid.*, 159.
[31] N. Wright, 'Geoffrey of Monmouth and Gildas', *Arthurian Literature* II, 1982, 1–40.

aid that Arthur is born. Uther falls violently in love with Igerna, wife of his enemy, Gorlois of Cornwall, and is magically transformed (by Merlin) into the latter's likeness. He enters the castle of Tintagel in Gorlois' absence, and begets Arthur by her. On his return, he learns that Gorlois has been killed a few hours earlier, and therefore marries Igerna at the earliest opportunity. Arthur thus enjoys the benefit of being miraculously and yet almost legitimately conceived. On his father's death, he succeeds to the throne, being then fifteen, and he is crowned by Archbishop Dubricius. His first campaign is against the Saxons, who had caused his father's death by poisoning him. He defeats their leader, Colgrim, in a series of battles based on the twelve described by Nennius. Arthur's chief allies are the Bretons, who play an important part throughout his reign, and whose leader Hoel is second only to Arthur himself.

Having defeated the Saxons with Hoel's assistance, he settles the internal affairs of his kingdom, and marries Guenhuuara daughter of a Cornish nobleman, who is of course the Gwenhwyfar of the Welsh and the Guinevere of Malory. His ambitions now rise to an imperial plane, and with little apparent effort he proceeds to conquer large areas of northern Europe. Ireland is his first objective, and its conquest is swiftly followed by that of Iceland, Gothland and the Orkneys. Norway is overcome and given to his brother-in-law; Dacia (Denmark), Aquitaine and Gaul have to be subjugated before his appetite is temporarily sated.

He then returns to Britain to hold his Whitsuntide crown-wearing; and it is here that Geoffrey waxes most eloquent over the glories of Arthur's court. However, immediately the festivities are concluded, there arrive messengers from Lucius Hiberius, the Roman Emperor, demanding tribute on the grounds that Britain was once a Roman province. Arthur convenes a council of kings, who unanimously agree that the only possible answer to so outrageous a demand is to march on Rome at once.

The kingdom is entrusted to Modred and the army prepares to embark. On the night before departure, Arthur has a foreboding dream which presages an imminent struggle between himself and either a bear or a giant. He proceeds to France, landing at Barfleur, where he hears that a giant has carried off and killed Hoel's niece. He makes a rapid detour to Mont Saint Michel, and disposes of the monster. Continuing his march to Burgundy, he hears that the Romans are encamped hard by. He sets off in pursuit, and, after various skirmishes, engages the main body of the army in a wooded valley near 'Sessia', perhaps Soissons in eastern France. Lucius is killed and the Romans defeated, though not without considerable losses on the British side; notable among the slain are Kay and Bedivere.

Having thus cleared the way to Rome, Arthur is preparing to march south again, when he hears that Modred has proved treacherous. He has usurped the crown and is about to marry Guinevere, having falsely spread the news that Arthur is dead. On learning this, Arthur immediately returns to Britain, dispatching the bodies of Lucius and various senators to Rome in lieu of the tribute.

At this point, Geoffrey interrupts the story to address his patron: 'About this matter, august consul, Geoffrey of Monmouth will be silent, but, as he found it in the aforementioned British treatise and heard it from Walter of Oxford, a man most learned in many histories, he will briefly set out in his own poor style the battle which that famous king, returning to Britain after his victory, fought with his nephew.' He deals with the remainder of

6 *Arthur fights the giant of Mont St Michel: an initial from a twelfth-century copy of Geoffrey of Monmouth's work. (Douai, Bibliothèque Municipale, MS 880, f.66v).*

7   *A very different version of Arthur's fight with the giant, from the* Chronicles of Hainault *illuminated by Guillaume Vrelant in 1468. (Bibliothèque Royale Albert Ier, Brussels, MS 9243, f.49v).*

Arthur's reign in one-tenth of the space allotted to the Roman campaign. When Arthur lands in Britain, Modred retires with his forces into Cornwall, where Arthur meets and engages him. In this final battle, Modred is killed with almost all his followers; but Arthur's forces suffer no less, Arthur himself being taken to the mysterious Avalon for his wounds to be healed. Guenhuuara retires to a convent and the kingdom passes to Constantine. Geoffrey's narrative, deliberately rhetorical up till now, becomes terse and factual.

The borderline between Geoffrey's own invention and the legendary material he has incorporated is hard to define. We have already compared the degree of historical fact and looked at the sources of some of the names he uses; but these are by no means so elusive as the incidental stories. The main outline of

8   *Arthur's last battle, from the* St Albans' Chronicle, *illustrated by a Flemish artist in about 1470. (Lambeth Palace Library, MS 6, f.66v).*

Arthur's career in the *History* is Geoffrey's own; but how much of the detail came from his fertile brain? One incident, a curious chapter on marvellous ponds in Britain, which Arthur describes to Hoel at the end of the Saxon campaign, is drawn from Nennius' *Marvels*. Similarly, the episode of Mont Saint Michel has little to do with the main military campaign; both this and another giant-killing recounted by Arthur afterwards come from a totally different atmosphere of personal strength and valour, and are found independent of Arthur himself in later Welsh legend. It seems as though Geoffrey had first exhausted the possible material in the Welsh traditions, and only then invented new stories. Even the idea of Arthur's expedition to Gaul may be a dim memory of the several usurpers who set out from Britain to claim the imperial title during the Roman occupation.

But Geoffrey has done a great deal more than simply combine the Welsh legendary and historical portraits of Arthur. He has formed an entirely new character, an emperor where there was once a 'hero without deeds'.

We have already noted the remark in a variant manuscript of the *History of the Britons* which says of Arthur that 'though there were many more noble than he, yet was he twelve times chosen commander'. Geoffrey takes this hint of mystery about Arthur's origins and uses it to elaborate his story. He may have had in mind the story of Alexander's birth. Greek and Latin romances had already been written about Alexander, in which he was the son of Nectanebus, not of Philip of Macedon. Nectanebus was a wizard and exiled king of Egypt, who arrived in Macedonia during Philip's absence and fell in love with his wife Olympiades. He told her that the god Ammon would come to her in the shape of a dragon which would then turn into a man; and a great hero would be born to her. However, Philip returned unexpectedly, but consented to receive the strange visitor and then retire. It was in fact Nectanebus himself who arrived under this disguise, and in due course Alexander was born. Other parallels are the story of Jupiter and Amphitryon and the Irish tale of the birth of the hero Mongan. The general idea of some mystery attached to the birth of a great hero is present in all three, and Geoffrey uses the story to raise Arthur to the status of Alexander and Hercules.

The idea of Arthur as emperor may well have developed from the French *chansons de geste* of the early twelfth century where Charlemagne appears as a kind of father-figure, invested with all the majesty of vigorous old age as well as the trappings of imperial power. Geoffrey's vision of Arthur is of a kind of younger, active version of Charlemagne, not only commanding his troops on campaign but fighting alongside them in the thick of the press. However, Geoffrey does not attribute to Arthur the

9 *Arthur fights the Roman champion Frollo; the fifteenth-century artist has shown the combat as a formal judicial duel, instead of an ordinary episode in a battle. (Bibliothèque Royale Albert Ier, Brussels, MS 9243, f.42).*

lands of the empire created by Charlemagne, for their history was too well known, and he is always careful not to make statements which could be contradicted. Instead he gives Arthur an empire whose nearest historical parallel is that of Canute, heavily biased towards the north of Europe, but with the addition of Gaul. Here Geoffrey may be remembering the usurpers who had claimed the imperial throne, such as Magnus Maximus, who succeeded in becoming emperor in 383 with the support of the Roman army in Britain. Magnus Maximus was remembered in Welsh legend as Macsen Wledig, and there were other echoes of an imperial past in the Welsh romances: in *Culhwch and Olwen*, Arthur's porter says: 'I was of old in … India the Great and India the Lesser …

in Africa was I, and in the islands of Corsica; I was there of old when thou didst conquer Greece unto the east.'[32] Such echoes of Britain's ancient links with the Roman world may be enough to account for Arthur's expedition to Rome.

Arthur's campaigns against the Saxons are described at great length. Again, parallels can be drawn between the English campaigns of William I and those of Arthur. But the main source of inspiration seems to have remained *The History of the Britons*, from which eight of the battles are adopted directly. Geoffrey has had to invent new sites for them, since the meaning of the original names was evidently already lost. Nonetheless, the events immediately following the campaigns offer one remarkable resemblance. In 1069 William spent Christmas at York, which had been laid waste by Normans and Danes in turn. He appointed a new archbishop, the former prelate having recently died, and drew up plans for the general restoration of the city. Arthur is specifically stated to have been at York for Christmas, and he similarly appoints a new archbishop.

Geoffrey seems to be attempting to provide the Britons with an emperor-hero to whose golden age they could look back with pride. France had Charlemagne; the Greeks, Alexander; and the Saxons, Beowulf and kindred heroes. Arthur's history is modelled, as has been shown, on the first two; but Geoffrey is no slavish imitator. It is the concept of the emperor-hero that he has adopted, rather than minor details. All these imperial chronicles lie on the borderline of history and romance, and Geoffrey is merely more obviously inclined to fiction than the others. It is a conscious attempt to create a national epic, in the same way as the *Aeneid*, or, a closer parallel, the *Franciade* of Pierre de Ronsard.

Geoffrey is also filling in the missing part of the history of Britain which Henry of Huntingdon and William of Malmesbury had been unable to complete. He provides a complete list of British rulers from the arrival of Brutus from Troy down to Cadwallawn in the seventh century: and he gives a clear account of how the British lost the sovereignty of their island to the Saxons, cleverly exploiting the gaps in Bede's account (whose work he undoubtedly knew) to push back the date of the final collapse of British rule, and inserting in the space thus created the climax of his history, Arthur's empire.[33]

Another object behind Geoffrey's work may have been to provide politically useful precedents. Even if his work as a whole is unhistorical, there is enough accurate material in it to make fact and fiction hard to distinguish, as we have seen. So his work could be quoted with reasonable safety in cases where a precedent was required. Brittany and Scotland are two examples of this. The Bretons play a considerable part in the *History*, but

[32] Tr. Jones & Jones, 98–99.
[33] R. W. Leckie, *The Passage of Dominion* (Toronto 1981), ch. 1

are rarely found in connection with Arthur elsewhere. A possible reason for this bias on Geoffrey's part is that a tenuous claim to overlordship of Brittany had been advanced by the Normans since the days of William the Conqueror, and this was confirmed only in 1113. The Duchy of Brittany was, however, still poised between independence and the feudal suzerainty of Normandy, and in any case was a valuable ally. So a reminder of the connection between the two countries was likely to go down well in the Norman court, and a little flattery of the Bretons would be regarded favourably. As for Scotland, Edward III in a letter of 1301 to the Pope actually quotes the *History* in support of his claim to it. Geoffrey, albeit rather belatedly, seems to have been successful in his object.

Given that it is almost certain that we can discount the 'ancient British book' as Geoffrey's direct source, the picture that emerges is of a writer who has plundered a wide range of written and oral sources, but whose chief genius lies in elaborating and fleshing out his raw material. A shadowy hint in Gildas, a line or two in *The History of the Britons*, a story heard in Wales or told to him by Oxford friends, all are grist to his mill, and emerge transformed as complete and well-shaped episodes in the history of the British people.

When Geoffrey's narrative turns to a description of ancient manners and morals, he simply draws on contemporary life. The passage describing Arthur's crown-wearing at the City of Legions immediately after his campaigns in Gaul against the Romans is the most elaborate of these episodes. The city is here described at length; its churches of St Julius and St Aaron, its monastery of canons and college of astronomers, until the magnificence of the court itself makes even the loquacious Geoffrey pause for words. He can hardly be thinking of the English court of the twelfth century as he describes this splendour; and a few lines further on, he relates a custom which betrays one source of his inspiration. When it comes to the church ceremony, the women go to a separate church; afterwards they hold their own banquet, at the same time as that of the men. These customs have a strong eastern flavour; and the only place where they were combined with Christianity was at Constantinople, a favourite stopping-place for the returning Crusader or pilgrim. It was regarded as the most luxurious city in the Christian world, and it is clearly one model for Geoffrey's City of Legions.

So Geoffrey, like the greatest Arthurian writers who followed, drew together themes and ideas and half-forgotten legends to create his masterpiece. He wrote at a time when the cultural aftermath of the Norman conquest was still in evidence, bringing the Celtic, Breton, Norse, French and classical cultures together, and thus had immensely rich resources on which to draw. The result is the greatest single contribution to Arthurian legend. The *History of the Kings of Britain* provided the entire historical part of the story of Arthur, and was more extensively known and used by later writers than any other part of the legend. It is a plausible account, and therein lies Geoffrey's greatest achievement. He produced an historical fiction, which, whether he intended it or not, was lifelike enough to be taken by his successors as history for some six hundred years after his death. Up to the beginning of the nineteenth century it was on Geoffrey of Monmouth's story, rather than on Malory's, that the English conception of Arthur was founded.

As an author, Geoffrey had an immediate success by medieval standards. Since the spread of written works depended on the laborious hand-copying of manuscripts, reputations in the literary field were slow in the making, but the huge number of surviving manuscripts (over 200) is the best evidence of its popularity.[34] Furthermore the *History* was accepted and enthusiastically read by most historians of the time, and there was very little opposition to it. Only very discerning writers detected Geoffrey's unreliability, such as William of Newburgh, who criticised *The History of the Kings of Britain* sharply, at the end of the twelfth century. In the introduction to his *Historia Rerum Anglicarum (History of English Affairs)*,[35] he attacks Geoffrey's excessive praise of the British race, his stories about Arthur and Merlin (which had of course been Geoffrey's own largest contribution) and his acceptance of the 'Breton hope' of Arthur's return implied in the departure of Arthur to Avalon in the *History*, and developed in the later *Life of Merlin*. William shrewdly sums up Geoffrey's method of working: 'taking the ancient fictions of the Britons and adding his own to them, by translating them into the Latin tongue he cloaked them in the honest name of history...' Giraldus Cambrensis, while often citing the *History* as though it were reliable, also tells a story of a man plagued by evil spirits, by which he was able to pick out false passages in books. When St John's Gospel was placed on his breast, the spirits vanished, but when by way of experiment it was replaced by 'Geoffrey Arthur's book' they returned, more horrible and numerous than ever before. He thus implies that he realised the true nature of the work.

But most chroniclers and historical writers followed Geoffrey without question. We have seen how Henry of Huntingdon, in his letter to Warinus in 1139, gave a summary of it to supplement his own Saxon history, and declared his astonishment at finding the work. Alfred of Beverley, in the 1140s, was the first to incorporate it into the standard form of historical work of the period, the monastic chronicle. Some fifty other chroniclers writing in Latin used it in the years up to 1420 to a greater or

[34] 212 at the latest count: see David N. Dumville, The Manuscripts of Geoffrey of Monmouth's 'Historia Regum Britanniae', *Arthurian Literature* III, 1983, 13–28 and subsequent updates.
[35] William of Newburgh, *Historia rerum Anglicarum* in *Chronicles of the reigns of Stephen*... ed R. Howlett (1884–5) i.11.

lesser extent, and it acquired the standing of the accepted authority on the period for British history.[36]

Nor were the poets slow to adopt it. By 1155, two translations of Geoffrey had appeared in French, and within half a century a Middle English version, taken from the French, followed. We no longer possess the first of the French versions, by one Geoffrey Gaimar, but we know something of it from his other work, *L'Estoire des Englés (The History of the English)* which forms a sequel to it. As far as we can tell, it must have been completed within a decade or so of the original, *c.* 1145–50.

Gaimar's work was, however, rapidly superseded by Maistre Wace's *Roman de Brut*, probably a much superior work from the literary point of view. In many manuscripts, Wace's *Brut* precedes *L'Estoire des Englés*, as though it were the recognised first part of the complete history of Britain. Wace was born in Jersey in about 1100, and in his youth lived at Caen, where he studied for some time, completing his education in the Ile de France. On his return to Caen, he wrote his first 'romanz' or tales in verse, including some saints' lives. Before writing the *Roman de Brut*, he seems to have visited southern England, possibly through a connection between the two great monasteries at Caen and Sherborne. In 1155, twenty years after the *History of the Kings of Britain* had been completed by Geoffrey, Wace finished his version of it in French; we learn from his English translator, Layamon, that a copy was given to Queen Eleanor, whose husband, Henry II, had ascended the English throne in the previous year. Wace soon received a commission from the king to write a history of the dukes of Normandy, and he started this, the *Roman de Rou*, in 1160. In 1169, he was appointed to a canonry at Bayeux as a token of royal favour, but since he had still not finished the commissioned work in 1174, Henry asked another poet, Maistre Beneeit, to complete it. Wace must have died shortly after 1174, when his name is found in records for the last time.[37]

The *Roman de Brut*, so named after Brutus, whom Geoffrey of Monmouth made the founder of Britain is largely based on *The History of the Kings of Britain*. Much of the apparent expansion (from 6,000 lines of Latin prose to 15,000 of French verse) is due to the shortness of the verse line. But Wace, like many medieval translators, has treated his material with some freedom. His personal knowledge of southern England led him to make some alterations, especially in the account of the campaign against the Saxons. The latest French literary fashions supplied him with the element of courtly love, which is absent from Geoffrey, and there is a definitely romantic tone to the work as a whole, in contrast to Geoffrey's drier and more historical approach. The same contrast appears in Wace's use of similes and direct speech,

[36] R. H. Fletcher, *The Arthurian Material in the Chronicles*, Boston 1906, ch. VI ff.
[37] I. D. O. Arnold & M. M. Pelan, *La partie arthurienne du roman de Brut*, (Paris 1962) 16–23.

heightening the dramatic and emotional effect. Vivid descriptions of scenes and events abound; the sea and nautical affairs, scarcely noticeable in Geoffrey, are much to the fore in the *Brut*, possibly because of Wace's childhood environment in Jersey. Lastly, and somewhat surprisingly, there is a rational and critical attitude on Wace's part towards the prophecies of Merlin: he omits them on the ground that they are entirely unintelligible.

There is, however, one major addition in the Arthurian section of the work, which was to become one of the central images of Arthurian romance. Wace relates how Arthur, because his barons could not agree on an order of precedence in seating,

> For the noble barons he had, of whom each felt that he was superior [to his companions] – each one believed himself to be the best, and no-one could tell the worst – King Arthur, of whom the Britons tell many stories, established the Round Table. There sat the vassals, all of them at the table-head, and all equal. They were placed at the table as equals. None of them could boast that he was seated higher than his peer.

10 *The Round Table at Winchester, probably made for a royal feast in Henry III's reign and painted with a portrait of Arthur and the names of his knights three hundred years later. (British Tourist Authority).*

It seems that the idea of this egalitarian round table may be Wace's own invention, reflecting the politics of the Angevin court under Henry II.[38] It is noteworthy that the king does *not* sit at the table himself: he sits on the dais, at a higher table, with his close friends, while the rest of the barons are prevented from claiming any special status. It is this insistence that no knight should have precedence, rather than its shape, that is the real distinguishing feature of the Round Table. Eventually Arthur himself was to join the company there, and the number of places was limited – in some later romances it is as few as thirteen. It becomes the forerunner of the great knightly orders of late medieval Europe, and for once life imitates literature: the order of the Garter can be shown to have arisen from Edward III's interest in Arthurian romance and his attempts to create an actual round table at Windsor.[39]

It was in Wace's work that Arthur himself reached his widest recognition as a heroic king in the mould of Charlemagne, and as the central figure of an epic poem. Later works might be more popular, or magnify Arthur to a greater extent, but the two factors never coincided again as they do here. No less than twenty-four manuscripts of the *Roman de Brut* survive, and, even if this figure palls beside the mass of manuscripts of its original, it is more than any other medieval French work save one. From it, all other subsequent chronicles of the legendary history of Britain were also known as Bruts, and several of these have much to say about Arthur.

The first of these is also the first English vernacular version of the Arthurian legend of which we have record. It is the *Brut* of Layamon, who, as he himself tells us, was parish priest of Areley Regis on the upper reaches of the Severn in Worcestershire. His name (pronounced Lawman) indicates Scandinavian origin, but it is unlikely that he was of Norse-Irish stock, as has been suggested. He completed the *Brut*, his only known work, between 1189–99:[40] it is a measure of Arthur's instant and universal appeal that a relatively humble priest should be moved to write about him, in a language which meant that there was almost no likelihood of patronage or reward.

It is a translation from Wace's French from beginning to end, in spite of his claim in the introduction that he had used an English translation of Bede and an otherwise unknown 'book of SS Albin and Augustine' as well as the *Roman de Brut*. Most of the additional material is his own, and just under one-third of the whole is concerned with Arthur. Where Wace had begun to draw Arthur into the world of courtly romance, Layamon moves in the other direction, back towards the Anglo-Saxon epic. He deliberately cuts out references to courtly manners and to love-making as one of a knight's accomplishments, and returns to the

[38] Beate Schmolke-Hasselmann, 'The Round Table: Ideal, Fiction, Reality', *Arthurian Literature* II, 1982, 41–75.
[39] Juliet Vale, *Edward III and Chivalry* (Woodbridge 1982) 67–69.
[40] A new edition of the Arthurian section, with translation, is being prepared by W. R. J. Barron.

40

antique virtues of *Beowulf*. This is reflected in his language and style: he uses simile extensively and effectively: dead knights in the river Avon are depicted as 'steel fishes lying in the stream … their scales float like gold-painted shields, their fins float as if they were spears'. His use of set phrases which recur with a particular character or situation, is a device borrowed from the 'kennings' of Anglo-Saxon literature. His vocabulary is largely Saxon, with not more than two hundred romance words in the whole work, and he has inherited a great variety of synonyms from earlier English poets.

In Layamon, the influence of chivalry is entirely lacking. The atmosphere is closer to the Welsh tradition which had been Geoffrey of Monmouth's starting point. He explains and simplifies situations rather than making them more complex, as would be only natural for a writer whose audience was the common people rather than the royal court. Although the French romances were in full spate, there is no trace of any of the later heroes, and the native characters retain their original qualities: Kay is still the brave and valiant knight of Welsh legend, and shares with Bedivere many of the adventures, which are military rather than knightly. Gawain is second only to the king, while Hoel's considerable part in the *History of the Kings of Britain* has been drastically reduced. Merlin's role is also a minor one, and the impact of his appearances is lessened. It is Arthur, and Arthur alone, who has any real importance; his character here reaches its zenith. He is neither the somewhat crude and vigorous leader of the Welsh tales — although it is to the barbaric rather than the aesthetic that his splendour inclines — nor the *roi fainéant*[41] of lascivious tendencies found in some French romances. His courage, generosity, sincerity and leadership are all brought out; but they are seen through the eyes of a simpler culture. Layamon's attitude is less refined and literary in style than that of his sources, and markedly less civilised altogether. Thus Arthur, although he laments his own fallen knights with great tenderness, is ferocious towards his enemies in a way that recalls the savage element in Anglo-Saxon heroic poetry, a ferocity which was commonplace in Layamon's time. Examples can be found everywhere in its popular tales and art: the doom paintings in almost every church in the country were scarcely less savage in spirit than Arthur's exultation over the dead Saxon leader, Colgrim: 'Even if you desired to go to heaven, you shall go to hell, ever to remain there, never to return.' It is perhaps an echo of an old Welsh tradition: *Arthur mab uthr* may mean, not Arthur son of Uther, but Arthur the terrible or cruel; and one version of the *Historia Brittonum* tells us that 'he was cruel from his boyhood'.[42] He has no compunction about hanging twenty-four children he has taken as hostages when the Saxons break a

[41] 'The king who does nothing'.
[42] Marie-Claude Blanchet, 'Le double visage d'Arthur', *Studi in onore di Italo Siciliano*, Biblioteca dell' 'Archivum Romanicum' 86, (Florence 1966), I 78.

truce. Layamon portrays Arthur in a series of contrasts, setting heroism against the supernatural and cruelty against magnificence.

The account of the Round Table is an embellishment of Wace's story. Layamon tells us how, at a Christmas feast attended by seven kings' sons with seven hundred knights, a quarrel over precedence arose, and several of them were slain in the ensuing fight. Arthur had the knight who started the quarrel and all his kinsmen beheaded; the knight's female kin had their noses cut off. When Arthur went to Cornwall shortly afterwards, he met a carpenter from foreign lands who had heard about the incident and offered to make him a table which could be carried anywhere, and at which sixteen hundred men could sit without one being higher than the next. He was provided with materials, and completed the table in four weeks.

The element of the supernatural introduced by Layamon was a natural part of many stories familiar to his audience; it adds an aura of mystery and of greater, hidden powers at work. Arthur himself is described as 'selcuth', strange or marvellous. Both at his birth and death, Arthur is attended by beings not of mortal race — 'elves' fails to translate the Saxon 'alven' adequately. These, it is implied, give him their support throughout his life, and Argante, their queen, carries him away at his death. The closing scene of Arthur's life in Layamon is only rivalled by that in Malory:

> 'Constantine, you are welcome. You were Cador's son. I entrust to you my kingdom; guard my Britons as long as you live, and maintain for them all the laws that have stood in my time and all the good laws from Uther's days. And I will travel to Avalon, to the fairest of all maidens, to Argante their queen, the most beautiful of the spirit-folk, and she shall make all my wounds sound and make me whole with healing medicines. And then I will come to my kingdom and dwell with the Britons with great joy.'
> Even as he spoke there came from the sea a little boat, driven by the waves, and two women in it, in wonderful dresses, and they took Arthur at once and carried him quickly and laid him down safely and went on their way. So what Merlin had said now happened: that there would be much sorrow at Arthur's departure. The Britons still believe that he is alive, living in Avalon with the fairest of spirit-folk, and they still continue to expect Arthur to come back. There is no man born, chosen by any lady, who can say for certain anything else about Arthur. But there was once a wise man, whose name was Merlin: he said in these words – and his words were true – that an Arthur should yet come to help the English.

Layamon alters another supernatural event in Geoffrey's last chapter. This is Arthur's dream presaging the conflict between him and Lucius Hiberius. In Layamon's version a different dream is described, and its import is different, for it concerns the treachery of Mordred and Guinevere. It is also more dramatically conceived: Arthur is sitting on the roof of his hall with Gawain, when Mordred appears with a throng of men and starts to cut down the posts supporting the building. Guinevere aids him by tearing off the roof. The building collapses, killing Gawain, but Arthur himself escapes, and beheads Mordred and the queen, to find himself alone on a wild moor. A golden lion approaches; he mounts it and is carried down to the sea-shore. The lion starts to swim out to sea with him, but he loses his grip on the lion's mane and is only rescued by a giant fish, which deposits him once again on the shore. Here Layamon uses the vein of symbolism found in the *Prophecies of Merlin* and foreshadows the coming events in his narrative even more vividly than in Geoffrey. The emphasis is now on Arthur's tragedy, rather than his triumph, an emphasis continued in later writers, for whom the Roman wars became almost incidental and the tragedy of Arthur was paramount. But this change of attitude was part of Arthur's role as a hero of imaginative literature; for the chroniclers wars took precedence over personal disaster.

The finest 'chronicle-version' of Arthur's story is in the alliterative Morte Arthure,[43] a poem written during the late fourteenth century revival of this ancient English form of verse; the need for alliterative words leads to a rich vocabulary, full of obscure words and resonant phrases, which draws heavily on Anglo-Saxon and Norse words, as opposed to the French bias of Chaucer's language. This makes it less accessible to a modern reader, but all the more rewarding once the language has been mastered.

The alliterative Morte Arthure is chiefly based on the *History of the Kings of Britain*, with some additions from later works, including the version of Wace on which Layamon's *Brut* relied, some *chansons de geste*, notably that of Fierabras (from which the encounter of Gawain and Priamus is drawn) and finally the romances of which Alexander is the hero. The vivid dramatisation that has taken place, in a different idiom, but on the same lines as that carried out by Wace and Layamon, requires no other source than the anonymous writer's own imagination. Many other departures from the original can be explained by what may be termed the contemporary reference process. Just as Geoffrey of Monmouth described Arthur in terms of the events and politics of his own times, and thus created parallels between his portrait of Arthur and the Norman kings, so the author of the *Morte Arthure* has portrayed Arthur as a Plantagenet king, fighting a fourteenth-century war. Nor was he the last to use this process, for in Malory's portrait of Arthur are traces of Henry V.

[43] No good modern version exists: there are several editions, of which that by Valerie Krishna (New York 1976) is the best.

A few instances from the poem may be used in illustration. The scene of the great battle against Lucius Hiberius exactly resembles that of Crécy. A sea fight is introduced, which appears to be a description of that off Winchelsea against the Spanish fleet in 1350; the author mentions Spaniards where the sense would require Romans, and this may well be a slip of the pen. Mordred and Roger Mortimer have several points in common, and the charges brought against Mordred are similar to those of Mortimer's impeachment. Hoel's niece, who in Geoffrey played a very minor role, becomes Duchess of Brittany and niece to Arthur, thus presenting an analogy with Jeanne de Montfort, who was similarly related to Edward III, and held the same title. Arthur's imperial ambitions reach their highest pitch yet in this poem: he is about to be crowned in Rome when he is forced to return by Mordred's treachery.

Before Arthur is forced to abandon his imperial pretensions, he has a dream in which he sees himself as one of the great emperors, bearing the symbols of imperial coronation, and seated on one of the nine chairs of Fortune's wheel. He reaches the highest point of the wheel, and, like his predecessors, is dashed down at the next turn of it. Finally, on his return from the Continent, Arthur

11 Arthur on the wheel of fortune: a miniature from a north French manuscript of about 1316 (British Library, MS Additional 10294, f.89).

44

engages Mordred in a sea-fight on the beach, in which Gawain is killed. Both Arthur and Mordred speak movingly of his greatness. The final battle follows, and Arthur, although victorious, is mortally wounded and buried at Glastonbury.

The portrait of Arthur himself makes him a tragic and towering figure, and there are conscious parallels with Alexander and Charlemagne which neither Wace nor Layamon had really explored. The 'fall of princes' which Arthur's story here exemplifies is less a human tragedy than the work of an unyielding fate, and, quite apart from their shared poetic tradition and language, there is much in common between the author of the *Morte Arthure* and Layamon. Arthur is cruel, and his battles are full of black humour and wry comments, less forthright and more self-conscious, perhaps, than his exultation over dead enemies in Layamon's work. By contrast the supernatural element disappears almost entirely, and the ending denies any possibility of his return: the mourners 'bring him to earth, with all the worship and richness that a man might deserve', and 'thus ends king Arthur.' That this was not a popular view is shown by an addition by the scribe, Robert Thornton. After the last line he wrote, in contrast to the lines he had just copied: 'Hic iacet Arturus rex quondam rexque futurus' – 'Here lies Arthur, the once and future king.'

This is one of the great medieval epic poems, but it has been overshadowed by Sir Thomas Malory, writing a century later, who draws heavily on the *Morte Arthure* in the early part of his work. The earlier poem has many merits: strong characterisation, which lends dignity to Mordred, often a mere villain, and enables him to command our sympathy; a sense of inescapable tragedy, again shared by Mordred, who is reluctant to become regent; powerful oratory in the speeches, particularly in Arthur's eulogy of the dead Gawain, who appears here in his early and untarnished character as Arthur's chief warrior. And there is a surging strength in the verse, particularly in the battle scenes: the following translation can only hint at the vigour of the original, evoking the confusion of a sea-fight:

Then the mariners gather, and masters of ships
Merrily each of the mates talks to the others,
Speaking in their language, telling how things were,
Drawing bundles on board, tying up sails,
Crowding on canvas, battening down hatches,
Brandishing brown steel, blowing their trumpets;
One stands stiffly at the bows, another steers aft;
Gliding over the water, the fighting begins.
The waving wind rises out of the west,
Blows its burly breath into men's sails,
Hurling together the stately ships

So that prows and strakes burst asunder;
The stern strikes so sharply against the stem
That the planks of the rudder are dashed in pieces!
Great ships and small crash against one another.
Grappling irons are thrown out, as they should be,
The stays are hewn down that held up the masts.
There is keen strife and cracking ships.
Great ships of battle are crushed into pieces!

The *Morte Arthure* is the last important piece in the tradition which treats Arthur's story as part of history. Many other writers had of course included him in their chronicles, in verse or prose, drawing to a greater or lesser extent on Geoffrey of Monmouth. There had been poetic versions of the bulk of Geoffrey's work by various writers, notably Robert of Gloucester, Peter Langtoft, and Robert Mannyng and even the most critical of late medieval historians had few doubts about the general accuracy of the *Historia Regum Britannie*.

But questions about Geoffrey's reliability were beginning to be asked. Writers whose country had supposedly been conquered by Arthur naturally took a less flattering view of his exploits. Thus in the Scottish chronicles, from John of Fordun in the fourteenth century onwards, Arthur is regarded with suspicion; Hector Boece's version of the story in 1528 is the most extreme, making Mordred the rightful heir who is supplanted by Arthur. This scepticism was soon to be found in England as well. Robert Fabyan, in his *New Chronicles* at the end of the fifteenth century, questioned Geoffrey's accuracy for the first time in three centuries, and omitted the romantic and supernatural elements of the *History*. A modified account of Geoffrey's work prevailed until Polydore Vergil took the critical approach further than the mood of the times warranted in his *Historia Anglica* of 1534. As a result, several writers came out in defence of Geoffrey, notably the antiquary John Leland in his *Assertion of Arthur*, and it was not until the advent of serious historical criticism in the seventeenth century that the obviously legendary parts were rejected. Even then, Geoffrey's version was so well established that it was the end of the eighteenth century before the whole outline was labelled as historically unacceptable. It says much for the merits of the *History* that it was able to deceive historians for six hundred years into a false view of the period it covered. The romantic history of Geoffrey of Monmouth has permanently coloured our idea of Arthur; and its writer could hardly have hoped for greater success than this.

Chapter 3

Arthur and his Court

Geoffrey of Monmouth took fragments of Welsh history and welded them into a narrative which ensured Arthur a central place in many chronicles. By a similar process, Arthur was to be given an even more important place in literature, in particular in the romances, which were to a medieval audience what the novel is to today's readers. Whether this flowering of Arthurian romance is entirely due to Geoffrey's portrait of Arthur or whether it is a parallel and separate development has long been the subject of scholarly argument, and is almost as great a mystery as the question of the historical Arthur.

We have already quoted William of Malmesbury and Ailred of Rievaulx, contemporaries of Geoffrey, who spoke of stories told about Arthur in a way that implied that romantic tales about him were in circulation in their day. There is other evidence of such tales, but it is exceptionally difficult to interpret. Before we look at the evidence about *how* Arthur, a Welsh hero, came to be one of the central figures in French romance, it may be helpful to look briefly at *what* was borrowed from Celtic sources by the writers of twelfth-century France.

The French romances and early Welsh literature have a number of characters in common, and a smaller group are found only in the French romances. Disregarding the varying degrees of transformation which the different characters undergo, the group common to both are Guinevere, Merlin, Kay, Bedivere, Gawain, Ywain and Mordred. The separate tale of Tristan and Iseult and King Mark was added to the Arthurian romance cycle and brought in three more Celtic figures. On the other side, Lancelot, Perceval, Galahad, Gareth and Bors are leading Arthurian knights who have no early Welsh counterparts.

In terms of plot, we can point to a large number of episodes throughout Arthurian romance which have parallels in Celtic folktale, Irish saga or Welsh literature. But here our ground is less sure: the diffusion of folklore is in itself a subject of immense difficulty. For example, there are several oriental stories which resemble closely episodes in the story of Tristan and Iseult: do we have to trace each one as it moves slowly by word of mouth or in manuscript round the Mediterranean and northward to France, or is there a common stock of human situations which are the basis of folktale, so that a similar story can be invented independently in France and Persia? All we can say is that some parallels between Celtic tales and French romances are so close that it is difficult to resist the conclusion that the French is a version of a Celtic original, but in very few, if any, cases can we point positively to the process by which the stories were transferred. Celtic literature was after all primarily an oral literature up to the twelfth century; the triads are *aides-memoire*, reminders of linked stories to prompt the bards with their next tale, and so our knowledge of what the plots were is very slight indeed. French literature was in the process of transforming itself into a written language: the word 'dit' at this period can mean both something spoken, a recital of a poem, or the poem written on the page of a manuscript. All we have is the last link in the chain, the French manuscripts of the poems, and a few hints of what might have happened on the way.

We have already noticed how, in the Welsh triads, Arthur's court became the accepted meeting-place of heroes. It is very difficult to date this development,[1] but it seems that Arthur's earliest companions, Kay (Cei) and Bedivere (Bedwyr), were augmented by other heroes of the sixth and seventh centuries well before Geoffrey of Monmouth's day. This process continued as the stories were transferred into the new context of French romance, and a number of Arthurian characters are first to be found as independent figures in the triads; Tristan and Iseult appear, under the names of Drustan mab Tallwch and Essyllt. Tristan himself was probably an historical north British king with the Pictish name Drust, of the sixth century. Essyllt is not specifically connected with him, but appears in the same triad. Merchyon, better known to us as king Mark of Cornwall, Iseult's husband, is also mentioned here. Another hero of the later romances, Ywain, is here too, under the name Owein ap Urien; there is reason to believe that he too was an historical prince of northern origin of the sixth century, absorbed into literature in much the same way as Arthur.

The first traces of Arthur's own personal tragedy are also present in the triads. Mordred is said to have raided Arthur's Court in Cornwall in one of the *Three Unrestrained Ravagings*, dragged Guinevere from her chair and struck her. But it is not clear that Mordred fought *against* Arthur at Camlann as a result;

[1] Bromwich, *Triads*, lxix.

all that we learn in another triad is that a blow 'struck upon Guinevere' by her sister Gwenhyfach resulted in 'the Action of the Battle of Camlann'.

Merlin also appears in the triads, as a bard: or rather, he appears twice, as 'Myrddyn vab Morvryn' and 'Myrddyn Embrys', who along with Taliesin are the three skilful bards of Arthur's court. The tradition of Merlin Sylvester or Celidonius and Merlin Ambrosius as separate figures is found in earlier Welsh poems;[2] they were eventually merged in Geoffrey of Monmouth's wonder-working prophet in the *History of the Kings of Britain*, whose later deeds he related in the *Vita Merlini*,[3] a poem written about two decades after the *Historia*. He was perhaps encouraged by the success of the prophecies of Merlin in the *Historia*, which, as we have seen, were circulated separately from the main work. Some of Geoffrey's story of Merlin comes from the account in the *Historia Brittonum* of the boy Ambrosius, whose history and prophecies provide the outline for those of Geoffrey's seer. From the fragments of his story contained in the early Welsh poems, we learn that the central characters were Myrddin himself, Gwenddolau, Gwendydd and Rhydderch. In the battle of Arfderydd (probably Arthuret near Carlisle) Rhydderch seems to have killed Myrddin's lord, Gwenddolau. This, and a vision in the sky during the battle, caused Myrddin to go mad. Gwendydd was his sister, but seems to have had some special part in the disaster which we know nothing about. In Geoffrey's *Life of Merlin* we meet all four again. Ganieda (Gwendydd) is in addition the wife of Rodarchus (Rhydderch), a detail which probably came from the lost part of the Welsh story.

Another source for these works comes from Scotland. Myrddin is connected with the Lailoken of certain legends preserved in the *Life of St Kentigern*. Both are associated with Rhydderch, and the Welshman is called 'Llallogan' at one point, suggesting a parallel with the name Lailoken. From these stories came Merlin's link with the Forest of Celidon, as a result of which Merlin Sylvester is sometimes known as Merlin Celidonius.

Early Welsh bards undoubtedly inherited something of the status of their pagan forebears, the druids, and both Merlin and Taliesin were reputed to be prophets. The success of the *Prophecies of Merlin* independently of the *History of the Kings of Britain* bears witness to the fascination of such utterances for medieval readers. The *Prophecies* have little to do with the biography of Merlin, and are in any case mainly based on the utterances of Ambrosius, though some remarks may come from other Welsh and Scottish tradition. They can be grouped under three headings: prophecies concerning a period in the past for Geoffrey; those concerning the near future for Geoffrey; and a

The evidence is usefully summarised in Nikolai Tolstoy, *The Quest for Merlin* (London 1985) 1–86, though the rest of the book is mainly speculation. Three of the early poems are given in translations by A. O. H. Jarman in the same book (251–255).
Ed. & tr. Basil Clarke, *Life of Merlin, Geoffrey of Monmouth, Vita Merlini* Cardiff 1973).

series of apocalyptic scenes. The first part, which would of course be the future for Merlin, is known as *ex post facto* prophecy; the predictions are composed after the event and attributed to someone who is supposed to have lived before it. Hence the references are clear in many instances, in spite of their cryptic form. The sinking of the White Ship in 1120 is alluded to as follows: 'The lion's cubs shall be transformed into fishes of the sea.' Henry I is, of course, the lion: his 'cubs' included the heir, Prince William, his only son, who was drowned in this disaster. Through this type of prophecy Merlin's reputation for accuracy in prediction was established, and Geoffrey goes on to make a number of vague allusions of great ambiguity in the second part. Occasionally he refers to projected schemes which have not yet come to fruition. These sketches of the future become more and more vague until they merge into the third section, the apocalypse, for which Geoffrey used the Bible and possibly classical sources for suitable imagery.

But we have digressed from our main theme, and in any event, the case of Merlin is an exception, as in this instance we can see the transition from Welsh to Latin taking place. It merely serves to underline the problem that faces us when we return to the question of the transition from Welsh to *French*. Geoffrey was probably working fairly closely with the original Welsh material: the French writers may have been learning their stories through a number of different intermediaries. It is possible that Breton storytellers had a hand in the process, though there were perfectly good contacts with Welsh bards through the courts of the Anglo-Norman lords in south Wales. A certain Bleheris is named in one source as a Welsh storyteller who had told an Arthurian story to the court of Poitou at some time before 1137, and is cited as an authority in several romances.[4] But we have to treat such comments with care. The distinguished late twelfth-century writer Walter Map is named as the author in two of the major prose romances, yet we know that they are not by him.

The most spectacular piece of evidence about the transmission of these tales is from a highly unexpected source, and has been the subject of much controversy.

On the north doorway, the 'Porta della Pescheria', of Modena Cathedral there is a carving on the semicircular frieze of the archivolt: it is generally agreed to be a scene from Arthurian romance. Reading from left to right, we have the following figures, identified by carved labels above them. First, an unnamed knight on horseback, fully armed, follows Isdernus, bareheaded but mounted and equipped with spear and shield. He is preceded by Artus de Bretania, armed and mounted, who is attacking Burmaltus, the latter on foot wielding a hammer, but without mail. A barbican and moated castle at the top of the arch contain

[4] *ALMA*, 57.

50

a woman, Winlogee, who is accompanied by an unarmed man, Mardoc. To the right of this, an armed knight, Carrado, rides out to attack Galvagin. There follow Galvariun and Che, with their lances on their shoulders. All the last three are armed and mounted: Artus, Galvariun and Che have pennants on the ends of their lances.

Neither names nor situation will be familiar; but a little interpretation will enable us to recognize them. A castle is being besieged by Arthur (Artus), Yder (Isdernus), a hero found in both French and Welsh romance, Gawain (Galvagin), Arthur's nephew, Galeron (Galvariun) and Kay (Che). The defenders are Durmart (Burmaltus), Caradoc (Carrado) and presumably Marrok (Mardoc), all of whom figure in the later Arthurian romances. Winlogee is probably Guenloie, Yder's beloved, rather than Guinevere, as has sometimes been argued.[5] The situation as a whole is similar to that found in two or three thirteenth-century romances, but no exact parallel has been found.

So far there is nothing remarkable in the carving; a not unfamiliar Arthurian scene, albeit rather far afield. But when it comes to the date of the work, there is much to explain. For though art historians cannot agree as to the exact date of the sculpture, and the style has been variously dated, the most likely dating of this work is between 1120 and 1140, earlier than any surviving evidence for written works about Arthur other than those in Welsh. This dating is confirmed by the record of the building of the cathedral, which tells us that a considerable part of the cathedral had been built and the sculptures placed in position by 1106. It is possible to trace a gradual development from the carvings of this first phase to the Arthurian frieze, but no more than a decade or two can separate them. And the possibility that the lettering was added later appears to be ruled out by the style of the alphabet used.[6] However, the theme of an attack on a castle is also to be found at the cathedral at Bari, on an archivolt with a frieze laid out in remarkably similar fashion, but much more archaic in style. It seems that the artist first chose his theme and then added names from a romance he had just heard, which had caught his imagination.

However incredible this sculpture may appear to be, and however difficult to accept, we have to explain how it came to be produced in Italy at a time when we have no recorded legends of any substance about Arthur on his native soil. Such slender evidence as we have already discussed shows that some sort of legend about Arthur was current among popular story-tellers of Wales, Cornwall and Brittany—in fact, among the Celtic races descended from the Britons of Arthur's day. And when the Continental romances of two or three decades later are examined, they are full of Celtic names and incidents. Furthermore, we

Maurice Delbouille, 'Guenièvre fut-elle la seule épouse du roi Arthur?' in *Mélanges de linguistique et de philologie romanes offerts a Monseigneur Pierre Gardette* (Strasbourg 1966) 129–32.

The literature on Modena is very extensive, notably a series of articles by R. S. Loomis. The best recent account is that of Jacques Stiennon and Rita Lejeune, 'La légende arthurienne dans la sculpture de la cathédrale de Modène'. *Cahiers de civilisation médiévale*, VI, 1963, 281–287.

12 The archivolt of the north door of Modena cathedral (Porta della Pescheria), one of the key documents in the history of Arthurian romance.

13 The archivolt at Bari cathedral: the scene is similar to that at Modena, but the labels are absent, and we have an everyday scene of feudal warfare instead.

have seen that there are parallels to some of these names and incidents in Welsh stories; but often there are bewildering and quite inexplicable discrepancies in an otherwise recognisable Welsh tale. Many hypotheses have been put forward to cover these facts and weld them into a rational whole, and long and complex arguments have resulted.

It has been argued that only one factor appears to reconcile the three points – Celtic tales, French romances, and Italian sculpture – namely, the Bretons. The Bretons came of Celtic stock, and had many points of contact with France and indeed throughout Europe. Records show that they travelled widely, and were found in Wales as well as in France at this time; and it seems that it must have been they who transmitted the tales. This would explain the strange discrepancies between the Welsh originals and the French versions. But there remains one major obstacle: there is no written trace of any Breton version of these legends.

This need not necessarily deter us; for most of the Welsh legends were only recorded in the memory of the bards, and told or sung at feasts. Similarly, the Bretons must have had their bards; their material may well have been the same as the Welsh, but they were free to wander beyond their own borders into France in search of an audience. The stories told by such bards would have attracted the writers and poets of the newly-developed French language, the vernacular tongue as opposed to the Latin of Church and Court officials, and in much elaborated forms the spoken tales passed into literature proper.[7]

Against this, it can be argued that at this period any distinction between Bretons and Welsh in cultural terms, is hard to make: the *Book of Llandaff* in the tenth century says that the men of Wales and of Brittany are 'of one race and one language', and it is very difficult to tell in a given text whether *Brito* means a Breton or a Welshman – the best translation is simply 'Briton'. Furthermore, if there is a distinctive Breton literary form at this period, it is the *lai*, a short poem about a single episode; the Welsh romances such as *Culhwch and Olwen* have a longer structure much closer to that of the French romances.[8] We may also ask why the Arthurian stories are first found in French in the twelfth century, when contacts between Bretons and French had been established since the eighth century by way of the Loire valley and Breton-Norman contacts had begun in the mid-eleventh century. It is only after the Norman conquest of south Wales that we have definite evidence of the Arthurian stories in languages other than Welsh, and this simple historical fact must take precedence over the problematic parallels between Breton material and the French romances.

To sum up, it seems that the figure of Arthur himself became known to the Normans and thence to the French through the

[7] R. S. Loomis in *ALMA*, 52–63.
[8] See Jean Marx *Nouvelles recherches sur la littérature arthurienne*, (Bibliothèque française et romane IX, Paris 1952) 10–11, 31–34, 77–84.

14 This mosaic at Otranto cathedral in Southern Italy is perhaps even more mysterious than the Modena sculpture: much restored, it may represent Arthur's fight with a giant cat, a story recorded as far apart as tenth century Wales, twelfth century Normandy and fifteenth century England. Alternatively, it may show Arthur riding on a goat, as a kind of supernatural figure.

Welsh; the concept of Arthur's court was also taken over into French, but the adventures of the Arthurian heroes were often embellished from other sources, among which Breton stories figured to some extent, but which included almost any oral or literary material which came to hand when the romances were being written.[9]

We have only fragments of the Celtic literature about Arthur, whether Welsh or Breton, so it is not always safe to generalise about the ways in which the French writers transformed the stories of Arthur and his knights. Some aspects merely reflected the transition from the spoken to the written word: the first French romances have a much clearer structure, and are often indebted to classical theories of literary form for the way in which they are shaped. Their writers are following the accepted rules of their art just as the Welsh poets were guided by their ancient traditions, but the results are very different. Furthermore,

[9] Frappier, n. 11 below, 39–41.

the social milieu in which the first French romances were created is totally unlike that of the Welsh poems: the old tribal values of the prince as giver of gifts, the loyalty of the war-band, the narrow world of the mead-cup and the battle axe, were replaced by a cosmopolitan and sophisticated setting, a world where courtly love and Greek philosophy, chivalry and the concept of universal empire all impinge on the Arthurian stories. The social function of the tales has changed and broadened: twelfth-century France is a country where the concept of leisure is familiar, and entertainment is accordingly more important. The men of the war-band have become *les jeunes* or *iuvenes*, the young men who, as younger sons in a society where inheritance goes to the eldest son, have to make their own way in the world by a mixture of charm, skill in arms and astuteness, perhaps in the shape of a shrewd but loveless marriage. The romances to a large extent reflect the hopes and aspirations of these men, as we shall see.

The earliest surviving Arthurian pieces in French are only marginally connected with Arthur, and are more an indication of the magnetic power of his name than a major contribution to the legends. They are the so-called 'Breton *lais*',[10] short poems which either tell a brief dramatic story or portray an episode from a larger tale. The most important are those written by Marie de France, who seems to have been a well-connected noblewoman possibly connected with Henry II's court. *Lanval* retells the familiar folktale of the fairy mistress whose existence must never be betrayed to any other mortal. Lanval, the hero, keeps his word until Arthur's queen tries to seduce him: he rejects her, boasting of his mistress's superior beauty, and is at once abandoned by his love and cast into prison for insulting the queen. At his trial, his mistress reappears to vindicate him and carries him off to Avalon. In Marie's hands, the simple appeal of the tale is enhanced by her skilled portrayal of Lanval's changing fortunes and the suspense of his mistress's reappearance, with vivid touches of life at court. Her other 'Arthurian' *lai*, *The Honeysuckle*, does not in fact mention Arthur, but is the earliest surviving piece about Tristan, whose story, as we shall see, was drawn into the Arthurian cycle. In it she sketches in a dozen lines the love of Tristan and Isolt, and describes Tristan's secret return from the exile into which king Mark, his uncle, has sent him because of his love for the queen. He leaves a message for her in the forest, alluding to the honeysuckle entwined round a nearby hazel, which cannot be separated without killing both: 'Fair friend, so it is with us; neither you without me, nor I without you.' They meet and part; and in memory of the meeting Tristan uses his skill as a harper to make a *lai*. In this handful of lines Marie captures the essence of the story, and creates in words a brilliant miniature

[10] Tr. Glyn Burgess, Penguin Classics, 1985.

akin to those which decorate the great medieval illuminated manuscripts.

The *lais* appeal by their brevity and lyric intensity; but the more leisured age of the late twelfth century demanded more extended works to beguile the hours. The adventures of Tristan were probably developed into a full-length romance (now lost) about the time that Marie wrote, and we shall return to the early Tristan poems when we see how this legend became attached to Arthur's court.

It is Chrétien de Troyes, who began to write soon after this, who represents the mainstream of strictly Arthurian literature. Born before 1130, Chrétien was closely associated with the court of Champagne and particularly with the Countess Marie, daughter of Eleanor of Aquitaine. From her mother Marie had inherited a taste for literature, particularly that of the Provencal troubadours; and the ideal of courtly love flourished in her circle. Chrétien may also have had connections with the Angevin court, and seems to have visited England. His first works seem to have been a translation of Ovid's *Art of Love*, a popular work in the Middle Ages, and a version of the Tristan legend. Both of these are lost, and the *Erec* is his earliest surviving piece. It was followed by the nominally Arthurian *Cligès*, drawn largely from classical legend and using Arthur's court merely as a backdrop. Three masterpieces followed: *Lancelot (Le Chevalier de la Charrette)*, *Yvain (Le Chevalier au Lion)*, and *Perceval (Le Conte du Graal)*, the last of which was left unfinished. Chrétien's works were written in the period 1170–1190, though opinions differ as to when, and it has been argued that his first work was as late as the mid-1180s.[11]

Chrétien's poems present two great problems for a modern reader. Because he laid the groundwork for so much of later Arthurian literature, the first problem is to realise just how extraordinary and innovative his work is, and to see how it challenges contemporary conventions as well as making use of them. Here is a writer trained in all the subtle arts of rhetoric, who knows his way through the mazes of medieval logic and philosophy, choosing as his material stories which seem the absolute opposite of the learning of the schools of Paris, and yet applying to these tales many of the devices which were the commonplaces of the learned world. Chrétien creates his masterpieces by drawing together three traditions which would seem to have nothing in common: the 'rhetoric' of the scholars, courtly love and Celtic folklore. And yet his verse is deceptively simple, his stories immediately attractive, so complete is the fusion of these unprobable raw materials.

The second problem is the role of Arthur himself in the stories. This is a crucial paradox in much of medieval 'Arthurian'

[11] The best works on Chrétien in English are L. T. Topsfield, *Chrétien de Troyes: a study of the Arthurian Romances* (Cambridge 1981) and Jean Frappier, tr. Raymond J. Cormier *Chrétien de Troyes: the man and his work.* (Athens, Ohio 1982). Claude Luttrell, *The Creation of the First Arthurian Romance: A Quest* (London 1974) pp. 26–46 argues for the late dating of the romances; he also concludes that Celtic influence was negligible (pp. 240–254).

la ueille ꝛ la pꞓntꞓou
ſtꝛ qꝛ̃t ꞇour li compaıg

15 *Arthur at a feast; as the most splendid kind of court ceremonial, feasts
figure largely in the romances, and it is at feasts that many adventures
begin. From a north French manuscript of c.1316 (British Library, MS
Royal 14. E.III, f.89).*

literature. Only two of the medieval poems and prose romances
which we shall be looking at give Arthur a central part, and these
are closely related, both concerned with the tragedy of Arthur's
end. Only in the chronicles does Arthur remain as large a figure
as he was in the *History of the Kings of Britain*. In literature,
from the moment the romances appear, the focus is elsewhere: on
his court and the knights who make up that court. Arthur himself

57

appears often only at the beginning and end of the stories, and in this respect becomes closer to the role of Charlemagne in the *chansons de geste*, a kind of remote and majestic figure whose aura is so tremendous that he cannot concern himself with mundane things. But once this role was established, writers sometimes took a less respectful view, depicting him as indolent and reluctant to involve himself in real action, 'the king who does nothing.' So while the lustre of his court remained undimmed, Arthur became an equivocal figure, resting on his laurels rather than ultimately involved in heroic deeds. He does on occasions

16 *Arthur enters Camelot: a magnificent parade portrayed by an Italian artist at the time of Edward III. (British Library, MS Additional 12228, f.221v).*

set out in search of the heroes of his court when they have vanished on their quest for adventures, but in only a handful of instances does he himself do anything to justify his reputation as one of the greatest of all knights.[12]

This paradox means that much of what follows is chiefly concerned with the individual knights of Arthur's court, rather than Arthur himself: but these heroes and their deeds are now regarded as an integral part of the Arthurian stories, and if at times we seem to have strayed far from Arthur himself it is because we are concerned with one particular thread in the vast tapestry of Arthur and his legend.

Chrétien's first romance, *Erec and Enide*[13], presents us at once with exactly the situation we have just outlined, and the handling of the subject matter in this poem sets certain patterns which were to endure throughout medieval Arthurian romance. The action begins away from Arthur's court, as Erec wins Enide as his bride by achieving two quests. He then brings her to Arthur's court, where she is received with great honour; and this affords an opportunity for Chrétien to describe the characters of the court and its splendours, and to display his own learning in Arthurian matters. The main psychological action follows: how Erec abandons knightly ways for Enide's charms, and, on hearing her reproach herself for this, mistakenly suspects her fidelity. The testing of both Erec's knightly prowess and his wife's faithfulness is worked out in a series of loosely-linked adventures, drawn from Celtic prototypes. When both Erec and Enide have been proved true, a last section forms the climax: Erec breaks an enchantment by which a king and his court are bound. It is as though the power to do this had only been established by his previous trials, though Chrétien does not make this explicit. The poem ends with the coronation of Erec and Enide as heirs to his father's kingdom.

The framework, with its three clearly defined divisions, betrays a mind trained in formal literary conventions, and is certainly Chrétien's own device. The actual content of the story is centred on the folklore theme of Patient Griselda, which accounts for the main action; and the individual adventures are drawn from the Celtic-French material already described, though only the last exploit, the so-called *Joie de la Cort*, has the characteristic fey quality of such adventures, with half-explained enchantments and disenchantments whose logic is not that of the rational world. The great appeal of this combination to contemporary audiences was its presentation of a familiar world with this fantastic surrounding of adventure. The familiar world is also transformed, but only by making everything more splendid and dramatic until it transcends reality. Arthur's court is like any ordinary court, but peopled with heroes and bedecked in the

[12] Rosemary Morris, *The Character of King Arthur in Medieval Literature*, (Woodbridge 1982) 80–93: B. N. Sargent-Baur, 'Dux bellorum, rex militum, roi fainéant: la transformation d'Arthur au xiie siècle', *Le Moyen Age* 90, 1984 357–73.
[13] Tr. W. W. Comfort, *Chrétien de Troyes, Arthurian Romances* (London 1914, rpd 1967) 1–90: new tr. in prep. D. D. R. Owen, Claude Luttrell's book cited above is specifically a study of this romance.

richest furnishings; Arthur himself is a king such as every knight dreamed of, generous and a great encourager of prowess, quite untrammelled by everyday considerations.

But these elements alone would not have been enough to establish Chrétien's place as one of the greatest writers of his day. He is also an expert in the subtler arts: he exploits the various tensions within his story very skilfully, opposing the demands of married love and the knight's calling as a warrior, setting the richness and companionship of the castle against the lonely and threatening magical forests where adventures are to be found. In his later works, he explored also the inner psychological stresses of his characters, and it is this sense of tension that gives his romances their dramatic power.

Chrétien's next romance, *Cligès*,[14] illustrates the way in which quite different stories could be drawn into the Arthurian web simply by using Arthur's court as a background. On this point, it is interesting that Chrétien, the first so to depict the Round Table as a great centre of chivalry, was also the first to name Arthur's capital Camelot, a name he may have found in *Camulodunum*, the Roman name for Colchester. *Cligès* tells of the love of Alexander and Fenice, and of their son Cligès for Soredamors; much of the action takes place in Constantinople. Chrétien uses witchcraft and the marvels of the East to supply the exotic element here, but these are no match for the less obtrusive mysteries of the Celtic world. As a result, none of the characters or episodes play an important part in later Arthurian stories.

In *Lancelot*, or as it is more often known, *Le Chevalier de la Charrette (The Knight of the Cart)*,[15] Chrétien introduced for the first time one of the most important elements of the romances: the idea of courtly love. It is important to distinguish between the passionate, unrestrained love of Tristan and Isolt and the carefully restrained code of courtly love, represented here by Lancelot and Guinevere. Courtly love (with which Chrétien does not seem to have altogether sympathised, since he firmly declares that he only wrote the tale at Marie de Champagne's bidding, and left it to another poet to finish) was derived from the literature of southern France, where, from the beginning of the twelfth century, the troubadours had elaborated on the theme of the superiority of the lady and the moral worth to which the worshipping lover could attain, investing the beloved with an aura of divinity which still lingers about Guinevere in Chrétien's tale. Utter obedience was required if the lover was to gain solace, though in the strictest schools such solace was no more than a chaste kiss. Hence Lancelot is rebuked for hesitating a moment in mounting an executioner's cart. The shame of appearing as though he was a condemned criminal should not have entered his thoughts when his duty was to rescue Guinevere at once.

[14] Tr. W. W. Comfort, (n. 13 above) 180–269; new tr. in prep. D. D. R. Owen.
[15] Ed. & tr. William Kibler: Chrétien de Troyes, *Lancelot or the Knight of the Cart* (New York 1981); new tr. in prep. D. D. R. Owen.

Chrétien does not hold to the principle of courtly love with its overtones of adultery – which in this case prove real: his own view of love was much more moral, as witness Fenice's proud rejection, in *Cligès*, of Isolt's fate: 'Never could I agree to live the life that Isolt lived; love was debased in her for her body was at the disposal of two, and her heart was wholly for one ... Let him who has the heart have the body and exclude all others.'

The story of *The Knight of the Cart* is that of Guinevere's abduction by Meleagant (otherwise the Melwas of the *Life of St Gildas*) while the all-important theme is that of Lancelot as lover and rescuer, whether performing heroic feats, falling into an ecstasy at the sight of his mistress's golden hairs on a comb she left behind, or playing the coward at a tournament at her command. The adventures are full of marvels and mysteries, of perilous beds and flaming lances; perhaps the most famous is that of the bridge made of a single sharp sword blade across which Lancelot has to crawl in order to reach Guinevere's prison. Lancelot is set apart from all other knights by his moral virtue, which derives not from religion but from his loyalty in love. Meleagant is his converse; violent, without respect for his beloved, he relies on the wrong kind of knightly prowess – sheer strength – to achieve his aims. However much Chrétien may disclaim his responsibility for both subject and moral, he has succeeded in combining all the essential ingredients of Arthurian romance for the first time, quite apart from his own masterly

17 Lancelot's adventures, from the opening page of a manuscript dated 1344: he crosses the sword-bridge, fights a lion, and jousts with Meleagant, Guinevere's abductor (Bibliothèque Nationale, Paris, MS Fr.122, f.1).

portrait of the lovelorn Lancelot and his distant, divine lady. Chrétien's unease with the work may have arisen from the fact that there was no neat ending within the compass of the story he was given; the tragic end of Lancelot's and Guinevere's love in the downfall of the Round Table was a later development, by a poet working on a larger canvas. Chrétien is still working on a scale which is not very much wider than that of the *lai*, in that he tells one story in each romance, centred on one hero.

Yvain or *Le Chevalier au Lion (The Knight with the Lion)*[16], which may have been written at the same time as *The Knight of the Cart* is generally accepted as Chrétien's finest work. Here the theme is a moral one, and harks back to *Erec*, to which it is in many ways a counterpart. In the first part, Yvain wins and marries Laudine by his prowess, but is lured away to Arthur's court in search of fame; promising to return in a year and a day, he breaks his pledge, and is rejected by his lady; and the second part describes his adventures in regaining her favour, in which he is assisted by a lion which he has rescued from a serpent, a theme which comes from the classical story of Androcles. The marvels are again Celtic, particularly the splendid episode of the fountain in the forest of Broceliande.

Like *Erec*, *Yvain* is a self-contained work and was never integrated into the later romance cycles, though its popularity is witnessed by Welsh and English translations. It is a beautifully coherent and balanced story which uses the adventures as part of the wider pattern of sin committed and forgiveness earned. Chrétien explores with great subtlety and richness of feeling the relationship of Yvain and Laudine, and gives a lovely portrait of Lunete, Laudine's maid, who as instigator of the match is punished when Yvain fails to return, only to be rescued by him in the second part of the tale.

Chrétien's last, unfinished work, *Perceval* or *Le Conte du Graal (The History of the Grail)* written for Marie de Champagne's cousin, Philip count of Flanders, once again points the way forward.[17] Just as *Le Chevalier de la Charrette* contains the essence of the courtly love of Lancelot and Guinevere, one of the crucial themes in later Arthurian romance, so *Le Conte du Graal* contains the germ of the spiritual side of the romances, the quest for the Holy Grail. The story is that of the simpleton whose innocence enables him to triumph, after initial misadventures, where more worldly heroes fail. Perceval is brought up by his mother in ignorance of chivalry, since his father and elder brothers have been slain while knights-errant. Perceval meets five knights by chance, and deserts his mother to seek knighthood, armed only with hasty advice from her on his conduct (which he misunderstands) and crude home-made equipment. His simplicity leads to his first adventures: he compromises a lady by kissing

[16] Tr. W. W. Comfort (n. 13 above), 180–269.
[17] Tr. Nigel Bryant, with parts of all the continuations and a linking summary: *Chrétien de Troyes: Perceval or the Story of the Grail* (Woodbridge 1982) new tr. of Chrétien's contribution only in prep. D. D. R. Owen.

18 *An early fourteenth century miniature of the second part of the story of Yvain: Lunete in prison, Yvain vanquishes a giant, and Yvain fights to rescue Lunete from the stake. (Bibliothèque Nationale, Paris, MS Fr.1433, f.90).*

her against her will, and slays a kinsman for his armour. He even fails to grasp the friendly teaching of Gorneman de Gohort, who tells him that to talk or question too much is ill-mannered. His only success is with the beautiful Blancheflor, whom he rescues from her enemies, though he quits her embraces to seek his mother again, not knowing that the latter has died of a broken heart.

On his quest, he meets a mysterious fisherman, who offers him shelter in his castle. He rides there, to find his host already reclining on a couch in the great hall.[18] The following morning the castle is empty; he learns from a girl whom he meets in the forest that his failure to enquire about the *graal* will be disastrous for the land around.

[18] Bryant, 35.

63

Perceval meets knights for the first time.

Perceval at Arthur's court.

Perceval departs on his adventures, leaving his mother distraught; he kisses a lady whom he finds alone in her tent.

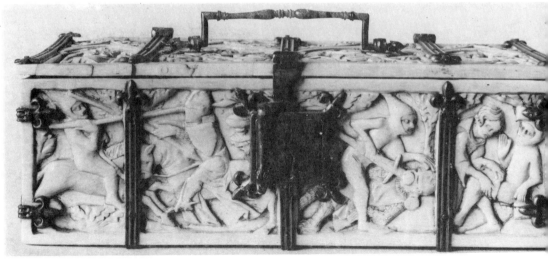

He fights the Red Knight, and takes his armour; and Gornemant tends his wounds.

19 *The four sides of a fourteenth century Parisian ivory box in the Musée du Louvre (OA 122), showing Perceval's adventures. Perceval can be identified by his fool's clothing in each scene.*

The remainder of the poem concerns Perceval's adventures in his search for the way back to the castle of the *graal* and Gawain's part in seeking the Bleeding Lance. As the story breaks off, Gawain's mysterious adventures have come to dominate the poem, though Perceval learns from a hermit that the Fisher King is his cousin, and is sustained by a single mass wafer served to him each day in the *graal*.

Chrétien's theme in *Perceval* is plain: he is exploring the spiritual element in knighthood, as Perceval proceeds from childish innocence through wordly failings towards the achievement of spiritual grace. It is clear that Perceval would have eventually found his way back to the Grail castle, and asked the crucial question as the culmination of the romance. Equally, Gawain is used as a foil to Perceval's adventures, to show how mere worldly prowess is not enough.[19] In *Yvain* and *Lancelot* Chrétien had showed the martial and moral development of a knight; here he adds the spiritual, and thus makes of his romance a work that transcends the boundaries of secular and religious literature. One of the most striking moments is Perceval's reappearance in the middle of a series of Gawain's adventures; the latter's deeds have been used to mark the passage of time as well as offering a counterpoint to those of Perceval:

Perceval, my source-book tells us, had lost his memory to such a degree that he no longer remembered God. April and May passed by five times – that's five whole years – without him entering a church or worshipping God or His cross: he lived like this for five years. That's not to say that he stopped seeking deeds of chivalry; he went in search of strange, hard and terrible adventures, and encountered so many that he tested himself well. In five years he sent sixty worthy knights as prisoners to King Arthur's court. That was how he spent five years, without a thought for God.

At the end of these five years it so happened that he was riding across a wilderness, fully armed, as always, when he met three knights and as many as ten ladies with them, their heads hidden in their hoods, all on foot, in hair-shirts and bare-footed. The ladies, for the salvation of their souls, were doing their penance on foot for the sins they had committed, and were astonished to see him coming in armour, holding a lance and a shield. And one of the three knights stopped and said:

'My good, dear friend, don't you believe in Jesus Christ, who laid down the New Law and gave it to the Christians? Truly, it's neither right nor good, but very wrong, to carry arms on the day when Jesus Christ died.'

And he who had no sense of day or hour or time, so tormented was his heart, replied:

'What day is it, then?'

'What day is it sir? Don't you know? It's Good Friday, the day when a man should worship the cross and weep for his sins, for on this day the one who was sold for thirty pieces of silver was nailed to the cross. He who was clean of all sins saw the sins with

[19] It has been argued that the Gawain passages are later interpolations, but this seems unconvincing: see Stefan Hofer in *Les romans du graal aux xiie et xiiie siècles* (Colloques internationaux du CNRS) Paris 1956, 15–30. This is only one example of the controversies which surround many aspects of *Perceval*.

which the whole world was stained and bound, and became a man to save us from them. It's true that He was God and man, for the Virgin bore a son conceived by the Holy Spirit, in whom God assumed flesh and blood, so that the Deity was housed in the flesh of man: that's certain. And those who will not believe it will never see Him face to face. That son born of the Virgin Lady, who assumed the form and the soul of man with His holy deity, truly, on such a day as today He was nailed to the cross and freed all His friends from Hell. It was a most holy death, which saved the living and brought the dead from death to life. With their spite the false Jews, who should be put down like dogs, did themselves great harm and us great good when they raised Him to the cross: for they damned themselves and saved us. All who believe in Him should be spending today in penitence. No man who believes in God should be carrying arms today, either in the field or on the road.'[20]

Stricken with remorse, he confesses to a nearby hermit, and it is then that he learns of his relationship to the Fisher King, and that it was his sin in causing his mother's death through grief that prevented him from asking the crucial question. This is the last we hear of Perceval in Chrétien's unfinished poem, but it is a vital clue to what would have followed. We do not possess, however, any real clue as to Chrétien's concept of the grail, nor do we know where he derived the images of the Grail procession. The grail or *graal* is a flat-serving dish, a not unusual word in twelfth-century French; but it evidently belongs to a magical or mystical world, as does the lance. A reasonable guess – and it can be no more – is that Chrétien had before him or had heard stories derived from Celtic tales of vessels of plenty, and that he had also heard of magical lances in Celtic lore. How far he intended to overlay this with Christian symbolism, and make the dish and lance the dish of the Last Supper and Longinus' spear from the crucifixion is impossible to tell: all we can say is that this was the interpretation offered by the writers who in the next half century completed his tale and provided the so-called *Elucidation* prologue to the work.

Chrétien is an exceptionally subtle writer, despite the apparent simplicity of his short eight-syllable verses and the clarity of so much of his descriptive writing. He is deeply learned in the learning of the great schools of Paris, and he uses the very elusiveness of his materials to lay allusion on allusion and to conjure up not only the magical and romantic but also deeply spiritual and moral meanings. The contrasts and tensions which drive his story along, particularly in *Perceval*, are at bottom the absolute contrast, that between Good and Evil, but on a variety of levels. His figures have multifarious guises: the Fisher King is at once the rich host, a distant cousin of the Celtic gods and a shadow of Christ, set in a trinity which comprises his father, the

[20] Bryant 67.

20 *The mysteries of the Holy Grail: angels bear the tapers, cloth and bleeding lance before Josephus, while Christ appears in the Grail to Galahad and the chosen knights. From the copy of the* Quest of the Holy Grail *written and illuminated by Pierart dou Tielt in 1351, perhaps at Tournai (Bibliothèque Nationale, Paris MS Arsenal 5218, f.88).*

holiest of men, as God, and the grail, the spiritual sustenance, as the Holy Ghost. *Perceval* sets out to explore the highest of themes, and it is a measure of Chrétien's success, despite the poem's unfinished state, that he created one of the most enduring of all spiritual images in the grail itself.

The other great achievement of the French romance-writers of the twelfth century was the creation of the earliest versions of the story of Tristan and Iseult. Chrétien, as we have seen, worked largely on material which he shaped in general outline and content, using details borrowed from Celtic tradition. With the story of Tristan and Iseult the reverse is true: the plot and events remain constant, deriving from Celtic and other, often exotic, material, while it is the details which tend to change for each new audience. We have already mentioned Marie de France's *The Honeysuckle*, and two of the troubadours mention Tristan as an ideal lover in the 1160s, while Chrétien's claim to have made a version of the legend supports the idea that it was already widely known. The earliest surviving fragments are of a poem by Thomas, who probably wrote at the Plantagenet court in England some time after 1150. A second Anglo-Norman version was produced by Béroul about 1190; meanwhile Eilhart von Oberge, working from a different French version translated the story into German some time after 1170.

The central theme of these romances, the love of Tristan for Iseult, wife of his uncle Mark, is found in outline, in Welsh literature and scholars have generally accepted that the original Tristan was Drust, son of the Pictish king Talorc who ruled in Scotland about 780, and that the legends were later relocated in Cornwall.[21] The so-called Tristan stone at Castledore refers to another character of similar name, and its only connection with the legend is that it may have suggested the new site of the stories: in Welsh legend, Essyllt's lover is always Tristan 'son of Tallwch' and the Cornish Drustanus' father is named in the inscription as Cunomorus. The shape of the legend was drawn by Welsh writers from Irish sources, adding the story of Diarmaid and Grainne to an episode about Drust which told how he rescued a foreign king from having to surrender his daughter as tribute by defeating a hero in single combat. This theme, similar to the story of Theseus in Greek myth, suggested the addition of other details from the Theseus legends: the half-bestial nature of his adversary (as with the Minotaur) and the use of the black and white sails as a signal of failure or success. Other incidents were drawn into the story from sources as far afield as India and Arabia, brought perhaps by travelling merchants; and merchants figure in the poem as the cause of Tristan's arrival in Cornwall from Brittany. In effect, the power of the central story has attracted all kinds of lesser folklore in which the same triangle of characters is repeated.

The story as given in the original version probably ran as follows. Tristan was the son of Rivalen and Blancheflor, the sister of King Mark of Cornwall. His father was slain in battle and his mother died in childbirth; hence his name, implying sorrow (*tristesse*). He came incognito to Mark's court, and soon distinguished himself by knightly feats, in particular by slaying the Irish champion Morholt, who came every seven years to demand a tribute of young men and girls from the Cornish king. Morholt's body was taken back to Ireland, where his niece, the Princess Iseult, removed a piece of Tristan's sword, swearing to use it to trace his slayer and exact vengeance. Tristan came to Ireland to search for a bride for King Mark and won Iseult by slaying a dragon, but he was overcome by the dragon's poison, and a seneschal falsely claimed to have achieved the exploit. As Iseult tended Tristan's wounds, she noticed the gap in the blade of his sword, but since only he could save her from the seneschal, refrained from killing him when he was unarmed. Tristan duly took her back to Cornwall as his uncle's bride, but on the voyage a magic philtre intended for her wedding night was given to the pair by mistake. Brangain, Iseult's faithful maid, took her place on her wedding night in King Mark's bed; and the lovers yielded to their passion, resorting to all kinds of trickery to deceive King Mark; when Mark, at last convinced of their guilt, made Iseult swear that she was faithful by the ordeal of holding a red-hot

21 Bromwich, ch. 2 n. 1 above, 329–333.

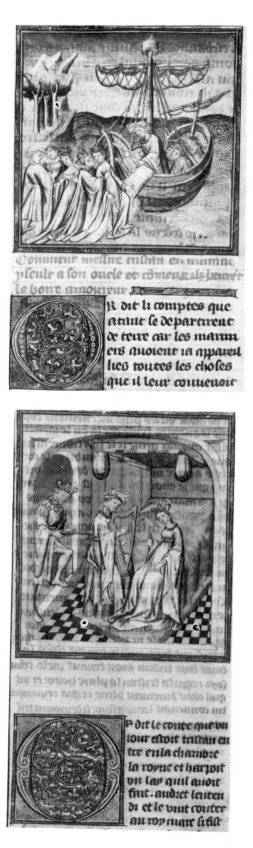

21 The adventures of Tristan, from a two-volume Tristan once in the library of Charles V of France. Iseult is prevented from slaying Tristan (top left); Tristan and Iseult leave Ireland (top right); Mark slays Tristan as he harps to Iseult (bottom right).

iron, she arranged for Tristan to disguise himself as a pilgrim. As she approached the place of the ordeal she stumbled into his arms, and altered the oath to swear that she had never been touched by any man save her husband and the pilgrim. She survived the ordeal unscathed, but Mark later banished the lovers. Hunting in the forest, he once came across them asleep, with a naked sword between them, which again persuaded him of their innocence. As a precaution, he banished Tristan, who crossed to Brittany and married Iseult of the White Hands, sister of Prince Kaherdin. However, he never consummated the marriage, and when this came to light, persuaded Kaherdin that he meant no insult and offered to show him the Irish Iseult. They travelled in disguise to Cornwall where Kaherdin fell in love with Brangain. They had to return to Brittany, where after a number of adventures, Tristan was wounded by a poisoned arrow. Sending for Iseult of Ireland to heal him, he instructed the messenger to hoist black sails if he returned without her, white sails if his quest was successful. Iseult of Brittany, jealous of the other Iseult, falsely told him that the sails were black; at which he died of grief, as did Iseult of Ireland on finding she had arrived too late.[22]

Eilhart and Béroul took this relatively sophisticated story, with its complex sequence of episodes, and did little more than retell it in their own way, making minor alterations but leaving the work of the tragedy of guilty love unchanged. Even though Tristan and Iseult stand in the same relation to Mark as the lover and lady in the stock situation of courtly love to the lord, neither poet takes a 'courtly' attitude towards them. Some of the episodes are of a primitive cruelty, as when Iseult is about to be burnt for adultery and a company of lepers suggest that a more fitting fate would be for her to be given to them as their whore. There are a few psychological elaborations, and the lovers' passion is neither praised nor blamed by either writer. Eilhart sees the love-potion as the one cause of their woe; once they have tasted 'the most unlucky drink', they are doomed. Béroul, on the other hand, apportions no moral blame but sees Mark's conduct towards the lovers in terms of strictly legal rights. Mark refuses Tristan the customary trial by battle and thenceforward is in the wrong, since Tristan is never legally proved guilty; and the episode of the ambiguous oath fits in with this legalistic attitude very well. In his version the love-potion only has effect for three years, but even when the enchantment ends, Tristan and Iseult continue to love each other. These two early versions of the legend are more realistic and down to earth than what followed, but the lovers lack fire and character: the mainspring of their actions is scarcely more than physical desire, however fierce or passionate.

Thomas's version, though perhaps the earliest in date of the

[22] Joseph Bédier's reconstruction of Thomas was translated by Hilaire Belloc, *Tristan and Iseult* (London 1913). Béroul's version was translated by Alan S. Fedrick, *The Romance of Tristan* (Harmondsworth 1970).

surviving poems, is much more sophisticated. The story is subordinated to the study of feeling, much in the manner of Chrétien's *Cligès*, and from physical realism we move into emotional realism. The crux is therefore the truth of Tristan and Iseult's love: the effect of the love-potion does not abate, as in Eilhart and Béroul, because it is not an external force but a symbol of an internal emotion and Tristan's marriage to the second Iseult becomes another of the tests of the lovers' fidelity. In similar vein, Thomas introduces the *Salle aux images* (hall of statues) to which Tristan retreats secretly to worship an image of Iseult of Cornwall, an idea which echoes the veneration accorded to their ladies by the troubadours. But there is none of the restraining *mezura* ('measure of all things') of the Provençal poets here, no holding back from the physical consummation of spiritual desire. But Thomas does not entirely achieve the glorification of love which he attempts, because he is too respectful of the original version. It was only his German translator, Gottfried von Strassburg, who realised the full possibility of the story.

Thomas does not set Tristan's story against an Arthurian background, for Mark is king of England. In Béroul and Eilhart, Arthur and his court appear and Mark is king of Cornwall. But we have seen that Arthur plays very little active part in the individual romances, either in the twelfth century or later. However, the next crucial development in Arthurian romance restored Arthur to his rightful place, by combining the individual stories into an epic cycle, framed by Arthur's career. Just as the evolution of the individual stories is obscure, so the transition from the romances of Chrétien de Troyes to the great sweep of the 'Vulgate cycle' is equally difficult to disentangle. It seems that the idea of extending a romance into a larger scale work was first conceived by Robert de Boron, a knight from Burgundy who was active for about two decades after 1190, just after Chrétien.[23] He began by taking the Grail story as told by Chrétien, and setting it in the context of Christian legend, notably the apocryphal gospels and similar fictitious accounts of Christ's life. The Grail becomes the cup used at the Last Supper, and the vessel in which Joseph of Arimathea caught the drops of Christ's blood after the crucifixion: it is the holiest of all holy relics. Joseph later set up the Grail table in memory of the Last Supper, and entrusted the Grail to his brother-in-law Bron, who carried it into the far west, to the *vaus d'Avaron* or vale of Avalon, by which Boron may have meant Glastonbury: the identification was certainly made very soon afterwards. With the Grail's transfer to the far west, the first part of Boron's cycle ends. The second part, entitled *Merlin*, links the history of the Grail with that of Arthur's court. Merlin, who knows the history of the Grail through his magical

[23] Fanni Bogdanow, *The Romance of the Grail* (Manchester & New York 1966), 2–4.

22 *A tournament between Meliadus and King Mark, from the thirteenth-century romance* Meliadus; *an Italian miniature of c.1367 (British Library, MS Additional 12228, ff.187v–188).*

powers, encourages Uther Pendragon, Arthur's father, to set up the Round Table on the model of the Grail Table; and the romance continues with the begetting of Arthur and his succession to the throne. Whether Robert de Boron completed the third part, telling of Perceval's achievement of the Grail and the downfall of the Round Table and Arthur's kingdom, is doubtful: just as Chrétien's last work was completed by other hands, so the prose romance known as the *Didot Perceval* may be the work of another writer taking up the threads of Robert de Boron's story, rather than a translation of Boron's 'lost' poem.[24] The end of the Grail adventure is followed by an account of Arthur's Roman wars and Mordred's treason, very much as in Geoffrey of Monmouth or Wace: there is no hint of Lancelot or Guinevere as actors in the final tragedy, and the last paragraphs tell how the news of Arthur's death reached Perceval and how Merlin withdrew from the world.

Although Robert de Boron apparently never completed his planned cycle, the concept of a series of linked romances which

[24]Tr. Dell Skeels, *The Romance of Perceval in Prose: A Translation of the E Manuscript of the Didot Perceval* (Seattle & London 1966).

would tell the whole story of the Grail and of Arthur was to inspire another unknown writer or writers to create an even vaster edifice, the so-called Vulgate Cycle, which became the most popular account of the Arthurian legend in the later middle ages. The new cycle is distinguished by the brilliant way in which it incorporates the love of Lancelot and Guinevere as a crucial element in Arthur's tragedy. What had until now been the tale of the rise and fall of a great ruler now became a deeply personal drama as well. In the Vulgate Cycle, the great symbols of the Grail and the Round Table are intertwined with the conflict between personal and public loyalties to create one of the masterpieces of medieval literature. For the modern reader, however, the cycle as a whole, printed in eight vast volumes,[25] is difficult to approach because of its sheer length. There are five sections or branches, beginning with a much enlarged account of the early history of the Grail based on Robert de Boron, which explains how the Grail leaves Britain after Joseph of Arimathea's death and is housed in a castle specially built for it in the 'terre foraine', called Corbenic. It is left at the end of the first romance in the guardianship of king Pelles, Lancelot's grandfather.

The story of Merlin forms the second section, taking the story down to the fourth year of Arthur's reign: and here the new version diverges sharply from that of Robert de Boron and his continuators, for Merlin is enchanted by his beloved, Nimue, and imprisoned under a rock. He vanishes from the romance at this point, and the next branch, recounting the story of Lancelot from his arrival at court, follows. This, the *Prose Lancelot*, is a huge assembly of adventures, for the interest is not confined to Lancelot alone. As in Chrétien de Troyes' *Perceval*, where Perceval and Gawain alternately share the limelight, the author of *Prose Lancelot* interweaves the adventures of a number of different knights. This device is carried to extremes: a knight may disappear from view for three hundred pages at a time, and the author expects us to know exactly who he is when he finally re-emerges. But the main theme, of Lancelot's career, is carefully sustained and worked into the pattern of Arthur's life. At Lancelot's knighting, Arthur forgets to gird on his sword; it is Guinevere who does this, thus creating a formal feudal bond between them, which is soon reinforced by that of love. And Lancelot and Guinevere become lovers on the night when Arthur sleeps with the enchantress Camille. Arthur then repudiates Guinevere in favour of the false Guinevere, a magical creation of Morgan le Fay, thus further weakening his claim to her loyalty.

Two techniques which Chrétien and Robert de Boron had begun to use experimentally are brought to fruition by the writer of the Vulgate Cycle: the interweaving of adventures which has just been described and the introduction of events which

[25] Ed. H. O. Sommer, *The Vulgate Version of the Arthurian Romances* (Washington 1908–16, rpd New York 1979).

foreshadow future developments, which the characters of the romance fail to recognise but which are evident to the reader. In the section leading up to the consummation of Lancelot's love for Guinevere, Lancelot's adventures are interwoven with those of Galehaut, who plays an important part in bringing the pair together. The abduction of Guinevere (much as described in Chrétien de Troyes' *Lancelot*) follows, considerably expanded and given a series of sequels, in which Lancelot is alternately sought by and seeking various other knights of the Round Table as they wander in pursuit of adventures. In the course of these, Lancelot is seduced by the daughter of king Pelles, keeper of the Grail, who has a son by him, named Galahad; and the action begins to foreshadow the Grail quest, making it clear through marvels that Lancelot will soon be supplanted as the best knight of the world because of his unchastity.

The events of *The Quest for the Holy Grail* show that the Round Table and the Grail are inextricably linked, and that the achievement of the Grail quest is to be the spiritual apogee of Arthur's rule. Once again, we can only admire the consummate skill of the unknown author in the creation of an overall structure using the individual existing romances. The Grail appears at Arthur's court at Pentecost, on the same day that Galahad arrives there and passes the test of the Siege Perilous, the seat at the Round Table which slays anyone who dares to sit on it unless he is destined to occupy it. But the events of the *Quest* are greatly altered from the Grail adventures in *Didot Perceval* and Chrétien, and concentrate as much on the failure of the once invincible heroes of Arthur's court, Lancelot and Gawain, as on the success of Galahad, Perceval and Bors. The Grail is entirely spiritual in meaning, and there is a strong ascetic feeling behind the attitude towards it which suggests that a monk of the Cistercian order may have shaped this part of the cycle. A new ideal has supplanted the secular chivalry in which the Lady of the Lake lovingly instructed Lancelot, and the knights are now judged by how nearly they approach sainthood. Above all, a new hero has replaced Perceval as the central figure. Perceval was a sinner in the earlier romances, and although he becomes a virgin in the *Quest*, sufficient remains of his original character for him to appear as only an approximation to the ideal. Galahad, who supplants him, is almost entirely free from sin, a perfect if somewhat unappealing figure in his cold purity.

The adventures draw heavily on Biblical tradition and symbolism; the ship which takes the knights to the accomplishment of the Quest is elaborately proclaimed to be an allegory of the Church, and there are echoes of the Messiah in the figure of Galahad. Each step in the progress of the knights is expounded by hermits, with whom they hold long conversations, and the doctrines they teach correspond closely to the ideals of the Cistercians. This radical rethinking of the idea of the Grail from the hints and half-thought-out ideas of earlier writers reaches its culmination in the scene at the Castle of Corbenic. What were once, long ago, Celtic mysteries are now translated into religious ectasy. The knights achieve, not the solution of a riddle or the breaking of a spell, but divine grace itself through the Grail as fount of the Eucharist; and the final scenes of the *Quest* achieve an irresistible power as a vision of man's aspiration towards a higher existence, that existence into which Galahad and Perceval pass, leaving Bors to ride homeward and bear the message of their success to Arthur's disheartened and depleted Court.

23 The knights swear to pursue the quest for the Grail, from an Italian manuscript of the Quest, c.1380–1400 (Bibliothèque Nationale, Paris, MS Fr.343, f.7).

24 *The magic sword Excalibur is returned to the lake by Bedivere; a hand rises from the water and seizes it. Arthur, mortally wounded, awaits Bedivere's return. From a northern French manuscript of c.1316 (British Library, MS Additional 10294, f.94).*

Just as the Grail has been given a high moral meaning, so the last part of the story, the *Death of King Arthur*, is changed from an illustration of the working of Fate, the fall of a great king in his hour of triumph, to the decay of a court where spiritual values are absent. The ideals of secular chivalry, however noble, are not enough. Lancelot, who has achieved a partial vision of the Grail in token of his sincere repentence, slides back into his old sin. In episodes which echo the story of Tristan and Iseult, Lancelot rescues Guinevere from the punishment that awaits her adultery, but in doing so breaks the bonds that unite the Round Table, and allows the self-seeking Mordred to rise to power: for the first time Mordred appears as Arthur's incestuous son and thus the king's doom is brought about by his own sin. The chain of causes seems endless and inevitable; only the spiritual way offers an escape from the toils of the flesh, and this is no longer open. Arthur, mortally wounded, is not carried to Avalon, but to burial at the Noire Chapelle; and here the remnant of his knights foregather to atone for the past in a religious life; among them is Lancelot, with whose death the tale ends.

We have spoken up to now of the 'author' of the Vulgate Cycle as though this huge work came from one pen. It seems likely that one man may have conceived the whole outline of the Cycle, but that it was executed by others, particularly the *Quest* and the *Death of King Arthur*. Only a single outline could have achieved the remarkable working together of so many conflicting themes and such diverse material into a unified whole. If Lancelot's pre-eminence is the most striking new feature, Arthur is nonetheless the figure who draws the whole work together. Here for the first time the Round Table acquires a definite purpose as a secular path to virtue in a chaotic world, a means of righting wrongs and combating evil. This sense of mission gives an overall purpose to the adventures which is lacking in the Arthurian world created by Chrétien. For much of the time, Arthur has no function in the story except as the central figure of the Round Table, and only in the opening and closing sections does he become a clear-cut figure. But his role is that of a great tragic figure rather than of a paragon of chivalry, and it is this which may have led the writer to elaborate the figure of Lancelot. For each character is in some measure a representative of a particular moral function: Arthur stands for royalty and leadership; Lancelot, human achievement through chivalry; Gawain, human nature which has not come to terms with chivalry. The three Grail knights correspond to varying degrees of spiritual perfection. Galahad attains to pure perfection; Perceval achieves redemption through innocent faith; while Bors reaches it through good works by which he expiates his one venial sin.

Yet had the Arthurian cycle been merely symbolic, it would never have reached such a wide audience. For the writers succeeded in making their heroes intensely human figures within their higher role. Lancelot's previously rather dutiful love for Guinevere becomes more real and passionate: the scene where Guinevere and Lancelot exchange their first kiss, encouraged by Galehaut and the lady of Malehaut, so impressed Dante that he made it the cause of Francesca da Rimini's downfall in the *Inferno*:

> One day we read for pastime how in thrall
> Lord Lancelot lay to love, who loved the Queen;
> We were alone – we thought no harm at all.
>
> As we read on, our eyes met now and then,
> And to our cheeks the changing colour started,
> But just one moment overcame us – when
>
> We read of the smile, desired of lips long-thwarted,
> Such smile, by such a lover kissed away,
> He that may be never more from me be parted
>
> Trembling all over, kissed my mouth. I say
> The book was Galleot, Galleot the complying
> Ribald who wrote; we read no more that day.

Among the other characters, Gawain's faults are not those of unrelieved wickedness, but of unrestrained passion; he cannot see the higher ideals, blinded by his immediate desires and hatreds. Even the passionless Galahad has a scene of great tenderness with his father Lancelot towards the end of the Grail quest.

It is this variety of qualities which raised the Vulgate Cycle above all other attempts at Arthurian romance on a large scale, and made the prose *Lancelot* immensely popular – over a hundred manuscripts survive. Fragments of a French reworking, the *Roman du Graal*, survive; this cut out the bulk of the 'adventures' in the prose *Lancelot*, and made the theme of Arthur and his kingdom more prominent. This version had a considerable influence on Sir Thomas Malory, as we shall see.

But although the Vulgate Cycle attempted to encompass the whole history of Arthur and the Grail, it was by no means the only Arthurian romance of its day. Stories in both prose and verse continued to flourish down to the fifteenth century. Of these individual romances, the *Perlesvaus*,[26] written about 1200–1210, is the most striking. It probably precedes the *Quest of the Holy Grail*, and develops the story of Perceval (Perlesvaus) in a very different way. By a series of allusions to the New Testament, it shows Perceval as a kind of knightly *alter ego* of Christ, and insists on the duty of knights to impose the New Law – as the author calls Christianity, in contrast to the Old Law of the Jews – by force if necessary. It is at once a reflection of the ethos of the crusades, which were at times represented as missions to bring the heathen into Christianity, and a call to knights to play their part in defending Christian society from the ever-present evil that besets it. Even the unresolved ending can be seen as a parallel to Christ's withdrawal from earthly life after the Resurrection. But *Perlesvaus* is far from being a sermon in disguise: it is also an immensely vivid work, where the constant background of threatening evil and darkness throws the deeds of Arthur and his knights into brilliant relief. There is a strong feeling of supernatural forces at work and mysterious destinies being accomplished. The romance begins with the story of how one of Arthur's squires commits sacrilege in a dream, but receives a real and mortal wound: the golden candlestick he had stolen from the altar in his dream is found by his bed as he awakes, tells his dream, and dies.[27] Again, in the closing pages of the story, Perceval meets his deadly enemy, the Black Hermit. They fight, watched by his followers: Perceval unhorses him: 'and when the men looking on saw him fall, they threw open the cover of a great pit in the middle of the hall, and staightway there rose from it the greatest stench ever smelt: and they took their lord and flung him into this chasm of filth.' Using St John's vision of Satan cast into the pit, the author of the *Perlesvaus* has created his own

[26] Translated by Nigel Bryant as 'The High Book of the Grail, Cambridge and Totowa 1978. The introduction is a useful summary of recent work on the romance.

[27] This strange episode is found in Latin in John of Glastonbury's *Chronicle* and independently in a number of other manuscripts, raising the possibility that a Latin original may lie behind the *Perlesvaus* or part of it.

78

25 *The adventures of Galahad, from the* Prose Tristan. *Galahad is an unexpected figure in the Tristan story, and his appearance shows how the romance gathered in all kinds of unlikely material. The miniatures show his knighting, the winning of his sword and a tournament. The manuscript, dated 1463, was written for the mother of Jacques d'Armagnac, duc de Nemours, a famous collector of manuscripts (Bibliothèque Nationale, MS Fr.99, f.561).*

26 *The single miniature from an unusual late manuscript (c. 1470) of the* Prose Tristan, *in which the original ending is restored. The artist has portrayed both the beginning and the end of the story in the miniature: in the foreground, Tristan and Iseult drink the love-potion, while in the background a ship with black sails bears their bodies away from Brittany. (Bibliothèque Nationale, MS Fr.103, f.1).*

equally powerful imagery; and it may well be that the romance was inspired by the apocalyptic views of Joachim of Fiore,[28] who saw history as a progression from the age of the Father or of the Law (the Old Law of *Perlesvaus*) to that of the Son or of the Gospel (the New Law of *Perlesvaus*) and finally to the Age of the Spirit, to which the end of the romance points the way. The unknown writer of *Perlesvaus* is highly skilled in creating a story which moves forward by recurrent themes, one event foreshadowing another; this is very much the technique of Joachim of Fiore's biblical commentary. Of all Arthurian romances, it is the most striking, moving within its own mysterious yet coherent world.

Coherence is not the strong point of the other great French prose romance outside the Vulgate Cycle, the *Prose Tristan*.[29] If the *Perlesvaus* stands at the religious extreme of Arthurian romance, the *Prose Tristan* is in its ways its secular opposite. It is a vast elaboration on the nucleus provided by the story of Tristan and Iseult; introduced by a long section on Tristan's ancestry, it includes an even longer passage of Arthurian adventures while Tristan is at Arthur's court. Among its original features are the introduction of Palamedes as Iseult's unrequited lover, and of the cynical Dinadan, whose quick wit excuses his cowardice, a kind of court jester to the ideal of chivalry. The ending, too, is altered: Mark slays Tristan with a poisoned spear as he sits harping to Iseult, and Iseult dies in Tristan's last embrace. There is no compelling and controlling theme and the technique of interweaving adventures, successfully used in the Vulgate Cycle, here meanders aimlessly: 'endless descriptions of jousts and tournaments, of knight-errant adventures and of love-affairs conducted in the fashion of a highly organized society.'[30] Yet this vast and rambling work achieved wide popularity, almost comparable to that of the *Lancelot*, and fixed the story of Tristan and Iseult for centuries: only in the early nineteenth century were the earlier poetic versions rediscovered.

Once the central framework of Arthurian romance was firmly established, later writers used it once more as Chrétien had done, as the starting point for independent stories to which it was no more than a backdrop. But few if any of these offerings have the power and consistency of his work, tending rather to immense repetitive length, in the manner of the *Prose Tristan*. Medieval audiences read such compilations with delight; works with a coherent theme and structure were not necessarily so admired as these formless tracts of knightly exploits. A few of the late romances might appeal to a modern audience, though Renart de Beaujeu's *Le Bel Inconnu*, a tale similar to Malory's *Tale of Gareth*, which has a simple dignity, is much less typical than the 30,000 verses of *Claris and Laris* or Jean Froissart's *Meliador*.

[28] See Norman Cohn, *The Pursuit of the Millenium* 3rd edn London 1970) 108–110.
[29] The first two-thirds have been edited by Renée Curtis (3 vols, Woodbridge & Dover, N. H. 1985); there is no translation.
[30] J. D. Bruce, *The Evolution of Arthurian Romance*, (Göttingen 913) i.484.

One of the stranger romances deserves a brief mention, as it is the only work to present Arthur as a knight-errant hero. *Le Chevalier du Papegau (The Knight of the Parrot)* offers the entertaining spectacle of the noble king led on his adventures by a talking parrot in a gilded cage. The usual gamut of fantastic creatures and happenings are encountered and duly overcome,

28 A woodcut from Dupré's printed editi Lancelot (1488) shou (right) Galahad arriv claim the Siege Perilo

27 A late fourteenth century painted tray from Italy depicting the great heroes of the Trojan stories and Arthurian romance adoring the goddess Venus, with Samson thrown in for good measure. Tristram (in the peaked hat) and, next to him, Lancelot are the two Arthurian lovers. (Musée du Louvre, Paris).

A Beille de la pen
thecouste que les
compaignons de
la table ronde fu
rent Benus a Ka
malot & ilz eurêt
ouy le service. Ai
si que on Bouloit
mettre les tables a heure de nonne: entra en la
court une moult belle damoiselle a cheual q̃
moult fort sestoit hastee/& bien y apparoit/car
son palefroy estoit tout tressuant. Elle desce̊

dit: puis mõta eη la sale ou estoit le roy/& tous
les compaignons. Si Bint deuãt le roy & le
salua/& le roy lui rendit son salut moult cour
toisemêt. Sire pour dieu fist elle dictes moy
se Lancelot est ceans. Ouy certes damoiselle
Beez le la. Si lui monstra/& elle ala inconti
nent celle part ou il estoit/ puis lui dist. Lan
celot ie Bous dy de par le roy pesles que Bous
Biengniez auec moy iusques a celle forest. Et
il lui demanda a qui elle estoit. Je suis fist el
le a celui de qui ie Bous parle. Et quel besoig
dist il auez Bous de moy/ce Berrez Bous bien

including such marvels as a Fish-Knight, whose armour, shield and horse are all part of his body and bleed when cut.

Even though few new Arthurian romances were written after 1400, they enjoyed a considerable vogue well into the sixteenth century, until the classical and Italian tradition came to dominate French literature. At the end of the fifteenth century, the French royal library contained more than thirty romances in a total collection of twelve hundred manuscripts. Huge illuminated versions were copied for Jacques d'Armagnac in the mid-fifteenth century and new compilations made for the Burgundian court. With the advent of printing, almost all the important romances appeared as books, and many were reprinted frequently until the mid-sixteenth century. But because these late romances, and even the Vulgate Cycle itself, were formidable in extent, once the fashion for them died away, revival was vastly more difficult in France than elsewhere, particularly since it was in France that the classical tradition took the deepest hold on literature. Rabelais, sounding the death-knell of so much medieval tradition, was not so wide of the mark in terms of their destiny in later French literature when he described the fate of the knights in Hell:

Lancelot of the lake was a flayer of dead horses. All the Knights of the round Table were poore day-labourers, employed to rowe over the rivers of Cocytus, Phlegeton, Styx, Acheron and Lethe, when my Lords, the devils had a minde to recreate themselves upon the water, as in the like occasion are hired the boatmen at Lions, the gondeleers of Venice, and oares at London; but with this difference, that these poor knights have only for their fare a bob or flirt on the nose, and in the evening a morsel of course mouldie bread.[31]

[31] *The Works of Mr Francis Rabelais* (London 1954), 297 = Bk ii, ch. xxx.

Chapter 4

The Arthurian Legend in Germany: Tristan and Parzival

When writers elsewhere in Europe turned their attention to the Arthurian legends, they accepted the great French poems and the Vulgate Cycle as a kind of standard version, and translated or adapted from the French when creating their own works. Their contributions lay less in the plot than in the interpretation of character, motive and moral, and here there were very considerable changes. Medieval writers did not value originality for its own sake as we do today, and the best of these 'translations' and 'adaptations' are masterpieces in their own right. It was a pattern already established by the German *minnesänger*, who had derived their ideas about courtly love from the French troubadours; once again, France was the arbiter of fashion.

So in the German romances the heroes and heroines and the main outlines of the plot are recognisably the same, but the details are often changed, the style is very different, and the ethos behind the poem may be totally at odds with that of the original. With the major poets, there is a considerable extension and development of the French original. In stylistic terms, the German poets tend – with one notable exception – to lay less stress on the virtue of *mesura*, the restrained classical style perfected by Chrétien de Troyes, and prefer a much more exuberant, almost baroque approach, revelling in the marvels and enthusing over their heroes' deeds.

Eilhart von Oberge's *Tristan* of about 1170, which has already been briefly discussed, is the earliest of the German poems to survive. He seems to have preserved the original story faithfully, with occasional alterations to the details, but without indulging in much elaboration on the lovers' feelings. He blames the plight of the lovers on the love-potion, and treats the tale as an adventure rather than a study of emotions. The poem's chief interest lies in its preservation of the bare outline of the first *Tristan*.

Ulrich von Zatzikhoven's *Lanzelet*[1] is likewise chiefly of interest for the story it preserves, the first account of Lancelot's youthful adventures. Written early in the thirteenth century, it is based on an Anglo-Norman romance brought to south Germany by Hugo de Morville, one of the hostages sent to Mainz in February 1194 as sureties for the fulfilment of the terms on

[1] Tr. Kenneth G. T. Webster and edited by Roger Sherman Loomis, (Records of Civilisation, Sources and Studies XLVII) (New York 1951).

which Richard I had been ransomed, after his capture on his way back from crusade in 1192. The romance may even have been written for a member of the Morville family. In Zatzikhoven's rather pedestrian retelling, Lancelot's adventures have nothing to do with Guinevere. He is brought up by a fairy, the Lady of the Lake of later romance, and undergoes a series of adventures before he can discover his name and parentage. He has a series of love-affairs, and finally marries Yblis, whose father he has killed in battle, though he appears to be married already to at least one other of his paramours. There is much emphasis on tournaments; the one adventure which involves Guinevere, her rescue from king Valerin, is accomplished largely by the enlisting of the wizard Malduc rather than by Lancelot's prowess. Themes which reappear in later romances include those of the 'fier baiser', where the hero kisses a dragon or snake and thus restores a princess to her own shape, and of the mantle which will only fit a faithful wife. The whole story seems to represent an Arthurian romance at an early stage of development, with a mixture of pure folklore and simple chivalric activities, and shows what the stories would have amounted to without writers of the stature of Chrétien de Troyes to shape them into masterpieces.

29 The remarkable thirteenth-century murals from Schloss Rodeneck in South Tirol, portraying the story of Iwein. *Discovered in 1972, these are among the finest surviving medieval depictions of Arthurian romance. They were painted within a few years of the composition of the poem, by an unknown master whose patron was probably the local bishop. The scenes depicted are:*

Above *Yvain meets the wild herdsman and pours water on the stone at the magic fountain, raising a storm.*
Below *Yvain fights Aschelon (Esclados) lord of the fountain.*
Right *Laudine mourns Aschelon, while Yvain observes her from his hiding place and falls in love with her.*

(Soprintendenza dei Monumenti, Bolzano)

Hartmann von Aue, too, simplifies the elaborate monologues of his source, Chrétien de Troyes, but enriches his material in other directions. He came from the borders of southern Germany and Switzerland, and probably wrote his *Erek* in the last decade of the twelfth century, some thirty years after Chrétien. It is the splendours of knighthood's estate which he prefers to Chrétien's poetic economy of detail, and he expands the text with long descriptions of the marvels of his hero's equipment or the luxuries of a great feast. The result is, curiously, simpler: Chrétien's subtle characterisation disappears under the elaborate trappings, and is replaced by an insistence on the high nature of knighthood and the glamour of its world. Hartmann followed this some years later with *Iwein*, a treatment in similar vein of *Yvain*; the details are perhaps less lavish, but more acutely observed, as though the composition of two romances of his own had in the meanwhile sharpened his vision. What we can admire is his technical skill, which was of a very high order. Hartmann's verse dazzled his would-be imitators; relying on poetic fireworks, they failed to see that his poems had a strong central plot.

If the German writers took over their matter relatively unchanged, the greatest of them infused into the romances a very different ideal of knightly behaviour from that presented by Chrétien. Wolfram von Eschenbach and Gottfried von Strassburg, in very different ways, share a spiritual approach to their subject which only the French *Quest for the Holy Grail* can begin to rival. Wolfram combines the highest philosophical themes and adventures in the manner of Chrétien with consummate skill in his *Parzival*,[2] written in the first decade of the thirteenth century. Within the framework of romance, he portrays a world in which chivalry becomes an ideal fulfilling all man's highest aspirations, crowned by its own religious order, the knights of the Grail, and which is nonetheless real and actual.

Wolfram was a Bavarian knight, from the village known as Wolframseschenbach. His family were *ministeriales*, knights in imperial service who remained officially serfs. Of his life we know only what he himself tells us: that he was poor – 'at home the mice rarely have enough to eat' – that he had various misfortunes in love (though he implies that he was happily married in the end), that he was widely travelled in Germany. He came at some point in his journeyings to the court of Hermann of Thuringia, where other great poets such as Walther von der Vogelweide had been honoured guests. His view of courtly life is not entirely approving; he has some sharp words for the disorderliness of Hermann's halls, where every insolent fellow who pretended to sing or make verses gained easy entrance. Addressing Hermann himself he says 'you would need someone like Keye [who appears in the romances as an uncompromising

2 Tr. A. T. Hatto (Harmondsworth 1980). See also D. Blamires, *Characterization and Individuality in Wolfram's Parzival* (Cambridge 1966); H. Sacker, *An Introduction to Wolfram's Parzival* (Cambridge 1963); M. F. Richey, *Studies of Wolfram von Eschenbach* (London 1957).

and forthright seneschal] to deal with an unruly mob like that'. And in another passage he attacks the morals that all too often lay behind the outward show of courtly love, saying that he would not care to take his wife to King Arthur's court, where everyone's thoughts were always occupied with love. 'Someone or other would have whispered to her that her charms were stabbing him and blotting out his joy, and that if she would end his pangs he would serve her before and after. Rather than that I would hurry away with her.'[3] Wolfram's wry humour marks him as a man with a down-to-earth view of life, at first blush an unlikely guide through the exotic forests and spellbound adventures of his chosen subject.

Wolfram gives the impression of being a fiercely independent character, beholden to no-one. We have little idea where his ideas were formed, and even whether he could write: he declares that he knows no letters, but as so often with this complex author, we cannot be sure what he really means. His great strength is precisely this originality and willingness to challenge accepted views: in another of his romances, *Willehalm*, he comes near to making a plea for religious toleration, a highly unusual attitude at a time when the Teutonic knights claimed that the heathen should be converted by force. Wolfram's learning is not that of the schools but, as far as we can tell, of a man who has made his own way in the world. In this he is nearer to another knight turned author, Sir Thomas Malory, than to his predecessors in the world of Arthurian romance.

Wolfram's central theme, Parzival's courtly and spiritual progress, is, the same as that in Chrétien, but the German poet both intensifies and alters the nature of this progress. The old folk-tale of the prince brought up in ignorance, the 'pure fool' of noble birth, was merely another inherited *motif* from the Celtic past which served as a starting point for the romance. Wolfram turns this into a deeply-felt heroic example, yet does not preach or point a conscious moral. Indeed, his portrait of Parzival's innocence is delightful and natural. The boy, kept from the ways of knighthood that have caused his father's death, is brought up by his mother in the depths of the forest with no knowledge of the glittering world that is his birthright, with no knowledge of even the simplest ideas about life: he has learnt who God is, and that 'his steadfast love never yet failed the world.' When he meets a knight who has fled deep into the forest to escape his pursuers, he can only imagine that this superior being is God: and though he is duly disillusioned, his natural instinct for knighthood has been aroused.

Wolfram makes great play with the idea that nobility is an inherited trait. Parzival's nature predisposes him to knighthood. From his father's family he inherits love as his destiny: from his

[3] Tr. A. T. Hatto (n. 2 above) 116.

89

30 *A sequence of four pages of illustrations from a German manuscript of* Parzival, *added about 1250 to an earlier text; they are possibly the remains of a much longer set of picture-pages. In the first, Arthur and king Gramoflanz are seen in their tents: they approach each other in the middle scene, and Gramoflanz is reconciled to Gawain's bride Orgeluse. The second page shows Gramoflanz's marriage to Gawain's sister. The story then turns to Parzival: he fights his half-brother Feirefiz, but in the bottom scene his sword breaks before he can kill Feirefiz. There follows, on the third page, Parzival and Feirefiz arriving at Arthur's court, and Kundry's announcement of Parzival's election as king of the Grail castle. Parzival, Kundry and Feirefiz ride to the Grail castle, where a feast is held; Parzival and Condwiramurs ride to meet each other, and in the last scene Feirefiz is baptised in the presence of Repanse de Schoye, his beloved. (Bayerische Stadtbibliothek, Munich, MS CGM 19, ff.49–50v).*

mother's, the service of the Grail. This idea of a place in life, at once fore-ordained and inherited, is at the root of Wolfram's concept of society, which he sees as a series of orders crowned by knighthood. Man should not question his appointed lot, even if it be a less honourable one than knighthood.

So Parzival sets out, dressed in fool's clothing and with the briefest of advice from his mother. She hopes that his attire will

draw mockery upon him and send him back to her; and he has misunderstood her advice. This provides the matter of his first adventures, and the wrongs he unwittingly inflicts will have to be atoned for later, including the killing of Ither, a knight who has done him little harm, but whose splendid armour he covets. It is not until he reaches the castle of Gurnemanz that he finds a mentor who is prepared to educate him in matters of chivalry. His fool's attire, which he still wears beneath the real armour, is taken from him, and with it his foolish ways. Gurnemanz instructs him in courtesy and, more important, in the ethics behind courtesy. 'Never lose your sense of shame' is his first precept, and the second to show compassion to those who suffer. Parzival remembers, but does not understand: he has learnt the outward forms but not the inner meaning.

His second series of exploits starts auspiciously. He wins the heart of Condwiramurs, and marries her. The contrast with Chrétien is sharp. Perceval and Blancheflor are deeply in love but their ties are only casual. Here Parzival and Condwiramurs are bound by the ideal love to which the concept of *Minne* or love-devotion aspires, the conjugal love of marriage and passionate physical love. When Condwiramurs comes to Parzival's room at dead of night to pour out her troubles to him, they do not even kiss; given that such nocturnal adventures have only one ending in every other romance, it is a remarkable scene. And when they marry, their love is so ethereal, 'they so shared togetherness', that Parzival does not think of making love to her for three nights after the wedding. The strength and joy of their earthly love shines clearly through the beautiful scene when Parzival, now at the end of his adventures, comes to meet his wife at the edge of the lands of Munsalvaesche, the Grail castle, in the grey light of dawn, and finds her asleep with their twin sons. The seneschal wakes the queen. Clad only in her shift, and a sheet hastily flung round her, with one impetuous movement she is in Parzival's arms. Parzival embraces her; their children wake, and he stoops to kiss them too. The old seneschal and the attendant ladies discreetly retire with the children, and leave the pair alone to prolong the night until the sun stands high in the heavens.

In this ideal marriage Parzival fulfils one half of his nature, the steadfastness in love inherited from his father. Most heroes of romance win their ladies only at the end of the tale. Even apparent exceptions such as Erec and Yvain, do not finally secure their beloved's affection until their adventures are over, and their deeds are always carried out with the idea of gaining favour in their lady's eyes. To Parzival, Condwiramurs is both the lady of his love-service and his sustaining hope in his adventures. At one moment, like Chrétien's hero, we find him sunk in ecstasy over three drops of blood in the snow, which remind him of the complexion of his beloved. If we remember that she is also his wife, the difference between Chrétien and Wolfram is evident. The idea for this relationship may well be evolved from Chrétien's married heroes, yet it is transformed by Wolfram's complete acceptance of the situation. Chrétien cannot quite believe that knighthood and marriage are compatible; for Wolfram they are the most natural companions in the world. Even Gawan, whose adventures occupy about half the romance, and whose deeds and character are much closer to his French counterpart, ends by marrying the proud Orgeluse. Orgeluse is in the French romance an irrational, scornful figure; and it would seem difficult for even Wolfram to make her a convincing character. Yet she becomes entirely human in his hands; her pride and scorn are partly the result of the loss of her lover, partly a test by which she will find the hero who can revenge her on her lover's killer.

Parzival's other inheritance takes us into the moral and religious spheres which are notably absent from Chrétien's unfinished poem. After a time, Parzival asks Condwiramurs to let him go in search of his mother; 'loving him truly, she could not disagree', and he sets out on a quest which, though he does not know it, is to lead not to his mother, but to his fulfilment of his part as guardian of the Grail. It is a task for which he is not yet ready: for though he comes to Munsalvaesche, the Grail castle, he heeds only Gurnemanz's warning that curiosity is rude, and does not ask the crucial question on seeing the Grail borne in procession, and the agony of the Grail-king, Anfortas. (It is noteworthy that Wolfram has his own ideas about the Grail, which he presents as a stone of strange powers which fell from heaven during the struggle between Lucifer and the angels, and which has the power to attract the highest and best in men.) The offence of the Grail-king has been to pursue an illicit earthly love, and he now lies wounded between the thighs in punishment, until such time as an unknown knight shall come and ask him: 'Sire, what ails thee?' Parzival observes the outward forms of courtesy but forgets its inward essence, humility and compassion: he fails to ask the question, and next morning awakes in a desolate castle – which had shone with all the show of a splendid feast on the previous night – to ride away in a dark and lonely dawn, with only the curses of the gatekeeper to speed him on his way. As if to show that ordinary men cannot judge between inward and outward courtesy, Parzival rides on to his greatest triumph yet at Arthur's court, only to have it shattered by the arrival of Cundrie, the hideous messenger from the Grail castle, who roundly curses him for his 'falseness', both to his nature and to his destiny.

However, Parzival can only ask the question when he is spiritually ready to do so: and his reactions to Cundrie's message show that he is far from such a state of mind or spirit. In the grip of black despair, he curses God for not rewarding his faithful service, and departs in search of the Grail again. He is now farther than ever from it, seeking it despite God; the lesson he has to learn is not only compassion and humility, but penitence and the real nature of man's relationship to God. He sees the latter only in feudal terms as a contract by which man's service earns God's favour. It is not until he comes, after long wanderings, to his uncle, Anfortas' hermit brother Trevrizent, that the way begins to clear. In Chrétien's version, Perceval is quickly brought to penitence, and goes on his way with no more than a brief lesson and prescribed penance.

Wolfram makes this scene the crux of his hero's development. The pilgrims who reproach him for bearing arms on Good Friday bring him out of the heedless, timeless mood in which he declares that 'I used to serve one named "God" till it pleased Him to ordain such vile shame for me'.[4] Though he gives his horse its head so that God may lead him to Trevrizent, he still defies and challenges: 'if this is his helpful day, let Him help, if help He

4 Tr. A. T. Hatto (n. 2 above) 229.

93

can!', and he only admits to his state of mind gradually, under Trevrizent's patient questioning. As his story unfolds, so does the seriousness of his offences appear: the killing of Ither, which he had dismisssed as something done while 'I was still a fool', proves to be the murder of a kinsman; and his equally thoughtless desertion of his mother has caused her death from sorrow. Finally, his failure to ask the redeeming question when he was the chosen knight to do this has condemned his uncle – for such Anfortas proves to be – to continued years of pain. Parzival now sees that though he has indeed been a skilful and valiant knight, his own sins are so great that he has no claim on God; the way lies not through deeds alone, but also through belief. 'God himself is loyalty', and cannot be disloyal, which had been the burden of Parzival's complaint against him. The spiritual world cannot be conquered by earthly virtues and services. He departs, chastened; the seeds of penitence and redemption are sown.

When 'the story comes to its rightful theme' again, Parzival and Gawan fight a duel as strangers, in which Parzival is victor, though he recognises Gawan before they have done each other serious injury. A similar combat ensues with Parzival's half-brother Feirefiz, in which the combatants are equally matched; again, they recognise each other in time. In the meanwhile, he has also fought and overcome a mutual enemy of his and Gawan's, Gramoflanz. Each of these battles at this stage of Parzival's spiritual progress must represent more than another episode in the romance, or they would reduce Parzival to the level of a mere knight-errant like Gawan again. But in the wider symbolism of the poem, Gawan represents earthly chivalry, and Gramoflanz pride; both earthly chivalry and pride must be overcome. And Feirefiz, Parzival's pagan half-brother from his father's marriage to the heathen Belakane, is the archetype of natural goodness; despite his strange black and white striped skin, he is as courteous as any of the knights of the Round Table, and as virtuous as any Christian. It is Feirefiz who is the one knight chosen by Parzival to go with him on his journey to claim the kingship of the Grail.

For Parzival's trials are now at an end; and on the day of Feirefiz's admission to the Round Table, a day of 'sweet pure clarity', the messenger from the Grail castle returns, to announce that he has been named as King of the Grail in letters which have appeared on the magical stone itself. He rides to Munsalvaesche; the compassionate question is asked, Anfortas healed. The story moves swiftly to its end, telling how Condwiramurs rejoins Parzival, how Feirefiz is converted and married to the bearer of the Grail, Repanse de Schoye, and how Loherangrin succeeds his father. The two ways are reconciled: earthly and spiritual chivalry move in harmony.

31 Wolfram preaches tolerance towards the Jews: a miniature from his romance Willehalm *which underlines his remarkably humane attitudes. (Bayerische Staatsbibliothek, Munich, MS CGM 193, III, f.iv).*

Wolfram's Parzival is at once the greatest and most human figure in the romances; in him the highest ideal of chivalry is shot through with a warmth and natural ease which owes little to convention. By contrast, Gawan, the secondary hero of the story, is a formal figure, moving within a limited world, but perfect within his own established limits. The idea of *orden*, levels of achievement according to each man's power, enables Wolfram to transcend the old ideals of knighthood, and to set a higher goal without contradicting these cherished images. For this is his real insight: that the chivalry underlying the stories is not merely a matter of rules of good behaviour, of a code of courtly love, or even of religious service. Its strength lies in its appeal to man's better nature while remaining in close contact with the realities of life. The marvellous is only an outward trapping, corresponding to the splendours of court festivals; what matters is the effect of these great ideals on the mind and soul. Chrétien had started to explore the effect of idealism in love on men's minds; in *Parzival*, Wolfram extends and completes the search, until his framework of an imaginary world contains the history of the way of Everyman to Salvation.

Wolfram's disrespect for courtly conventions, his inventiveness, sly humour, and obscure and uneven style – in short, his startling originality – won him harsh words from his great contemporary, Gottfried von Strassburg. In the middle of his *Tristan,*[5] Gottfried breaks off to discuss his fellow poets, and the

5 Tr. A. T. Hatto (Harmondsworth 1960, corrected rpt 1967) 'with the surviving fragments of the Tristran of Thomas'. See also W. T. H Jackson, *The Anatomy of Love* (New York 1971).

95

only one whom he cannot praise is 'the friend of the hare', as he calls Wolfram: the tumult of Wolfram's ideas, from his mastery of high ideals to his weakness for strange pieces of second-hand alchemists' lore, earned him that title. Gottfried is single-minded by comparison, and his purpose is quite different, so different as to be almost diametrically opposite.

The versions of the story of Tristan and Isolde we have looked at so far have been largely unpolished, relying on the elemental power of the tale for their effect. From this rough stone, Gottfried carves and polishes one of the masterpieces of erotic literature. Wolfram raises chivalry's idealism to its highest peak: Gottfried takes courtly love and infuses it with pure passion. The result is a work which professes the highest respect for tradition and convention, but which breaks some of the conventional rules by the very nature of the subject matter.

Like *Parzival, Tristan* begins with an account of the hero's father and his exploits. But as soon as Tristan himself appears, there is a great gulf fixed between the two tales. Parzival is potentially perfect, and seeks to fulfil that perfection; Tristan can do no wrong from the moment he is born. Image beyond all words of the perfect courtier and knight, every skill is at his command, no virtue is too taxing. Strong, handsome, gay, he turns his hand to chess, harping, the arts of venery or war, speaks several languages, is at ease from the moment he sets foot in a strange court.

With such a beginning, we might well expect to find ourselves back in the world of Chrétien, amidst yet more extravagant fantasies. Instead, the fantasies are kept to a minimum; the descriptions are extraordinarily real, yet none the less beautiful for it. The courtly world needs no apology, no excusing ethos; for Gottfried it is normal and natural. Tristan's loyalty to Mark, his duty to his subjects as ruler of Parmenie are part of this world; his adventures, until he meets Isolde, are purely chivalrous and of a very simple type. The slaying of Morold is treated in an antique heroic manner, as is the theme of the poisoned sword whose wounds only the dead man's relatives can heal.

Gottfried uses this perfect, self-contained world only as a starting-point. As with Wolfram, there are higher ends in view. Wolfram looks to a perfection to be gained by striving and effort, and spiritual pilgrimage; Gottfried's higher world is very different. Tristan and Isolde are already perfect. It is this that qualifies them for the transcending experience. The mysticism of love is his theme, and he speaks only to those of 'noble hearts' who can understand his message.

The crux of the story, the famous scene where Tristan and Isolde drink the love-potion, thinking it is common wine, has been given many different meanings. Gottfried uses the idea skilfully. He leaves us uncertain whether the drink merely confirms a love already begun, or is in itself the *coup de foudre*. For his own purposes he is well enough content to let it be regarded as a supernatural force; with this excuse he can tell his story of open adultery, treachery and broken oaths as a special case, and invoke magic as the cause of each transgression. On the other hand, the 'noble hearts' who understood his true meaning could see the potion merely as surrogate of love's power, a symbol of its workings.

Tristan and Isolde's love puts their relationship above the everyday ways of the world. They are no longer subject to the ordinary laws of men, and can only be judged in terms of their fidelity to each other and to love's ideals. The conflict and tension that arises between the two worlds, their unresolved discontent, shows that this is not an intensified version of courtly love, but a more disturbing force. Passion is the word we have now come to use for this force, and it is a commonplace of our view of love. But to Gottfried's contemporaries, despite Chrétien's tentative descriptions of the symptoms, this was novelty indeed. The romances offer a balance between social responsibility and sensual pleasure: *Erec* and *Yvain* are particularly concerned with this theme, the *mesura* or moderation praised by the poets of courtly love. For Gottfried, 'love in the sense he understands it, the total merging of one being with another, is incompatible with society as it was constituted in the romances or in life. If real love exists – and he wrote the *Tristan* to prove that it could – then it is not a succession of halcyon days of enjoyment but a demanding power which forces its subjects to love whatever sorrow it puts upon them.'[6]

Tristan and Isolde are equal in love. There is no question of knight serving lady; instead, they are both servants of *Frau Minne*, Lady Love. Caution becomes impossible, compromise unthinkable once her mystic joys have been tasted, Love becomes the fountain of all goodness, and even provides them with physical sustenance. The climax of the poem is the episode in which the lovers, banished by Mark, take refuge in the '*fossiure à la gent amant*', the Cave of Lovers. In this symbolically perfect retreat, whose every feature corresponds to one of Love's qualities: 'Their high feast was Love, who gilded all their joys; she brought them King Arthur's Round Table as homage and all its company a thousand times a day! What better food could they have for body or soul? Man was there with Woman, Woman there with Man. What else should they be needing? They had what they were meant to have, they had reached the goal of their desire.'

But if love is a higher ideal than those of the courtly world in which the lovers move, it affords them no protection. Its joys are

6 Jackson (n. 5 above) 54.

97

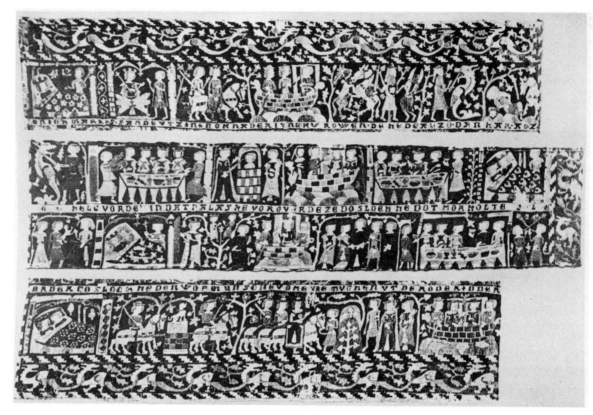

32 *Embroidery of c.1340 from Kloster Wienhausen in Hanover, telling the story of Tristan: the first row deals with the fight with Morholt, the second with Isolde's journey to Cornwall and the love potion. The third row shows Tristan and Isolde in the forest, and Tristan's exile in Brittany. The bottom row is concerned with Tristan's marriage to Isolde of Brittany.*

balanced by its sorrows; and its sorrows stem from the lovers' concern for their reputation. When Mark discovers them lying with a naked sword between them and is persuaded of their innocence, they return to court 'for the sake of God and their place in society'. Mark represents the opposite side of love: lust and appetite aroused by Isolde's beauty. As such he cannot find peace either; a pitiful figure, he wavers between the unpalatable truth and the comfort of illusion. Despite its outward gaiety, the court of Cornwall which he rules is similarly tainted; suspicion is everywhere, misunderstanding and distrust abound. Only Brangane and Kurvenal remain loyal; and even their steadfastness is tested. Isolde, fearing lest Brangane should reveal their secrets, tries to have her killed, but repents as soon as she fears the deed is really done. For loyalty only exists between the lovers themselves; all external claims are brushed aside and there is left.

> A man, a woman; a woman, a man:
> Tristan, Isolde; Isolde, Tristan.

Their true world is an enclosed, charmed garden, the garden of the Cave of Lovers; in the every day world, no matter how splendid and gay, they move guiltily, forced to deny their desires, and the air grows thick with sorrow and evil.

Gottfried did not complete his poem; whether by design or accident, we cannot tell for certain. It ends with Tristan's thoughts as he is torn between the idea of marrying Isolde of the White Hands, whose love he has won during his self-imposed exile from Cornwall, or remaining single for Isolde of Ireland's sake; and it seems likely that Gottfried was similarly torn between following faithfully the story as given in his original, and the loyalty in love which had become both his main theme and the excuse for his hero and heroine's misdeeds. That this ideal meant a great deal to him is plain enough, and there are veiled references to personal experiences of such a love throughout the poem. Yet, even as a guiding light for those 'noble hearts' to whom he addresses himself, it is an uncertain star. Gottfried makes sensual love sublime by his artistry; it is the one way in which the great tale he tells can come to life, but the philosophy of it is incomplete and less subtle than that of the troubadours and *minnesänger*. Indeed, it is scarcely a philosophy at all, though Gottfried would like us to think it was; it is a mysticism without a goal, the exaltation of emotion to the level of the divine through the element of suffering that emotion arouses. What he does tell us a great deal about is the psychology of love, how lovers behave and how their minds work; and his audience of 'noble hearts' are lovers who seek to find distraction for their own sorrows and perhaps a reflection of their own dilemmas.

In this lies the sharp distinction between Gottfried and Wolfram. Gottfried is a superb poet, a master of style whose cadences ring true, describing the deepest secrets of the emotions in a story well suited to his ends; Wolfram is less technically accomplished, but has a far broader view of life, which he expresses amidst the unlikely paraphernalia of knightly romance. Both, however, have risen too far beyond the conventions of the world about which they were writing for their successors to do more than admire their lofty concepts and produce imitations of the outward forms from which the inner spirit is lacking. Wolfram and Gottfried represent a *ne plus ultra*. All that is left for later writers in this genre is to compile immense fantasies, drawing on the inherited stock-in-trade of endless combats, strange adventures, mysterious beautiful damsels, prolonged quests that never seem to reach an end.

The later German romances, like the French, became lengthy and repetitive, with the additional handicap of being in verse. Although the bulk of the Vulgate Cycle – Lancelot, the *Queste* and La Mort Artu – was translated into German in the mid-thirteenth century, in a stylish and assured version, it had little or no influence on later writers.[7]. What we have instead are conscious attempts to invent new Arthurian romances, rather in the spirit of *Durmart le Gallois* or *Le Chevalier du Papegau*. Wirnt von Grafenberg's *Wigalois*, written *c.*1200–10, is based on Hartmann and Wolfram, taking a definite moral attitude in the same way as the latter, but lacking his firm control of the matter in hand; the result is naive and rather inconsequential. *Diû Krone*, written in Austria about 1220–30, by Heinrich von dem Türlin, comes under the heading of compendium romances: it is an *omnium gatherum* of all kinds of Arthurian themes, including a Grail quest with Gawain as its unexpected hero. It is notable that in all the German romances, Arthur and his court play a lesser part than in the French originals, though it is clear that Arthur was a familiar figure and that the romances were undoubtedly regarded as belonging to the Arthurian tradition, rather than as independent creations.

The immense vogue which Arthurian literature enjoyed in thirteenth-century France spread outwards to the very edges of Europe. A series of Dutch romances of the late thirteenth and early fourteenth century were chiefly based on the Vulgate Cycle, though there is one surprising work, *Walewein*, which includes Gawain's adventures with a talking fox. Three Latin romances contain some original material, but for the most part these far-flung translations were taken more or less directly from the French, whether in the Portuguese *Demanda do Santo Graal* or in the poems translated by Brother Robert for King Haakon of Norway about 1230 from Chrétien's poems, the *Erex saga* and *Ivens saga*, and from the *Tristan*. There is even a Hebrew translation of a variant of the Vulgate Cycle dating from 1279. The English romances, discussed in the next chapter, offer a mixture of direct translation, with a few pieces which seem to draw again on the Celtic stories from which all this literary activity had sprung.

As a result, the Arthurian heroes became household names throughout Europe, their adventures read by nobles and aspiring bourgeois alike. In Italy, the French romances were well known, and we have already quoted Dante's reference to them; but there is little trace of Italian versions of the legends, except at the relatively popular level of ballads and recited poems in the repertory of the *cantastorie*. The epics of the early Renaissance include many references, direct and indirect, to the Matter of Britain, but it was Roland and Godfrey de Bouillon who provided Ariosto and Tasso with their subject-matter in *Orlando Furioso* and *Gerusalemme Liberata*, while Arthur languished in the obscurity of Alamanni's *L'Avarchide*.

[7] Ed. Reinhold Kluge, (3 vols, Berlin 1948–1974). Only about a tenth of the French *Lancelot* is omitted.
[8] General introductions to Italian and Spanish Arthurian romances: E. G. Gardner, *Arthurian Legend in Italian Literature* (London & New York 1930); W. J. Entwistle, *The Arthurian Legend in the Literatures of the Spanish Peninsula* (London & New York 1925).

33 Head of King Arthur, perhaps from a set of statues of the Nine Worthies, produced in Germany in the thirteenth century. (Germanisches Nationalmuseum, Nuremburg, PL 251).

A similar late flowering of heroic themes took place in Spain, the form being the romance rather than the epic. The most famous of the Spanish romances is *Amadis de Gaula*, which, in the course of its immense length and many sequels has references to Arthur; and it was as popular as it was long-winded in the telling, for the tables were now turned and the French took their reading from the Spanish, and *Amadis* was admired throughout Europe. The Catalan romance *Tirant lo Blanc* has a substantial episode set at Arthur's court, and admiration for Arthur as the central figure of the chivalric world is evident in many other Spanish sources.

When Cervantes came to 'smile Spain's chivalry away', he had something to say both about the romances and about Arthur, who appears in a very unexpected guise; he is said to survive in the shape of a raven. As for the romances,

When they want to describe a battle, first they tell us that there are a million fighting men on the enemy's side. But if the hero if the book is against them, inevitably, whether we like it or not, we have to believe that such and such a knight gained the victory by the valour of his strong arm alone. Then what are we to say of the ease with which a hereditary Queen or Empress throws herself into the arms of an unknown and wandering knight? What mind not totally barbarous and uncultured can get pleasure from reading that a great tower, full of knights, sails out over the sea before a favourable wind, and that one night it is in Lombardy and by dawn next morning in the land of Prester John of the Indies...? If you reply that the men who compose such books write them as fiction, and so are not obliged to look into fine points or truths, I should reply that the more it resembles the truth the better the fiction, and the more probable and possible it is, the better it pleases.... What is more, their style is hard, their adventures are incredible, their love-affairs lewd, their compliments absurd, their battles long-winded, their speeches stupid, their travels preposterous, and lastly, they are devoid of all art and sense, and therefore deserve to be banished from a Christian commonwealth, as a useless tribe.[9]

And on this disenchanted note, we bid farewell to Arthur's European career, for the moment, and turn to his fortunes in England.

[9] Miguel de Cervantes Saavedra, *The Adventures of Don Quixote* tr. J. M. Cohen (Harmondsworth 1950, rptd 1968) 424–5.

Chapter 5

The English Poems

The earliest of the English romances was composed at about the time when the Arthurian matter began to go out of fashion in France, halfway through the thirteenth century. The last English romance is perhaps two decades later than Malory's 'noble tales'; thus they cover a span of two hundred and fifty years, from 1250 to 1500. None are on the same scale as their French counterparts, and of the twenty-three that survive, only five have any degree of originality; five are simply direct English renderings of complete French works.[1]

So most of the English Arthurian poems are translations, but English writers, perhaps handicapped by the lower level of literary development of their language, rarely manage to match the courtly and polished style of the French. And the English writers also prefer a more rapid progress through the plot, instead of the leisurely pace of the French; the story is invariably shortened and simplified, and there are only rare glimpses of the innate dramatic or psychological potential of the stories they are telling. The lack of English romances on the grand scale is largely due to a lack of demand: the upper classes could read the French in the original, as could any of the merchants and rich citizens; and the rise of English as the predominant language coincided with the decline of the romances. So when we do come to the one masterpiece of our native medieval Arthurian literature, *Sir Gawain and the Green Knight*, its splendours impress us all the more deeply.

Only the directness and naïve poignancy of the minor English romances save them from total oblivion. Unlike their French counterparts, the English poems seem more designed for recital than reading, and the approach to the subject is changed accordingly. Gone are the heartsearchings and lengthy soliloquys of Chrétien's heroes and heroines; instead, the English audiences

[1] Most of the English romances exist only in the medieval original, and their interest is largely specialist; the interested reader will do much better to turn to modern versions of the French originals.

demanded adventures and marvels; and these were supplied in abundance. The English romances are in general much briefer, and deal in single episodes rather than the complex interweavings of the French stories.

With this simplification goes a marked lack of taste and sophistication. Love is little discussed, and the physical side of it is more in evidence than the psychological. The wealth of kings and princes, on the other hand, is not tacitly assumed or indicated in a discreet phase, but is described with obvious amazement and wonder. The exaggerated and grotesque are greatly in demand, and there is a marked preference for combats with giants and monsters rather than mere human opponents. We are back in a much simpler world, nearer to folktale than literature.

The surviving English Arthurian repertoire includes versions of the Tristan legend, the story of Perceval's boyhood (omitting all reference to the Grail), an interesting version of Chrétien's *Yvain*, parts of the Vulgate Cycle in translation, and the story of the Fair Unknown, which is best known as the basis of Malory's *Tale of Sir Gareth*. The most impressive of this rather miscellaneous bunch of translations and adaptations is the stanzaic *Le Morte Arthur*,[2] which draws on the last section of the Vulgate Cycle to tell the story of Arthur's death with a simple and sometimes haunting poignancy; Malory used it in his account of Arthur's end, borrowing some of its more effective images.

Two groups of poems are distinctively English, harking back to the days when Arthur and his nephew Gawain were the chief protagonists in the Arthurian legends. A small group of poems contains adventures found only in English Arthurian literature. Arthur himself is one of the heroes of *The Avowing of King Arthur, Sir Gawain, Sir Kay and Sir Bawdewin of Britain*.[3] It is from the north of England and is dated to the mid-fourteenth century. The story opens at Carlisle, where Arthur hears of a great boar nearby, which, with the help of the three knights mentioned, he hunts to a lair in Inglewood Forest. There they all make vows: Arthur to kill the boar single-handed before dawn, Gawain to watch all night at the haunted Tarn Wadling, Kay to ride through all the forest until daybreak, and to slay anyone who opposes him, Bawdewin never to be jealous of his wife or any other lady, never to refuse food to any man, and not to fear the threat of death. All the vows are fulfilled except Kay's; Gawain rescues him, and the poem ends with Bawdewin's explanation of the events in his life which led to his triple vow. Such vows are paralleled in the so-called 'literature of boasting', where similar oaths lead to adventures, and serve, as here, to knit together a series of knightly exploits by means of an artificial central theme.

[2] *Le Morte Arthur* can be read with relatively little difficulty: ed. J. D. Bruce, Early English Text Society, Extra Series lxxxviii, (Oxford 1903).
[3] Ed. W. H. French and C. B. Hale, *Middle English Metrical Romances* (New York 1930).

The same characters and places are common to two other stories, the *Awntyrrs of Arthur (Adventures of Arthur)*[4] and *The Wedding of Sir Gawain*. In all three, Carlisle, Inglewood Forest (near Hesketh) and Tarn Wadling, a small lake in the forest, occur. It is conceivable that in their original form all three were by the same hand, although the extant versions are very different in construction and style. The title of the *Adventures of Arthur* is misleading, for Gawain is its true hero. The ghost of Tarn Wadling proves to be Guinevere's mother, who foretells Mordred's treachery and Arthur's end; this episode is loosely linked with a joust between Gawain and Galeron, which ends indecisively, but results in Galeron's admission to the Round Table.None of these episodes appear in the French romances, and the poems are imaginative variations on well-known themes by a local writer. An old and persistent tradition links Arthur with Carlisle, and Camlann, the site of his last battle, has been identified in recent years with Camboglanna, a fort on the Roman wall.[5] An echo of these associations may have been the inspiration for these poems.

Poems about Gawain form the most substantial group of English Arthurian romances. In the early French romances he is indeed of great knightly skill, but he is also lascivious, and not always courteous. To the English, he represents the flower of all courtesy and gentleness, and the figure of every virtue; the other knights, excepting only Arthur himself, are usually foils to his prowess and nobility. In maintaining this high opinion of Gawain, the English poets are echoing an older tradition, that of the first histories of Arthur.

Gawain first appears in Geoffrey of Monmouth's *History of the Kings of Britain* where he is called Gualganus, and in William of Malmesbury's reference to the discovery of his grave at Walwyn's Castle in Pembrokeshire. He resembles the Gwalchmai of Welsh legend and Cuchulainn in the Irish epics. Like the latter, he possesses many of the properties of a sun-hero, such as the increase of his strength until midday and its decline thereafter. Of all the knights of the Round Table, he has the longest connections with Arthur, save for Kay and Bedivere; and in Geoffrey of Monmouth he appears as Arthur's nephew. As a folk-tale hero, he remains the central figure of primitive stories, sometimes scarcely altered from their crude originals. Perhaps for that reason, Gawain cut a less imposing figure as the stories became the raw material for poets anxious to demonstrate their familiarity with a more sophisticated world.

Yet the first of the poems of which he is a hero, *Sir Gawain and the Green Knight*, is the outstanding literary accomplishment of medieval English Arthurian writing, one of the great masterpieces of the poetry of this period.[6] Both in its treatment of the

[4] Ed. R. J. Gates (Philadelphia 1969)
[5] K. H. Jackson, 'Once Again Arthur's Battles', *Modern Philology* xliii (1945) 57.
[6] The most accessible translation is by Brian Stone (*Sir Gawain and the Green Knight*, second edition, Harmondsworth 1974, rptd 1984). For studies, see (among a vast literature) J. A. Burrow, *A Reading of Sir Gawain and the Green Knight* (London & Boston 1968, repr. 1977) and A. C. Spearing, *The Gawain-Poet, A Critical Study* (Cambridge & New York 1970), chs 1 & 5.

subject-matter and in the strength of its style and imagery, it represents the climax of English alliterative poetry. The unique manuscript contains in addition three other poems of the same period and probably by the same writer: all are in the dialect of the north-west Midlands, with a strong Scandinavian influence, which is at its most marked in *Sir Gawain and the Green Knight*. Our poem seems to have been the first of the group to be written, at some time between 1360 and 1390. It has been suggested that it was commissioned by John of Gaunt, and there is evidence for some connections between him and the poet, if not for the actual commission. The identity of the unknown genius has long been a matter for debate. No suggestion yet put forward has gained more than a handful of supporters; attempts to marshal internal evidence, whether in the form of puns or numerology, all fail to make a convincing case for the author's identity. All that can be said with certainty about him is that he was well acquainted with courtly life, with feasting and hunting; he could read Latin and French, and was probably a scholar of some merit. He might well have been, or have become, a clerk in minor orders, since his later poems are distinctly religious in tone.

His chosen medium, alliterative verse, is a peculiarly English phenomenon at this period, the last flowering of a tradition going back to Anglo-Saxon times. Instead of rhyme, the verse-lines are marked by alliteration, the majority of words in each line beginning with the same sound. Only the stanzas are separated by rhyme, in a four-line 'bob' of short rhyming lines. Alliterative poetry is essentially a form for recital rather than reading, a medium for a minstrel at the feast rather than for a poet on the page; but in the hands of a writer such as the Gawain-poet it is powerfully pictorial, able to capture a scene or a situation more vividly than rhyming verse.

Arthur is at Camelot one Christmastide, and on New Year's Day, in accordance with his custom, does not eat until some adventure has taken place. Soon a gigantic knight, green from head to foot, duly appears to propose a bargain: any one of Arthur's knights who is bold enough to strike off his head with the axe he has brought, may do so – provided he will accept a return blow in a year's time. The knights, awed by the visitor's appearance, hesitate, and the Green Knight taunts them with cowardice. Arthur angrily leaps forward to take up the challenge himself, but Gawain restrains him, and asks permission to undertake the adventure himself. Arthur agrees, and Gawain beheads the Green Knight. To the astonishment of the onlookers, the latter picks up his head, which admonishes Gawain to meet him at the Green Chapel in a year's time, and gallops away with it under his arm.

Next All Hallows Day, Gawain is armed in preparation for his

34 *Arthur awaits an adventure, from a Flemish manuscript of c.1280. (Bibliothèque Nationale MS Fr.776, f.231).*

departure in search of the mysterious trysting place. He rides through the kingdom of Logres to north Wales, and eventually reaches the wilderness of Wirral, by way of Anglesey, Holyhead and the coast. By now it is Christmas, and he finds himself in a vast, dreary forest. He kneels and prays, and shortly afterwards, a splendid castle appears. Here he finds shelter for the night, and learns that the Green Chapel is but a few miles distant. The lord of the castle invites him to remain until the New Year, now only three days away, and proposes a bargain: he will go hunting each day, and Gawain shall remain at the castle with his wife. At the end of each day they will exchange their spoils.

The hunts take place, with all the ceremonial that medieval huntsmen loved; and meanwhile the lady visits Gawain each morning while he is still abed and tries to seduce him in her lord's absence. He, however, turns aside her advances with courteous but artful speeches. At the end of each day, the winnings are duly exchanged: Gawain gives one kiss for several deer on the first evening, two kisses for a boar on the second. However, on the third day, the lady gives him three kisses and a magical green lace girdle which protects the wearer from all harm. Gawain, by keeping this and giving the lord only the three kisses, in exchange for a fox's skin, breaks the pact.

Early next morning, Gawain makes his way to the Green Chapel with one of the lord's servants, who warns him of the fearful strength of the Green Knight and advises him to turn back. Gawain refuses, but finding the Green Chapel deserted, is about to go, when he hears the sound of an axe being whetted, and discovers the Green Knight preparing for the encounter. Gawain bows to receive the blow, but the Green Knight accuses him of flinching when he lifts the axe. He promises to keep still, and the Green Knight lifts the axe again, but lowers it without striking. Finally he lifts it again and lets it fall in such a way that it slightly grazes Gawain's neck. He then reveals that he is the lord of the castle at which Gawain had stayed, and that his wife had tempted Gawain in accordance with his instructions. The two feints were in payment for the kisses, and the graze was for the magic lace girdle which he had kept in breach of the terms of the bargain. Gawain is ashamed at being found out, and offers to give back the girdle, but is made to keep it and wear it in memory of his disgrace. The Green Knight tells him that his name is Bercilak de Hautdesert, and that it was Morgan le Fay who had arranged the adventure in order to test the knights of the Round Table and frighten Guinevere. Gawain returns to Arthur's Court, and, although much abashed, relates his adventure. The King decrees that all knights of the Round Table shall wear a green baldric in memory of his adventure.

In this tale there are two distinct themes which have been skilfully welded into one. The Green Knight's challenge to Gawain is an example of a Celtic episode that we may call the Beheading Game. The earliest form of this story is to be found in the Irish epic *Bricriu's Feast*, in which it is part of the contest for the championship of Ulster, with Cuchulainn as its hero. From Ireland it passed to France, perhaps via Wales and Brittany. Three French romances made use of this theme: in two cases Gawain is the hero, in the third Lancelot. The common feature of all versions is a supernatural being who is beheaded without apparent harm and who returns his half of the bargain with a harmless blow. The Temptation story is also Celtic in origin, the nearest parallel being found in *Pwyll*, one of the stories in the Welsh *Mabinogion*. This offers three major points of resemblance: a noble huntsman who introduces the hero as guest, a temptation scene in which the huntsman's wife is repulsed by the hero, and a year's interval between a challenge incident and its sequel. The huntsman is also the same colour as his horse, grey as opposed to green in the English poem. Two episodes in French romances offer a similar story.[7]

These two themes have been interwoven with great skill by the author of *Sir Gawain and the Green Knight*. Whether they were already associated we cannot tell, but it is his detailed working-out of the way in which the outcome of one text depends on success in the other adventure which is one of the delights of this very subtle poem. All we can say is that there seems to have been a French story of this type which was known to the Gawain poet.

The crux is the exchange of spoils during the three days' hunting, which provides a motive for the slight blow given to Gawain by the Green Knight. Gawain conceals the girdle out of fear of his encounter on the following day, which would have passed off without incident otherwise. Thus, while the Temptation arises naturally enough out of the Challenge, this addition makes the issue of the Challenge depend on the outcome of the Temptation.

But such a plot is as nothing unless matched by structure, verse and language. And here at last is an English poet writing an Arthurian romance who is capable of the task. The poet exploits skilfully complex dramatic devices: in particular, he uses suspense to great effect, leaving his audience with a host of conflicting possibilities about the nature of the Green Knight as he departs, head under arm, uttering his defiant reminder of Gawain's doom. These uncertainties are mirrored in the landscape of Gawain's northward journey, until he comes again to named and familiar places and then to the welcome comfort of Hautdesert. As soon as he leaves the castle on the last stage of the quest he plunges again into a threatening and mysterious terrain, akin to the magical world of the Mabinogion romances.

[7] In *Yder* and *Le Chevalier à L'Epee*. For translations of these stories see L. E. Brewer, *From Cuchulainn to Gawain: Sources and Analogues of Sir Gawain and the Green Knight* (Cambridge 1973).

[8] A hideous helmet-smasher for anyone to tell of;
The head of that axe was an ell-rod long.
Of green hammered gold and steel was the socket,
And the blade was burnished bright, with a broad edge,
Acutely honed for cutting, as keenest razors are.
The grim man gripped it by its great strong handle,
Which was wound with iron all the way to the end,
And graven in green with graceful designs. (Stone, n. 6 above, 29).

[9] He rode far from his friends, a forsaken man,

The structure is matched in power by the alliterative verse, which is a mirror of mood and imagination. The least description is turned into a jewel of language, whether it be the details of Gawain's arming before his departure or the loving portrayal of the Green Knight's magical axe:

> A spetos sparthe to expoun   in spelle whoso might
> The hede of an elnyarde   the large lenkthe hade,
> The grain al of grene stele   and of golde hewen,
> The bit burnist bright   with a brode edge
> As wel shapen to schere   as sharp rasores.
> The stele of a stif staf   the sturne hit bi gripte
> That was wounden with iron   to the wandes ende,
> And al bigraven with grene   in gravios werkes.[8]

But the greatest passages are those in which the poet depicts Nature and her ways, a theme which underlies the poem in several aspects. Two stanzas at the opening of the second part describe the changing seasons between Christmas and Michaelmas, and surpass all conventional poetry of this kind. They are followed by the harsh weather which Gawain encounters on his journey northwards, where in the sound of the words and in the rugged rhythms the very spirit of winter echoes and re-echoes:

> Mony clif he overclambe   in contrayes straunge,
> Fer floten fro his frendes   fremedly he rides.
> At eche warthe other water   ther the wighe passed
> He fonde a foo him before,   bot ferly hit were,
> And that so foule and so felle   that feght him behode.
> So many mervayl bi mount   ther the mon findes,
> Hit were to tore for to telle   of the tenthe dole.
> Sumwhile with wormes he werres,   and with wolves als,
> Sumwhile with wodwos,   that woned in the knarres,
> Bothe with bulles and beres   and bores otherwhile
> And etaines that him anelede   of the heghe felle;
> Nade he ben dughty and drighe,   and Drighten had served
> Douteless he hade ben ded   and dreped ful ofte.
> For werre wrathed him not so much,   that winter was wors,
> When the colde cler water   fro the cloudes shadde,
> And fres er hit falle might   to the fale erthe;
> Ner slain with the slete   he sleped in his yrnes
> Mo nightes then innoghe   in naked rokkes,
> Ther as claterande fro the crest   the colde borne rennes,
> And henged heghe over his hede   in hard iise-ikkles
> Thus in peril and paine   and plites ful harde
> Bi contray cayres this knight,   til Kristmasse even,
>   all one;
>   The knight wel that tide
>   To Mary made his mone,
>   That ho him red to ride
>   And wisse him to sum wone[9].

Scaling many cliffs in country unknown.
At every bank or beach where the brave man crossed water,
He found a foe in front of him, except by a freak of chance,
And so foul and fierce a one that he was forced to fight.
So many marvels did the man meet in the mountains,
It would be too tedious to tell a tenth of them.
He had death-struggles with dragons, did battle with wolves,
Warred with wild men who dwelt among the crags,
Battled with bulls and bears and boars at other times,
And ogres that panted after him on the high fells.
Had he not been doughty in endurance and dutiful to God,
Doubtless he would have been done to death time and again.
Yet the warring little worried him; worse was the winter,
When the cold clear water cascaded from the clouds
And froze before it could fall to the fallow earth.
Half-slain by the sleet, he slept in his armour
Night after night among the naked rocks,
Where the cold streams splashed from the steep crests
Or hung high over his head in hard icicles.
So in peril and pain, in parlous plight,
This knight covered the country till Christmas
Alone;
And he that eventide
To Mary made his moan,
And begged her be his guide
Till some shelter should be shown. (Stone, n. 6 above, 49).

The northern countryside in which the poet lived rises up before us in its most severe and impressive beauty. Across this background sweep past the three days' hunting, in which the essence of the chase is exactly caught: days of exhilaration, danger, triumph and noble ritual, at the end of each a homecoming to a warm welcome and a blazing fire when the last horn has been blown. On the day of the tryst at the Green Chapel, the countryside grows grim once more; the hills are mist-mantled, there is hoar-frost in the oakwoods, snow in the valleys. But perhaps the finest picture of all is that of Gawain lying awake on New Year's Day, waiting for dawn and listening to the gale outside:

> Now neghes the New Yere   and the night passes,
> The day drives to the derk   as Drighten biddes;
> Bot wilde wederes of the worlde   wakned theroute,
> Cloudes kesten kenly   the colde to the erthe,
> With nighe innoghe of the northe,   the naked to tene;
> The snawe snitered ful snart,   that snayped the wilde;
> The werbelande winde   wapped fro the highe,
> And drof eche dale ful   of driftes ful grete.
> The leude listened ful wel   that ley in his bedde,
> Thagh he lowkes his liddes,   ful littel he slepes;
> Bi ech kok that crue   he knew wel the steven.[10]

The people of this harsh, real world are equally alive; the poet makes us feel that we are partaking of their feasts and merry-making, gaiety and good cheer. Indeed, to heighten this feeling of realism, he deliberately places his story in an identifiable setting and the court and castle of Bercilak may be intended to reflect the household of the northern lord for whom he wrote, while the landscape of the Green Chapel has been plausibly identified with natural sites in the Peak District, which answer the poet's description.[11]

But just as Nature dominates the real world, so natural magic dominates the spiritual plane of the poem. The Green Knight is a superhuman being with strange powers, who moves in an aura of mystery, the shadow of his ancient role as the incarnation of spring who must be slain in winter in order to renew life for the next year. In the Temptation, he becomes a gay, friendly lord, owner of a fair castle; but this is only a disguise. The strange legendary world of Norse and Saxon literature never seems far from the poet's mind; Gawain encounters dragons, trolls and giants on his journey northward. The contrast between the Green Knight's two shapes is cunningly exploited to heighten the climax of the poem, and the Green Chapel itself may be a barrow, a mound haunted by a fearsome 'wight' as in Scandinavian stories.

The poet handles his romance with such high intent that it becomes a complex moral and didactic example. Gawain, the

[10] Now the New Year neared, the night passed, Daylight fought darkness as the Deity ordained. But wild was the weather the world awoke to; Bitterly the clouds cast down cold on the earth, Inflicting on the flesh flails from the north. Bleakly the snow blustered, and beasts were frozen; The whistling wind wailed from the heights, Driving great drifts deep in the dales. Keenly the lord listened as he lay in his bed; Though his lids were closed, he was sleeping little. Every cock that crew recalled to him his tryst. (Stone, n. 6, 96).

[11] See Martin Puhvel, 'Art and the Supernatural in *Sir Gawain and the Green Knight*', *Arthurian Literature* V (1985), 45–57.

35 Two possible sites for the Green Chapel: Weston Mill, near Buxton and Lud's Church, also in north Staffordshire. (Photos: Martin Puhvel).

model of knighthood, only escapes the fatal return blow because he holds out against the lady's adulterous temptations. This is a far cry from the easy acceptance, indeed exaltation, of the immorality of courtly love found elsewhere in Arthurian romance. For courtly love, the English poet substitutes courtesy: not our mere surface forms of politeness, but its combination with a deeper, inner truth, so that outward show and inward heart correspond. The English poet takes even these worldly ideals onto a higher plane: Gawain's device, the pentangle, borne on his shield, is a religious rather than armorial symbol, and he is frequently called 'Mary's knight'. There is an idealism throughout that raises the poem far above the level of the other English romances, and reminds one of Wolfram von Eschenbach. Gawain is an idealised hero who makes one error that cannot be redeemed; Parzival, on the other hand, although he almost fails in the Grail quest when he does not ask the question at his first visit to the Grail castle, gains a second opportunity by long years of atonement. The common subject of Wolfram and the Gawain poet is the search for perfection; for Wolfram it is typified by the achievement of the mysterious Grail, and in the other by the more realistic preservation of knightly honour in face of temptation. And the Gawain poet is more pessimistic than Wolfram, who sees perfection as eventually attainable; here the hero's reputation for perfection is contrasted with the harsh reality of his failure in the face of temptation. Some writers have seen *Sir Gawain and the Green Knight* as a poem with a didactic moral; but it is rather a moral reflection on human weakness.

In this poem, the Arthurian legend leaves its realms of isolated fantasy to become natural and human; the result has the same power and pathos as the closing pages of Malory. Here language, style and a subtle framework combine into a magnificent achievement, and beside it all but a handful of Arthurian poems pale into literary insignificance.

The Arthurian tradition in medieval England remained independent of the French romances in a number of ways, even if translations of the latter were the most common form of Arthurian literature of the time. There is evidence of a cycle or group of poems with Gawain as hero, preserved only in late ballads of extraordinary feebleness. It is only the fortunate survival of a single manuscript which reveals that behind the pedestrian rhymes of *The Green Knight* there lies the sublime poetry of *Sir Gawain and the Green Knight*. The poems all seem to be localised in the north-west of England, and Gawain evidently had some kind of local following here. We also find translations of Gawain-poems at a date when his star in the French romances had long since eclipsed. One ballad, *The Gest of Sir Gawain*, is an incident from one of the continuations of Chrétien's *Perceval*, of which Gawain was the other hero.

The progress of Gawain's character is an interesting commentary on the changing values of Arthurian romance. From an unimportant role in the *History of the Kings of Britain*, he appears to rise rapidly in the French romances. But even in the first sources he is Arthur's nephew; and in certain societies a man's sister's son was regarded as more important than a son. So his position in the stories is perhaps assured from the outset: he quickly becomes the first knight of Arthur's court, skilled in knightly arts, courteous and gentle. But he was by no means perfect in the French romances, and as Lancelot rose to become the chief Arthurian hero, so Gawain's faults were dwelt on in proportion. It was the English writers who raised him to the standing of the perfect knight, and made it possible to fashion a masterpiece around him. By contrast, the French version of

Arthur's downfall places a good deal of the blame for the disintegration of the Round Table on Gawain, and Malory, drawing on this, includes him among the 'murtherars of good knightes', a portrait redeemed only by his moment of greatness in his last letter to Lancelot. Tennyson, ignoring the earlier English tradition, depicts him as one of the worst elements in Arthur's court, a sad ending for the great hero of medieval literature.

The English romances as a whole are no match for the Continental works about Arthur and his court. A steady mediocrity, with occasional lapses into crudity – always excepting one towering masterpiece – is the sum of their literary achievement. Yet they reflect the taste of a rather different audience which also enjoyed the Arthurian stories, and the plots that the English writers chose are much more coherent than their French and German counterparts. The diffusion of the English romances was slighter than elsewhere, even when they were of considerable literary quality, and there are far fewer reworkings of the material.

Like their Continental counterparts, the English Arthurian stories enjoyed a great vogue immediately after the introduction of printing; but the book that brought this about belongs to our next chapter. The ballads also continued to be read, printed and recited in Elizabethan times, and the early ballad collections, such as Percy's *Reliques*, contain a number of examples, drawn from Malory or the French romances. But we are in the land of Sir Marramile and Sir Bredbeddle, a distant descendant of the Green Knight, and with these faintly ridiculous characters our survey of medieval Arthurian romance in England might well end. Yet before it finally passed, there was to appear one of the most masterly versions of the legends in any language, which was also one of the great works of English prose. It is largely due to Sir Thomas Malory that the Arthurian tradition survived in England long after it had become a mere antiquarian curiosity elsewhere; the last flower of medieval romance was also one of the finest.

Chapter 6

The Flower of Chivalry

The French Vulgate Cycle, although it contained the entire story of Arthur, was a vast and unwieldy work, and even in France itself attempts were made to reduce it to a coherent form. The best of these, made by Michel Gonnot for the book-loving Duc de Nemours, Jacques d'Armagnac, was completed in 1470, but was unduly learned in tone and concentrated on chivalric adventure rather than Arthur himself.[1] In Germany, Ulrich Fuetrer attempted the same kind of summary of the romances for duke Albrecht of Bavaria in his *Lantzelot* (1467) and *Buch der Abentever* (1481–4, in verse), but reduced the adventures to a series of separate tales, scarcely linked to one another. It was only when Sir Thomas Malory came to put the same material into English that a true masterpiece embracing the whole story of Arthur and his knights was created. The translation alone was a formidable task: indeed, only one other anonymous writer had attempted a similar work by producing an English *Prose Merlin*. But interest in a complete version of the legend in English at this period is shown by the existence of amateur efforts to render the Merlin and Grail stories into English verse, by Henry Lovelich, a London merchant, which date from 1460–70. Just as the French romances had attained their greatest popularity in the prose versions, so it was in Malory's works that the romances reached their highest esteem in England.

Malory himself is an enigmatic figure. Four men bore the name Thomas Malory, and were probably knights, at the period when *Le Morte Darthur* was written. Of these, only three are serious candidates. The first is the man usually accepted as the author; but there are, as we shall see, serious difficulties and objections. Sir Thomas Malory of Newbold Revel in Warwickshire was born in about 1410. At the age of twenty-three, he inherited the family estates, and in the following year may have served at Calais

[1] The superbly illuminated manuscript survives in the Bibliothèque Nationale, Paris (MS fr.112).

114

under the Earl of Warwick, with one lancer and two archers. He married in about 1440, and had one son, who died within his father's lifetime. So far there is little problem; but at the age of about forty he apparently embarked on what a biographer has called 'an orgy of lawlessness'. If we accept the records at face value, between June 1450 and July 1451 he was accused of a dozen crimes, including attempted murder, theft, rape and extortion. He was arrested and imprisoned at Coleshill in July 1451, but escaped within a day or two by swimming the moat. His recapture took place, after further robberies, in the following month, and he spent the next three years in prison, save for a brief interval in 1452. However, on his release on bail in May 1454, he continued his career of crime in Essex. In October of the same year he was imprisoned in Colchester Castle, and was unable to appear at the expiry of his bail. He was handed over to the Marshal in November, and we know nothing more until February 1456, when he produced a writ of pardon issued by the Duke of York during his period of office as Lord Protector in November 1455 in answer to the charges against him. The following month he borrowed a sum of money, and sat for his shire in Parliament. He apparently failed to repay the debt, for he was imprisoned in Ludgate until October 1457, when he was once more released on bail. At the end of two months he returned to prison. The date of his release is not certain, but in 1459 he was apparently at large in Warwickshire. In Lent 1460 he was recaptured and imprisoned in Newgate.

In 1462 he accompanied the Earl of Warwick on Edward IV's expedition to Northumberland, and was at Bamburgh and Alnwick (to which reference is made in *Le Morte Darthur*) during the sieges. There is reason to believe that he joined the Lancastrians when Warwick broke with Edward IV, and was active in the campaign against the latter, for he is excluded specifically from two general pardons to the Lancastrians granted in 1467. His final imprisonment seems to have been in 1469–70; it is this period that coincides with the production of *Le Morte Darthur*. Whether he was released before his death on 14 March 1471 we cannot tell, but he was buried not far from Newgate prison, in Greyfriars Church.[2]

Such a turbulent career accords ill with the noble sentiments of the book to which the name of Sir Thomas Malory is attached; and this has turned scholars' attention to the other candidates. An ingenious case has been made for Thomas Malory of Hutton and Studley in Yorkshire, who, although never actually described as a knight, was certainly of sufficient standing for the title. Equally, he is not known to have been a prisoner, though in an age of frequent warfare there is no reason why he should not have been an honourable captive, and there is a possibility that

[2] Edward Hicks, *Sir Thomas Malory: His Turbulent Career* (Cambridge, Mass. 1928).

he was imprisoned in a place where he might have had access to the duke of Armagnac's manuscripts. Furthermore, there is a possible link between the Yorkshire Malory and a French manuscript of the *Merlin* on which *Le Morte Darthur* seems to have been based, and of which only this one copy is known. The use of the alliterative *Morte Arthure*, again in northern dialect and with a unique manuscript coming from Lincoln, would also be more plausible in the case of the Yorkshire Malory.[3]

The third candidate is Thomas Malory of Papworth St Agnes in Cambridgeshire, about whom little is known: it is argued that he too could be linked with the use of the *Morte Arthure* and the French *Merlin* manuscript. But the records consistently refer to him as 'esquire', with the exception of one doubtful posthumous record of the inquiry into his estates.[4]

There is, however, a further possibility, which I personally find the most convincing. Sir Thomas Malory of Newbold Revel, apart from his criminal record, seems to have the right background, with contacts in high places. It has been suggested that his criminal record is in fact the result of political intrigue, and that these were trumped-up accusations brought against a leading supporter of the duke of York; his imprisonments were thus entirely political, and there is no difficulty in reconciling the high sentiments of his book with the author's own life. Indeed, some of the concerns of his lesser characters – to find a good lord and financial security, and to see the kingdom well-governed – would thus have been Malory's own.[5]

Scholars are equally divided about the exact intentions of the author of *Le Morte Darthur*.[6] In its original version, it was divided into eight separate books. For some three and a half centuries, Caxton's edition of 1485, which welds them into one, albeit not very coherent, single composition, was regarded as being a more or less faithful reproduction of the original. In 1934, however, there came to light in the Fellows' Library at Winchester College a unique manuscript of the eight tales, which for the first time revealed the earliest form of Malory's composition. But the question of whether Malory intended from the start to produce a complete cycle in separate parts, or whether he progressed by adding to his existing work until he reached the point where an attempt at completeness was almost inevitable, is still the subject of fierce debate. It is true that the chronology is not continuous throughout the work, and the tales may have been intended to have some degree of independence, perhaps dictated by the sources from which Malory worked. For example, the birth of sir Tristram is related three hundred pages after his appearance, which argues a *prima facie* case for the independence of two of the books at least, as does the injunction at the end of the first book to 'seke other bookis of kynge

[3] See William Matthews, *The Ill-Framed Knight* (Berkeley 1966).
[4] R. R. Griffith, 'The Authorship Question Reconsidered: A Case for Thomas Malory of Papworth St Agnes, Cambridgeshire' in *Aspects of Malory* ed. T. Takamiya and D. S. Brewer (Cambridge & Totowa 1981) 159–178.
[5] P. J. C. Field, 'Sir Thomas Malory, M. P.', *Bulletin of the Institute of Historical Research* XLVII (1947) 24–35.
[6] Edited by Eugène Vinaver as *The Works of Sir Thomas Malory* (2nd edn, Oxford 1967, 3 vols) and (in Oxford Standard Authors) as *The Works of Sir Thomas Malory* (Oxford 1977).

I. *Lancelot, carrying a white shield, carries off Brandus, Lord of the Dolorous Garde, and is challenged by Sir Kay, who claims the right to take Brandus to King Arthur. They fight and Sir Kay is left wounded. Arthur and his knight ride to where Sir Kay is lying, while Lancelot, bearing his prisoner, gallops into the wood. This and the following miniatures are all from a magnificent copy of the Prose Lancelot produced in northern France c.1300–1320. (Pierpont Morgan Library MS 805, f.39)*

II. *The War with Galeholt. Guinevere, the Lady of Malohaut and three attendants survey the battlefield. Lancelot approaches, awaiting a message from the Queen. On the right, Lancelot unhorses Galeholt with a lance given to him by Gawain. (f.60).*

III. *Lancelot, Galeholt and Guinevere are seated on a bench. Galeholt encourages the Queen to kiss Lancelot. Under three trees, the seneschal converses with the Lady of Malohaut and another noblewoman. (f.67)*

IV. *Gawain and the daughter of the King of Norgales. He enters the anteroom of her bedchamber, in which twenty knights keep guard: four are shown asleep in their full armour. By the couch is a tall candlestick with a lighted taper, which Gawain is about to put out with an extinguisher. On the right, he kisses the lady, who is lying naked in bed. (f.99)*

V. *Lancelot's madness. Guinevere has hung around Lancelot's neck the shield sent to her by the Lady of the Lake. Lancelot regains his senses and recognises the Queen and the Lady of Malohaut. On the right, the Lady of the Lake, having divined his condition, arrives and anoints Lancelot with unguent, so that he sleeps and recovers. (f.109)*

VI. *Lancelot fights with three companions of the false Guinevere: two are slain and he is engaging in the third. On the right, the false Guinevere and the old knight Bertolais are bound to a stake and burnt. (f.119v)*

VII. *Lancelot breaks the spell of 'Escalon the dark' by opening a little door within the church, which is magically defended by swords which attack him of their own accord. When he wrenches the door open, the light returns, but he faints before the altar, and Yvain and the damsel who has led him into the adventure rush in to revive him. (f.135)*

VIII. *Lancelot enters the valley of False Lovers. He is attacked by two dragons, but overcomes them and arrives at a river to be crossed only by a narrow plank. The way is barred by three knights: the first he throws into the river, the other two disappear by enchantment, as do the river and the plank when he uses the ring given to him by the Lady of the Lake. He passes through a wall of fire and comes to steps defended by two knights. He wounds the first, so that he falls into the flames; the second fares likewise. (f.139)*

IX. *Karadoc, an evil knight of great strength, had captured Gawain, and put him in the Dolorous Tower. Lancelot attacks Caradoc by raising his sword: it will be shivered on the steps, but a maiden stands above, holding out a sword fated to provide Karadoc's death. Karadoc knows this, but has entrusted the sword to the maiden, believing her to be true to him. Within the battlemented wall of the Tower, Lancelot throws the headless Karadoc into a pit, while Gawain escapes from his prison. (f.148v)*

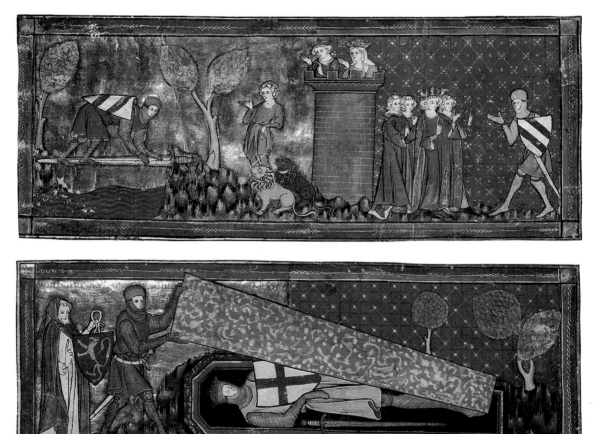

X. Lancelot, in disguise, undergoes the disgrace of being drawn in a cart by a dwarf on horseback. The dwarf has promised Lancelot that if he submits, he will take him in sight of Guinevere, who has been captured by Meleagant, son of King Baudemagus of Gorre. They approach the castle, followed by Gawain and two squires. Gawain is also in search of the Queen and does not recognise Lancelot, because, according to the conventions of knighthood, Lancelot would never allow himself to be driven in such a shameful way. (f.158)

XI. Lancelot, on his way to rescue Guinevere, crosses the Sword Bridge. His way is barred by a youth and two lions, against which his sword has no effect. Therefore he uses the ring given him by the Lady of the Lake, and they vanish. Guinevere, who is watching with Baudemagus from a tower, recognises Lancelot's ring and rejoices. (f.166)

XII. Lancelot arrives at an ancient house of religion, and is led by a monk to the cemetery in which are the tombs of twenty-four knights, one far richer than the others, Lancelot learns that it has been foretold that the deliverer of the subjects of Arthur held captive in the land of Gorre would be able to raise the heavy marble covering fixed with lead and cement. Lancelot raises it easily, disclosing a knight in full armour. This is the son of Joseph of Arimathea. When Lancelot wishes to replace the stone, it remains suspended. (f.161v)

XIII. *Gawain and Ector enter a cemetery, despite a warning inscription on a tomb at the entrance. They see a tomb from which flames leap up to the height of a lance, surrounded by an upright sword. Gawain enters first, but cannot reach the burning tomb because swords rise up of their own accord and strike him. He retires and Ector is depicted falling on one knee, struck by five swords on his shield and helmet. (f.207)*

XIV. *Lancelot ends the enchantment of the Lost Forest and a magic chessboard is brought to him. The pieces, of gold and silver, move of their own accord and hitherto nobody has won a game. Lancelot plays and wins, so the chessboard is declared his. He sends it as a gift to Guinevere, who is shown sitting with King Arthur. She plays her best, but loses. (f.253v)*

XV. *The Tourney at Camelot. Lancelot has been maligned by certain knights of the Round Table. He receives a message from Guinevere to take the side of King Baudemagus. Bearing a red shield so that nobody should recognise him, Lancelot overthrows all his opponents until he comes to the Queen, watching the tourney with her ladies. At the sight of the Queen, he falls into a swoon, and has to be rescued and carried into a wood by Baudemagus. Here he sleeps and recovers. (f.262)*

XVI. *Arthur fights a Roman general, from a collection of historical narratives called* The book of the treasure of histories, *written and illuminated about 1415, possibly for Prigent de Coetivy, later admiral of France, when he was a young man. The artist is one of the associates of the 'Boucicaut master', one of the finest of all French miniature painters. (Bibliothèque nationale, Paris, MS Arsenal 5077, f.298)*

XVII. *The marriage of Arthur and Guinevere, a miniature from a copy of the* Chronicles of Hainault *prepared for Philip the Good of Burgundy and illuminated by Guillaume Vrelant about 1468. The architectural setting and brilliantly coloured clothes are typical of Vrelant's work. (Brussels, Bibliothèque Royale Albert Ier, f.39v)*

XVIII. *A damsel comes to Arthur's court: one of the seventeen surviving leaves of a magnificent copy of* Guiron le Courtois *written for a Knight of the order of the Golden Fleece, the count of Nassau in Flanders, in about 1480. Arthur is shown as an elder statesman, seated alone in splendour at a canopied table. (Oxford, Bodleian Library, MS Douce 383, f.1)*

XIX. *Hospitality by William Dyce, from the set of four frescoes in the Royal Robing Room in the House of Lords. This depicts the admission of Sir Tristram to the Round Table in Malory's Morte Darthur, where Arthur welcomes him 'for one of the best knights, and the gentlest of the world, and the man of most worship.' The fresco was completed by C. W. Cope after the artist's death in 1864. (Department of the Environment Photographic Library)*

XX. The Damsel of the Holy Grail *by D.G.Rossetti. The tradition that the Grail was carried by a damsel goes back to the original Grail romance, Chretien de Troyes' Perceval. Rossetti has emphasised the religious symbolism by adding the dove as symbol of the Holy Spirit. (Tate Gallery)*

XXI. Guinevere *by William Morris. The details of this painting actually correspond more closely to the story of Iseult: the lapdog on the bed and the figure harping in the background both recall Tristram rather than Lancelot. (Tate Gallery: photo John Webb)*

XXII–XXIII. *Two of the set of Arthurian tapestries produced at the Royal Windsor Tapestry Manufactory to designs by Herbert Bone (1879). Although technically of a very high standard, the Windsor tapestry venture was short-lived, and only half a dozen sets of designs were woven. These show the arrival at Camelot of the barge bearing Elaine's body and the departure of Arthur for Avilion. (Vigo-Sternberg Galleries)*

XXIV. La Morte D'Arthur *by the Scottish artist, James Archer (1823–1904), exhibited at the Royal Academy in 1861. It shows the dying king attended by three queens, while the barge that is to bear him to Avalon lies offshore. To the right, an angel hovers with the chalice of the Grail, an original addition to the scene. (City Art Galleries, Manchester)*

XXV. The Lady of Shalott *by J.W. Waterhouse (1849–1917), exhibited at the Royal Academy in 1888, perhaps the most popular of all Arthurian images. (Tate Gallery)*

> *Down she came and found a boat*
> *Beneath a willow left afloat …*
> *And at the closing of the day*
> *She loosed the chain and down she lay;*
> *The broad stream bore her far away …*   *Tennyson*

XXVI–XXVII. Tapestries woven by Morris and Co. to designs by Edward Burne-Jones. Burne-Jones had been a consistent Arthurian enthusiast, and when Morris and Co. were commissioned to decorate Stanmore hall in Middlesex, Morris consulted him. They chose the subject of the quest of the Holy Grail for a set of tapestries for the dining-room. The two largest are illustrated here: The Knights of the Round Table summoned to the Quest by a Strange Damsel, (above) and The Attainment: The Vision of the Holy Grail (below). These are from later sets to the same designs woven in 1898–9 and 1895–6 respectively. The Attainment does not follow any recognisable literary source, but The Knights … summoned to the Quest is close to Malory. (City of Birmingham Museum and Art Gallery)

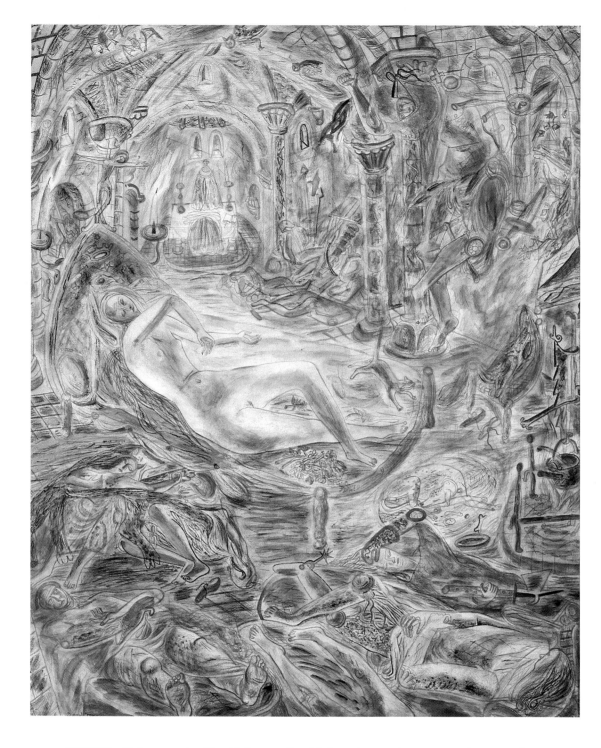

XXVIII. Guinevere *by David Jones. David Jones' complex approach to myth in his poetry is mirrored by the mass of detail which surrounds the central figure of Guinevere. The sleeping figures hint at the folktale of Arthur and his court in enchanted slumber in a cave; in the background is an altar, at Guinevere's feet a realistic fireplace and cooking-pot. The picture conveys the magic and absence of logic of myth and the unconscious mind, an essential undercurrent of Arthurian romance. (Tate Gallery)*

Arthure or of sir Launcelot or sir Trystrams...' if the reader wishes to know more. The most reasonable solution seems to be that Malory did not intend to continue his task at this point; but when he changed his mind, he produced a work which conforms to medieval rather than modern ideas about logic and consistency of approach. After all, these are romances, not works of schoolmen or philosophers, and it would be foolish to expect an exacting regard for consistency from an author whose very subject is full of incidents which defy the rational order of things.

So we must reject both the unity praised by earlier critics – 'of this vast assemblage of stories only Malory makes one story and one book' – and an absolute division between the tales. It is possible that the second tale, *The Tale of King Arthur and the Emperor Lucius*[7] may be Malory's first literary effort, antedating even *The Tale of King Arthur* with its dismissive remarks implying that there was no more to come. *Arthur and Lucius* is an almost straightforward reworking in prose of the alliterative *Morte Arthure* already mentioned. This epic-heroic work had a great influence on his style, and there is virtually none of the reordering and recomposing found further on; the narrative of the poem is direct and uncomplicated, and needs no simplification. Malory does, however, omit the great descriptive set-pieces which are among the glories of the original poem, as well as monologues and conversations which are not directly concerned with the action; of the remainder, some of the lines are quoted in full without alteration. Perhaps for this reason it was here that Caxton made his most considerable abbreviations; his version bears little resemblance to what Malory actually wrote.

In view of this close translation of the French, it is strange to find here another example of the insertion of contemporary references, parallel with those in Geoffrey of Monmouth and in the alliterative *Morte Arthure* itself. Malory does not go so far in this direction as his predecessors, of whose efforts at alteration he was in all probability unaware. Arthur is modelled in some respects on Henry V, as is suggested by his route through France, which is reminiscent of the campaign preceding Agincourt. Instead of Mordred, two chieftains are left as regents, in much the same way as Henry appointed Bedford and Beaufort. Other changes were made for the purpose of the narrative form: Arthur is actually crowned by the Pope, a detail found in contemporary chronicle accounts of Arthur's career: Malory wished to end the tale at a climax rather than anticipate the dark tragedy of Arthur's end. And Lancelot is given a new prominence, supplanting Gawain as the main hero, an alteration which looks forward to Malory's later books.

It seems likely that it was after this adaptation from an English poem that Malory turned his attention to the French romances.

[7] I have followed Professor Vinaver's short-title references: Malory's full title is 'The tale of the noble King Arthur that was emperor himself through dignity of his hands.'

He seems to have used the version of the *Merlin* known as the Huth Merlin, which differs substantially from the *History of Merlin* in the Vulgate Cycle, although it is perfectly compatible with the latter. On reading the French, he must have discovered very rapidly that a totally different story-telling technique was involved, as complex as that of the English poet had been direct and simple. A number of themes were interwoven in an almost inextricable mesh, giving a tapestry-like effect to the whole. Quite frequently, the themes or their sequels extended between separate romances, thus giving the cycle its unity. Malory succeeded in both isolating many of the incidents, often told in passages many pages apart in the French, and in strengthening such links as remained, especially if they offered a point of contact between his own tales. This process is well illustrated by *The Book of Balyn le Sauvage* where Malory has added to the original story of a knight who slays, and is slain by, his brother, the incident of the Dolorous Blow, by which an entire country is laid waste. The latter forms a quite separate incident in the original, but by adding it, Malory heightens the portrayal of Balin as a fated knight, who is destined to do harm. It is chiefly changes of this kind that distinguish *The Tale of King Arthur* from a mere translation, and which enable Malory to reduce the prominence of Morgan le Fay and Merlin, concentrating instead on Arthur himself.

Lancelot, as we have seen, first appears in the *Tale of King Arthur and the Emperor Lucius*, and this puts his story in a different light. He now rises to fame by his military exploits in the Roman Wars, and goes on to become first knight of the Round Table in deeds of chivalry thereafter, whereas the reverse was true in the French cycle. His position as Guinevere's lover, the role in which his character first became of importance, is given less emphasis by Malory, who did not entirely sympathise with the point of view of the French writers on this.

The Tale of Sir Launcelot du Lake falls into three sections. The first of these is the third part of the French *Lancelot*. Malory has reduced it by about a half, while retaining the outline of the original. He then moves to the next reference to the theme of Lancelot and his nephew Lionel, separated by many pages of material on other themes in the French version, which he omits *en bloc*. The third section has no known source, but it is probable that Malory followed with the same degree of closeness a version of the romance now lost. The Chapel Perilous episode is similar to an incident in the French romance *Perlesvaus*, but it is unlikely that this is the direct original, since so much of the rest of the story in it is violently at odds with the Vulgate Cycle. The sections chosen from this unknown work deal entirely with adventures pure and simple, without any underlying theme. The conclusion, as so often, is Malory's own, and probably cuts short his source well before the end.

For *The Tale of Gareth* there is again no known source. The romance *Sir Libeaus Desconus* bears some resemblance to it, and an incident in the French *Prose Tristan* may have contributed to it. It was from this latter that Malory learnt of Gawain's evil reputation, and it is not until the last section of *Le Morte Darthur* that he regains his old character. *The Tale of Gareth* is the shortest unit of Malory's works; the next, *The Book of Sir Tristram de Lyones* represents over one-third of his entire output, and is drawn from one source, a version of the *Prose Tristan* which does not correspond exactly to any surviving manuscript. Here Malory begins to treat his material with increasing freedom and confidence. He firmly omits the whole of the third book of the original, which dealt with some of the Grail adventures, saying: 'Here endyth the secunde boke off syr Trystram de Lyones, whyche drawyn was oute of freynshe by sir Thomas Maleorré, knyght, as Jesu be hys helpe. Amen. But here ys no rehersall of the thirde booke.' The introduction dealing with Tristram's parentage has also been omitted, and the whole is divided into sections, each with an introduction and ending in the Winchester manuscript.

Malory alters both the literary style of the French and the essence of the tale itself. His language, particularly in dialogue, is realistic and direct, while the Tristram story is not presented here as a tragedy: we only learn of the death of the lovers – in a version very different from the earliest and most familiar one – by a chance remark in the last part of *Lancelot and Guinevere*. The tragic undertones disappear with the blackening of Mark's character; Iseult is thus represented as in great measure justified in turning to Tristram. Tristram becomes above all a knight-errant; his love for Iseult seems to be less the prime motive of his existence than an adjunct of his chivalry. The return of the lovers to Joyous Gard is invented by Malory to replace the ending of the original, and we leave them in domestic bliss there. This replacement of earlier attitudes by his own realistic brand of chivalry is typical of Malory; yet he fails to remove entirely Sir Dinadan, whose mocking counterpoint questions the very ideals he cherishes, in the manner of a privileged jester.[8]

Malory's overall theme in *The Book of Sir Tristram* is to chart Sir Tristram's career as a knight.[9] The use of apparently unconnected episodes such as the story of Alexander the Orphan (from the fourteenth-century *Prophécies de Merlin*) and that of Lancelot and Elaine (from the Vulgate *Lancelot*) are part of a calculated pattern by which Tristram's career is compared and contrasted with those of other knights. He traces Tristram's progress from unknown knight to his final rank as one of the

[8] Vinaver, *Works* (1967) i.xxxiv.
[9] L. D. Benson, *Malory's Morte Darthur* (Cambridge, Mass & London 1976) 109–34 gives a good account of the merits of *The Book of Sir Tristram*.

four best knights in the world, and it is perhaps for this reason that he leaves the end of the tale alone, wishing to finish with his hero at the high point of his achievements.

The original of the *Tale of the Sankgreall*, the French Vulgate *Quest for the Holy Grail*, follows the *Lancelot* section to form the fourth branch of the cycle. No surviving manuscript exactly corresponds to the passages selected by Malory, but there are no substantial differences in the actual material. His skill here has been directed at omissions calculated to alter considerably the character of the quest. The French work was virtually an exposition of the doctrine of grace and salvation, and to emphasise and interpret the lesson of each adventure hermits appear on every other page, moralising or preaching over the unfortunate knights whose injuries they tend. Malory ruthlessly excises most of the hermits, and abbreviates the moralisings of those who remain. In doing so, he manages to make Lancelot, and the chivalry which Lancelot represents, emerge with much greater credit from the Grail adventures. He seems to have been concerned to diminish the distinction between religious and secular chivalry, and to remove the religious atmosphere of purification and repentance as a keynote of the quest. It is Lancelot's relative success which he emphasises rather than his eventual failure at the vital stage. The result may not always be sound theology, but it brings the story more into line with the rest of the cycle.

For the last two of his eight tales, Malory combined English and French romances, but depended less and less on his sources. The two works he used were the English *Le Mort Arthur* and the conclusion of the Vulgate Cycle, *La Mort Artu*. In the *Book of Sir Launcelot and Queen Guinevere*, the first two parts are careful selections taken almost directly from the sources. Thereafter he departs from any known version of either French or English. In *The Great Tournament*, for example, the actual description of the tournament is Malory's own work, and *The Knight of the Cart* is very much rewritten: whereas Chrétien long ago had made Lancelot's journey in the cart so shameful that Guinevere seemed almost divine in her power over him, Malory passes it over as merely another adventure. In *The Healing of Sir Urry*, he presents his own contribution to the legend, the apotheosis of Lancelot. After a vast procession of knights, whose names are a roll-call of Malory's by now extensive reading, have failed to heal the stricken Sir Urry, Lancelot succeeds, and movingly, weeps 'as he had bene a chylde that had bene beatyn'[10] when this private miracle is granted him.

Until now, in spite of *The Tale of the Sankgreall*, Malory had had relatively little difficulty in making Lancelot his hero. But when he came to the tragic conclusion of the cycle, he found that

[10] Vinaver, *Works* (1967) iii.1152.

the French writers had made Lancelot the main agent of Arthur's downfall. Malory could not blame him for this without bringing down the whole carefully-constructed edifice built around the idea of Lancelot as the flower of chivalry; nor did the blunt statement at the end of the previous tale actually resolve the problem: 'and now I go unto the morte Arthur, and that caused sir Aggravayne'.[11] He had to make a major alteration to the emphasis of the old tale, and he effected this by standing back from all moral judgements, thus shifting the focus onto character and situation rather than cause and effect. The feeling throughout this last book is that of a series of unhappy chances, combined with regret and longing for what might have been. By heightening the intimacy of the relationship between Lancelot, Guinevere, Arthur and Gawain, the tragedy is intensified. Loyalty plays an important part: Lancelot's loyalty to Guinevere is brought into implacable opposition to Gawain's loyalty to kith and kin.

Malory's handling of the end of the Round Table and Arthur's death is his masterpiece. Where the author of *La Mort Artu* became over-florid and the English poet insipid, Malory's prose reaches its majestic climax of greatness and grief. His revision of the incidents of the last stages of the disaster is done with much finesse and feeling. The premonition of disaster before the last great battle is skilfully developed, until the storm breaks when, at the moment of truce, one of the handful of knights alone with Arthur and Mordred between the armies draws his sword to kill an adder which has just bitten him; both sides see the flash of his weapon, and take it for treachery. As we might expect, the great set piece of these final pages is not Arthur's mysterious disappearance and apparent burial, but the death of Lancelot, brought on by grief for Guinevere and Arthur.

Throughout the later books, Malory's growing mastery over his material is evident. Earlier writers had been unduly concerned with meanings as well as events, a trait seen at its worst in the French *Quest for the Holy Grail*. The romances became either fantasies irrelevant to real life or moral illustrations; both types abound in earlier Arthurian literature. Malory achieved a reality that required no moral standpoint as its excuse or purpose, and turned to the interplay of character and situation instead. Yet this absence of moral does not mean that he had no hero, but that his hero was all too fallible. And this also works in reverse; for he does not seem to have set out with the conscious intention of writing a story without a moral standpoint. He arrived at this effect by a process of evolution. It would be no great exaggeration to say that, having chosen Lancelot as his ideal, he altered everything to harmonise with this, and to show him in a better light where necessary. Hence it was chivalry rather than

Ibid., iii.1154.

121

courtly love in which his practical nature was interested, and he did his best to divorce the two. This led him into major difficulties, for in the French romances the two are quite inseparable. Lancelot is challenged by a damsel whom he has just rescued, who says: 'But one thyng, sir knyght, methynkes ye lak, ye that ar a knyght wyveles, that ye woll nat love som mayden other jantylwoman' and repeats the rumour that he loves Guinevere. Lancelot, instead of protesting his single-minded adoration of his lady, defends himself on quite different grounds:

> For to be a weddyd man, I thynke hit nat, for that I muste couche with hir and leve armys and turnamentis, batellys and adventures. And as for to sey to take my pleasaunce with peramours, that woll I refuse: in prencipall for drede of God, for knyghtes that bene adventures sholde nat be advoutrers nothir lecherous, for than they be nat happy nother fortunate unto the werrys; for other they shall be overcom with a simpler knyght than they be hemself, other ellys they shall sle by unhappe and hir. cursednesse bettir men than they be hemself. And so who that usyth peramours shall be unhappy, and all thynge unhappy that is about them.[12]

Knighthood is a vocation from which there is no respite, and love has become an obstacle on the knight's road, as Iseult points out when Tristram refuses to go without her to Arthur's court: 'For what shall be sayde of you amonge all knyghtes? "A! se how Sir Trystram huntyth and hawkyth and cowryth within a castell wyth hys lady, and forsakyth us. Alas!" shall som say "hyt ys pyté that ever he was knight, or ever he shulde have the love of a lady" '.[13] The High Order of Knighthood is the great theme of Malory, and its code his ideal; knighthood can only survive as long as it remains the supreme ideal. Once the knights put their personal feelings before all else, the darkness of tragedy descends. Indeed, it is arguable that the decline begins with the overthrow of Lancelot by his son Galahad in *The Tale of the Sankgreall*. In the light of the earlier part of the work, this reverse seems scarcely credible, and Lancelot himself is stunned by it. But Malory never gave Galahad pride of place. His code of knighthood has become involved with forces above it and beyond it; and he merely accepts the moral offered by the French author and continues on his own path, putting the earthly worship attached to the Grail quest before its religious and spiritual benefit. His lack of enthusiasm for Galahad and Perceval is noteworthy and springs from the same cause as his rejection of the legacy of *amour courtois*: he exalts the practical over the ethereal and spiritual.

Malory's preference for Lancelot is underlined by his account of Lancelot's deeds in the quest for the Grail. In the French original, Lancelot's unworthiness and failure is emphasised, while

[12] *Ibid.*, i.270.
[13] *Ibid.*, ii.839–40.

122

Malory stresses his partial success in achieving the vision of the covered Grail at Carbonek. Malory accuses Lancelot only of instability, but does not specify his sinfulness more explicitly. And the grave and noble pages which tell of the achievement of the quest belong to a separate world, where secular knighthood still has its representatives in the nine knights of Gaul, Ireland and Denmark, and in Sir Bors; but as Sir Bors returns to Camelot from Sarras, bearing Galahad's greeting to the court, we feel that it is the Round Table above all else that has made this achievement possible. In Arthur's command that 'grete clerkes ... shulde cronycle of the hyghe adventures of the good knyghtes'[14] earthly worship is once again to the fore.

But the ultimate effect of the Grail story is to produce a hero who fails, an important step towards the modern novel; for Lancelot is still the hero after his failure. Malory might have preferred to make Arthur the central figure, but the French stories did not provide enough material on which to build his reputation. As it is, he is the hero of the first two parts, and Malory pays him the highest compliment he knows: 'of him all knights may learn to be a knight'. Arthur is again to the fore in the closing pages, and for all Malory's partiality for Lancelot, it is the image of the king himself, faced by personal and political tragedies which are inextricably intertwined, that is the most haunting vision of all. It was Malory's portrait of Arthur, rather than his treatment of Lancelot, which was to attract later readers. Guinevere, like all Malory's female characters, lacks life and conviction; her main function in the French romances, to be Lancelot's lady and mistress, is played down, and Arthur's interest is concentrated on his company of knights rather than her. In the final stages of the tragedy he declares: 'And much more I am soryar for my good knyghtes losse than for the losse of my fayre quene; for quenys I myght have inow, but such a felyship of good knyghtes shall never be togydirs in no company.'[15]

The remaining characters are chiefly the knights: Galahad and Perceval, the unearthly seekers after spiritual perfection, for whom Malory does not greatly care; the imitators of Lancelot, who cannot quite attain his level of knightly prowess; and the group of whom Gawain is the chief representative, meaning well but unfortunate in their actions. Gawain is a strongly drawn character: impetuous, quick to repent, courageous yet misguided and obstinate, he is in some ways more human and sympathetic than Lancelot, and his farewell letter to the latter is one of the most moving moments of the story. The magical characters, Merlin and Morgan le Fay, are reduced in stature by Malory, who has less time for the grotesque and incredible than his predecessors; and since Morgan le Fay's plots served largely to complicate the French romances, Malory's simplifications sweep

[14] *Ibid.*, ii.1036.
[15] *Ibid.*, iii.1184.

away many of the episodes in which she appears.

Malory's singleness of purpose in following out his chosen themes and characters is all the more remarkable when one turns to the French and observes how widely separated the component parts often are. This unravelling of the threads of the Vulgate Cycle and the gathering of them into simpler patterns must have been Malory's hardest-won achievement; out of its diffuseness, recurrent themes and unwieldy branches, Malory forged relatively coherent sections, cutting away the multiplication of incidents that have no real value as far as his main plot is concerned, and drastically abbreviating the wordy disquisitions on love, religion and chivalry which had encumbered the story. The prose of the French was, like the frame of the work, an unwieldy tapestry. Out of this Malory drew phrases with a clear cadence. His prose is crisp, lucid and rhythmic, varying in tone with the events it describes, quick and fierce for a combat: 'So when Sir Launcelot saw his party go so to the warre, he thrange oute to the thyckyst with a bygge swerede in his honde. And there he smote downe on the ryght honde and on the lyffte honde, and pulled down knyghtes and russhed of helmys that all men had wondir that ever knyght myght do suche dedis of armis.' Or it can become elegiac and solemn in grief:

'And now I dare say, thou sir Launcelot, there thou lyest, that thou were never matched of erthely knyghtes hande. And thou were the curtest knyght that ever bare shelde! And thou were the truest frende to thy lovar that ever bestrade hors, and thou were the trewest lover of a synful man that ever loved woman and thou were the kyndest man that ever strake with swerde. And thou were the godelyest persone that ever cam emonge prees of knyghtes, and thou was the mekest man and the jentyllest that ever ete in halle emonge ladyes, and thou were the sternest knyght to thy mortal foo that ever put spere in the reste.
Than there was wepyng and doloure out of measure.[16]

Within the ponderous elaborations of the Vulgate Cycle, there lay hidden a great epic drama, ranging through every human passion, joy and grief. Malory drew out the noble tragedy of Arthur from the mass of adventures and marvels in which it had become entangled, and gave to it a new unity and clarity. He made its protagonists real people once more, stripped off the moralising to restore the unrelenting onset of the tragedy, and gave to the climax a befitting majesty and grandeur which it had never before attained. It needed Malory's skilful hand to reveal the full force of the 'noble chyvalrye, curtosye, humanyte, frendlynesse, hardynesse, love, frendshyp, cowardyse, murder, hate, vertue and synne'[17] which in Caxton's words the epic contained. By doing so he ensured that the Arthurian tradition, at

[16] *Ibid.*, iii.1259.
[17] *Ibid.*, i.cxlvi.

least in England, did not become a mere literary curiosity like the medieval stories of Charlemagne and Alexander, but would re-emerge to inspire new masterpieces.

Chapter 7

Arthur and Popular Tradition

So far we have been concerned with the writers who created the Arthurian romances, and have looked only at the literary world which Arthur and his knights inhabited in the middle ages. But the spread of Arthur's fame depended not only on the forging of the great stories about him out of the most diverse materials, but also on the appeal of the resulting works to an audience. Who were the listeners when the Welsh poets recited their verses, or when a volume of romances was read? They had as much influence on the shape of the Arthurian stories as the writers; yet they are often ignored, if only because they are so elusive.

Arthurian literature was above all courtly literature. From the political recreation of Arthur in a resurgent Wales in the tenth century to the marvellous illuminated manuscripts of the romances made in the fifteenth century, the stories are always to be found in the context of a royal or baronial court. Arthur is the ruler of the court of courts, the most glittering assembly of knights ever seen, whether in the references to *Llys Arthur* in the triads or in Malory's closing pages. So the audience was always made up of men and women highly placed in the secular world: even in the most lax of monastery or cloister libraries it was unusual to find a copy of a romance, even those of the Grail, and although authors of the romances might be clerics, their audience was not intended to be their fellow-clergy. Some of the romances undoubtedly appealed to a fairly narrow and sophisticated audience: we have noted Gottfried von Strassburg's invocation of the 'noble hearts' who would understand his theme, and Chrétien de Troyes' poetry employs a considerable range of rhetorical devices and philosophical themes more familiar to the scholars of Paris than to the country knights of Champagne.

126

By concentrating on the masterpieces which have the power to speak directly to today's reader, we do paint a slightly false picture of the romances. For one *Sir Gawain and the Green Knight* there are half a dozen lesser translations direct from the French; for one *Prose Lancelot* or one *Parzival* there are a dozen fantastic concoctions of meaningless adventures. But these works underline the fact that there was a wider Arthurian audience whose standards were less exacting and who simply wanted a story in the fashionable style about their favourite hero. In England we can define this audience by language, the non-French speaking knights and merchants of the later fourteenth and fifteenth century; in Germany, France and Flanders the city merchants acquired the tastes of their noble counterparts, a process we can first observe in the Flemish cities, with their bourgeois tournaments, as early as the thirteenth century. For the merchants, the world of chivalry was an unreal and usually unattainable one, and this may explain in part the increasing element of fantasy in the later medieval romances. Chrétien's and Wolfram's poems are rooted in a society where the knight is paramount, and where the audience could easily identify with the hero. In works such as *Le Chevalier du Papegau* and even *Amadis de Gaula* or *Tirant lo Blanc* there is a much stronger mixture of the purely fantastic. It is true that in Chrétien Celtic magic is transmuted and is used to create a world beyond the castle walls where the strangest adventures are possible, and in Wolfram the fantastic is turned to the service of the highest ideals; but there is a reality about their heroes which is much harder to find in the later works, as the subject matter of romance became divorced from the world in which its readers lived.

The spread of the romances was vastly increased by the advent of printing, and huge folios containing versions of the Vulgate Cycle, Tristan and later stories issued from the French presses from the late fifteenth century onwards. Malory's work was immortalised by Caxton, without whom it would have remained unknown until the discovery of the manuscript in Winchester College Library in 1934. In Spain, the romances poured out in a flood: we have already quoted Cervantes' wry dismissal of most of them. But manuscripts and books were not the only means by which the stories spread. There was a long tradition of 'Arthurian' tournaments from the thirteenth century onwards, where themes from the romances were re-enacted to provide the setting for courtly spectacles. Edward III's 'Round Table' of 1344 is perhaps the most famous example, but the Arthurian influence can still be traced in court entertainments mounted for Philip II of Spain when he was acknowledged as Charles V's successor in 1549. The medieval orders of knighthood themselves owed not a little

36 *Manuscripts with decorated initials and small miniatures which illustrate sequences of events in the cycle of Arthurian romances first appear in the 1230s and 1240s; this example, with its rather grander pictures, dates from 1274. Lancelot has a vision of a sick knight healed by the Grail (top left); Perceval hears mass in a hermitage with the maimed king (centre left). At the beginning of the* Death of Arthur *section, Bors is shown returning from the Grail quest, and king Henry II instructs Walter Map (who was supposed to be the author of the romance) to continue his work by writing the book of the* Death of Arthur *(bottom left). Finally, Lancelot rescues Guinevere from being burnt at the stake (above). (Bibliothèque Nationale MS Fr.342, ff.77, 84v, 150, 186).*

to the ideal of the Round Table: that imaginary order, as depicted in the Vulgate Cycle, antedates the first real secular order of knighthood by nearly a century.

The stories of the Arthurian heroes were also recorded in art from the early twelfth century. We have already looked at the mysterious carvings at Modena: after these, the earliest surviving work other than illuminated manuscripts with occasional miniatures, is the cycle of frescoes at Schloss Rodeneck in the Tirol, painted soon after the beginning of the thirteenth century. These remarkable late Romanesque paintings are a powerful evocation of Hartmann von Aue's *Iwein*, a German version of Chrétien's *Yvain*. Gothic frescoes survive at Schloss Runkelstein nearby, portraying scenes from Gottfried's *Tristan* and two lesser German romances. That such frescoes were by no means unusual is witnessed by the badly damaged cycles to be found as far apart as S. Floret in the Auvergne, Schmalkalden in Thuringia, and a set of Parzival frescoes (now destroyed) at Lübeck, the great Hanseatic trading town on the Baltic. If Arthur and his knights flourished on the walls of medieval houses, they were also to be found on household objects, tapestries and embroideries and especially ivories. The earliest of this is a casket showing scenes from *Tristan* carved at Cologne in the first part of the thirteenth century, but the bulk of the Arthurian ivory caskets were made about 1300–1340 in Paris, and portray the adventures of Tristan, Perceval, Gawain and Galahad. The tryst of Tristan and Iseult also appears on mirror backs. The caskets were probably intended to hold jewels or as a part of a toilet set, a reminder that many of the first patrons and later enthusiasts for Arthurian romance were ladies of high birth.

The greatest Arthurian works of art from the middle ages are of course the miniatures in illuminated manuscripts. An artistic tradition of how the cycle of romances should be depicted developed from the mid-thirteenth century; many manuscripts have illuminated initials showing scenes from the passage in question, but the most striking are those where the miniaturist has been allowed free reign, and among these one stands out for its intense affinity with the spirit of the romances, a *Prose Lancelot* now in the Pierpont Morgan Library, New York. Produced in northern France in the early fourteenth century, perhaps about 1316, it is the epitome of one of the best periods of manuscript production, as the reader can see for himself on colour plates I to XV. The delicately drawn yet expressive figures of the lovers, the drama of the adventure scenes (worthy of an Apocalypse manuscript), the brilliant colouring and gilding, the careful heraldry and attention to pictorial detail, all make it an outstanding work.

Only in the early fifteenth century do we find other French manuscripts to rival this *Lancelot*; among these the most striking are the Arthurian volumes which belonged to that great connoisseur, Jean, duc de Berry. If they cannot compare with the marvels of the books of hours created for him by the Limbourg brothers, the great *Lancelot* which he bought from a Parisian bookseller must have been a handsome volume: but it was evidently so popular that the miniatures became worn, and were repainted by a lesser artist later in the century. Flemish manuscripts of this period, created for the court of Burgundy, are equally resplendent: a notable set of pictures adorns the Arthurian section of the *Chronicles of Hainault*, painted in 1468 by Guillaume Vrelant. And a handful of full page miniatures survive from a superb version of the romance *Guiron le Courtois*, commissioned by a knight of the order of the Golden Fleece about 1475, one of the last and richest of Arthurian manuscripts.

But beside the Arthur of these aristocratic and luxurious volumes of romances, there existed also a very different figure, the Arthur of popular tradition. When Malory came to the end of *Le Morte Darthur*, and to the end of his French books, he turned to his own memories of stories about him, and to sources which mentioned other traditions about Arthur's end:

> Thus of Arthur I fynde no more wrytten in bokis that bene auctorysed, nothir more of the verry sertaynté of hys dethe harde I never rede, but thus was he lad away in a shyp wherein were three quenys...

Now more of the deth of kynge Arthur coude I never fynde, but that thes ladyes brought hym to hys grave, and such one was entyred there whych the ermyte bare wytnes that sometyme was Bysshop of Caunturbyry. But yet the ermyte knew not in sertayne that he was veryly the body of kynge Arthur: for thys tale sir Bedwere, a knyght of the Table Rounde, made hit to be written.

Yet some men say in many parts of Inglonde that kynge Arthure ys nat dede, but had by the wyll of oure Lorde Jesu into another place; and men say that he shall com agayne, and he shall wynne the Holy Crosse. Yet I woll nat say that hit shall be so, but rather I wolde sey: here in thys worlde he chaunged hys lyff. And many men say that there ys wrytten uppon the tumbe thys:

HIC IACET ARTHURUS, REX QUONDAM REXQUE FUTURUS[1]

Caxton, coming to print Malory's manuscript, wrote in the preface of his own doubts as to whether Arthur existed, saying that 'dyvers men holde oppynyon that there was no suche Arthur and that alle such bookes as been mad of hym ben but fayned and fables'. But he was told 'that there were many evydences of the contrarye. Fyrst, ye may see his sepulture in the monasterye of Glastyngburye...'[2]

So in the fifteenth century the doubts about Arthur's death, raised so long ago by the unknown poet of the *Stanzas of the Graves*, were still rife. Malory was unsure whether his body lay in the grave said to be his, while for Caxton Arthur's grave was one of the few pieces of certain evidence about him. Even today the same doubts linger. Was the discovery of Arthur's grave at Glastonbury in 1191 a stage-managed propaganda coup or one of the great archaeological finds of the middle ages? We have an apparently eye-witness account, and a number of chroniclers of the period mention the event. It made a considerable impression at the time, and yet we cannot be really sure what happened. I believe that the most authentic account is to be found in a chronicle written at the abbey of Margam within a decade or two of 1191; the writer probably had before him a copy of a letter sent out by the monks of Glastonbury to announce their discovery, and this is what he says:

At Glastonbury the bones of the most famous Arthur, once King of Greater Britain, were found, hidden in a certain very ancient coffin. Two pyramids had been erected about them, in which certain letters were carved, but they could not be read because they were cut in a barbarous style and worn away. The bones were found on this occasion. Whiie they were digging a certain plot between the pyramids, in order to bury a certain monk who had begged and prayed the convent to be buried here, they found a certain coffin in which they saw a woman's bones with the hair

[1] Vinaver, *Work:*, lii 1242.
[2] Ibid., i.cxliv.

still intact. When this was removed, they found another coffin below the first, containing a man's bones. This also being removed, they found a third below the first two, on which a lead cross was placed, on which was inscribed, 'Here lies the famous king Arthur, buried in the isle of Avalon'. For that place was once surrounded by marshes, and is called the isle of Avalon, that is 'the isle of apples'. For *aval* means in British an apple. On opening the aforesaid coffin, they found the bones of the said prince, sturdy enough and large, which the monks transferred with suitable honour and much pomp into a marble tomb in their church. The first tomb was said to be that of Guinevere, wife of the same Arthur; the second, that of Mordred, his nephew; the third, that of the aforesaid prince.[3]

Soon after the discovery was announced, Gerald of Wales, well known as a writer and courtier, visited Glastonbury and was given a detailed account of the discovery: he was shown the lead cross, and handled the huge thigh-bone which was said to be Arthur's. This has deceived many later writers into calling him an eye-witness: but the account is rather what a distinguished visitor might have been expected to write, particularly as the monks were well aware of his achievements as an author.

Arthur, the famous British king, is still remembered, nor will this memory die out, for he is much praised in the history of the excellent monastery of Glastonbury, of which he himself was in his time a distinguished patron and a generous endower and supporter.... His body, for which popular stories have invented a fantastic ending, saying that it had been carried to a remote place, and was not subject to death, was found in our day at Glastonbury between two stone pyramids standing in the burial ground. It was deep in the earth, enclosed in a hollow oak, and the discovery was accompanied by wonderful and almost miraculous signs. It was reverently transferred to the church and placed in a marble tomb. And a leaden cross was found laid under a stone, not above, as is the custom today, but rather fastened on beneath it. We saw this, and traced the inscription which was not showing, but rather turned in towards the stone: 'Here lies buried the famous king Arthur with Guinevere his second wife in the isle of Avalon.' In this there are several remarkable things: he had two wives, of which the last was buried at the same time as him, and indeed her bones were discovered with those of her husband; however, they were separate, since two parts of the coffin, at the head, were divided off, to contain the bones of a man, while the remaining third at the foot contained the bones of a woman set apart. There was also uncovered a golden tress of hair that had belonged to a beautiful woman, in its pristine condition and colour, which, when a certain monk eagerly snatched it up, suddenly dissolved into dust. Signs that the body had been buried here were also found in the records of the place, in the letters inscribed on the

[3] Richard Barber, 'Was Mordred buried at Glastonbury? Arthurian Tradition at Glastonbury in the Middle Ages', *Arthurian Literature* IV (1984) 37–63: the major texts are given in an appendix. The translations here are my own.

37 The cross preserved at Glastonbury in the late sixteenth century which was said to be that found in Arthur's tomb. From William Camden, Britannia (London 1610), p. 228.

pyramids, although these were almost obliterated by age, and in the visions and revelations seen by holy men and clerks; but chiefly through Henry II, King of England, who had heard from an aged British singer of stories that his [Arthur's] body would be found at least sixteen feet deep in the earth, not in a stone tomb, but in a hollow oak. This Henry had told the monks; and the body was at the depth stated and almost concealed. lest, in the event of the Saxons occupying the island, against whom he had fought with so much energy in his lifetime, it should be brought to light, and for that reason, the inscription on the cross which would have revealed the truth, was turned inwards to the stone, to conceal at that time what the coffin contained, and yet inform other centuries. What is now called Glastonbury was in former times called the Isle of Avalon, for it is almost an island, being entirely surrounded by marshes, whence it is named in British Inis Avallon, that is the apple-bearing island, because apples (in British, *aval*) used to abound in that place. Whence Morgan, a noblewoman who was ruler of that region and closely related to Arthur, after the Battle of Camlan carried him away to the island now called Glastonbury to be healed of his wounds. It used also to be called in British Inis Gutrin, that is, the isle of glass; hence the Saxons called it Glastingeburi. For in their tongue, *glas* means glass, and a camp or town is called *buri*. Knowing the size of the bones of Arthur's body that were discovered we might see in this the fulfilment of the poet's words:

Grandisque effossis mirabitur ossa sepulchris.

[When the graves are opened, they shall marvel at the great size of the bones. (Virgil, *Georgics I* 497)]

The thigh bone, when put next to the tallest man present, as the abbot showed us, and placed on the ground by his foot, reached three inches above his knee. And the skull was of a great, indeed prodigious, capacity, to the extent that the space between the brows and between the eyes was a palm's breadth. But in the skull there were ten or more wounds, which had all healed into scars with the exception of one, which made a great cleft, and seemed to have been the sole cause of death.

Between the original announcement and Gerald's arrival, some modifications had been made to the story. There is no mention of the third body, probably because the presence of Mordred, Arthur's betrayer in the romances, had been greeted with disbelief. The inscription on the cross had been amended to include Guinevere: and it is this which is the weakest point in any argument which claims that the discovery was genuine. The cross, or what purported to be the cross, survived into the seventeenth century, to be engraved by William Camden, and only disappeared at the end of the eighteenth century, if local tradition is correct. This gives the simpler wording, not the elaborate wording which Gerald saw on the cross shown him by the abbot, Henry of Sully: 'Here lies buried the famous king Arthur in the isle of Avalon, with Guinevere his second [*or* fortunate] wife.' Setting aside the differences in the spelling of names, either Gerald's account is unreliable, or the cross described by the Margam annalist and drawn by Camden is wrong; or the monks were adjusting the evidence while they decided which was the best story. And there is one more flaw: not until the eleventh or twelfth century was Arthur ever described as a king, *rex* in Latin, as on the inscription on the cross: the early Welsh references are to Arthur primarily as a leader or commander, possibly a prince.

It is perfectly possible to brush aside the discrepancies and argue that the find was genuine: but many scholars, myself included, believe that it is more likely that the discovery was stage-managed to a greater or lesser degree. I would suggest — and it can be no more than a suggestion — that the sequence of events was as follows. In 1184, a disastrous fire devastated the abbey, destroying its buildings including the ancient church which had become a legendary shrine. The monks said that they had recovered many of their precious relics, but without the old church, they no longer had the focal point which they needed to maintain the abbey's great prestige. It has been argued that the idea of finding Arthur's tomb preceded the discovery itself,[4] and a writer in the 1240s with some knowledge of west country affairs said that the whole cemetery was excavated in the search. But the archaeological excavation in 1962 showed that only a small excavation was made, probably disturbing three stone coffins between the two pyramids. I believe that the discovery was indeed fortuitous, and the inspiration of labelling the bodies came afterwards: hence the confusion over their identity, and the withdrawal of the claim to have found Mordred. The suggestion that it was Arthur's grave may have been inspired by Henry II himself: the hope of Arthur's return was still a political rallying-point for the Welsh, and the discovery neatly destroyed a propaganda weapon used to good effect by the king's enemies, while at the same time offering the prospect of renewed interest in Glastonbury itself.

The medieval chroniclers, preferring the certainties of a known grave to the vague rumours of Arthur's return, by and large accepted the Glastonbury burial as genuine, and used it either to round off their account of Arthur's career, or as a separate entry under the year of the discovery. It eventually penetrated to the romances: at the end of *Perlesvaus* the author says that the Latin original of his story 'was taken from the Isle of Avalon, from a holy religious house which stands at the edge of the Lands of Adventure; there lie King Arthur and the queen, by the testimony of the worthy religious men who dwell there...'[5] And the

[4] R. F. Treharne, *The Glastonbury Legends* (London 1967) 101.
[5] Tr. Nigel Bryant, 265.

38 Arthur's last battle, from Jacob van Maerlant's Mirror of History, *written in the early fourteenth century in Flanders. An unusual touch is the departure of the dying king in a cart, at the right. (Koninklijke Bibliotheek, The Hague, MS XX, f.163v).*

discovery of Arthur's tomb in the Vulgate *Mort Artu*, which Malory follows, seems clearly influenced by the discovery at Glastonbury, even though the site of the hermitage is never specifically named.

However, not all romance writers were satisfied with either Geoffrey of Monmouth's deliberately enigmatic account of Arthur's end on the one hand, or the cut-and-dried factual burial reported by the monks of Glastonbury. At some time before the end of the thirteenth century a learned author wrote a Latin version of Arthur's death, which offers a very interesting mixture of imagination and apparent folk traditions.

His account begins at the end of the battle between Arthur and Mordred. Arthur withdraws from the battlefield, seriously wounded, and sits down to recuperate. As he is resting, an unknown youth rides up and hurls an elm spear poisoned with adder's venom, which strikes the king. Arthur slays him, but it is clear that the new injury will be fatal for him. He is taken to Gwynedd (North Wales) 'since he had decided to sojourn in the delightful isle of Avalon'. Here he dies; and the author describes the despair of the Britons in highly rhetorical terms. The next day his body is taken for burial to a certain chapel dedicated to the blessed Virgin Mary; but the entrance proves too narrow to admit the body, which is left outside. An extraordinary storm and mist descends, so that the attendants of the royal corpse can see nothing at all: thunder rolls continuously for six hours, and when the air at last clears there is no sign of the king's body. But there is a sealed tomb, which seems as though it is made of a single piece of stone. Those who believe that Arthur will come again say that he was carried off during the storm; those who say he is dead argue that he is within the recesses of the tomb – 'and even up to the present time shadows of ignorance are discerned, as to where King Arthur was destined to find his place of rest.'[6]

The origins of this strange story are as mysterious as the events it relates, but internal evidence points to a Welsh-speaking cleric or monk from north Wales, with a knowledge of Welsh romances and folklore, from which the youth with the elm spear and the magic mist and storm, as well as lesser details, seem to be drawn. And Arthur was undoubtedly a figure in popular lore by the beginning of the thirteenth century, as the sleeping warrior who will one day reappear as leader when called by the breaking of a spell. Such stories have been told of every great national hero, and are readily adaptable to new names and characters as events provide them. The earliest appearance of Arthur in this role is recorded in Gervase of Tilbury's *Otia Imperialia (Imperial Trifles)* (after 1214). Gervase quotes the disappearance of Arthur to Avalon, but also describes the recent adventure of the groom of an Italian bishop, who, while following a stray horse on

[6] Richard Barber, 'The *Vera Historia de Morte Arthuri* and its place in Arthurian tradition', *Arthurian Literature* I (1981) 62–78.

Mount Etna, came across Arthur in a sort of Earthly Paradise, entered by a cleft in the rock. There are other similar stories of Arthur and Etna of this period which are undoubtedly explained by the presence of the Normans in Sicily, which they ruled from the early twelfth century onwards.

In Britain, there are two versions of the story, the best known being attached to Craig-y-Dinas near Snowdon and some other Welsh caves. On London Bridge, a Welshman with a hazel staff meets a stranger who tells him that a treasure lies hidden under the tree from which the staff was cut. They return together to Wales, and find the tree, and a cave beneath it. In the passage leading to the cave hangs a bell which must on no account be touched. If it rings, the warriors in the cave, among whom is Arthur, waiting to lead the Welsh to their former glory, will awake and ask, 'Is it day?' The answer must be, 'No, sleep thou on.' This happens: but the correct answer is given, and the Welshman is able to take some of the treasure. On his next visit he forgets the formula, and is beaten until he is crippled by the warriors. He is never able to find the cave again.

The other version is found at Sewingshields on the Roman wall, and at Richmond in Yorkshire. The visitor finds Arthur, Guinevere and his Court sleeping by a table on which lie a garter, a sword and a bugle. The garter must be cut and the horn blown, at which Arthur will arise and lead the Britons to victory. But the visitor only does the first and Arthur wakes only to fall asleep again. The Richmond version concerns one Potter Thompson, who is dismissed with these words by Arthur:

> Potter Thompson, Potter Thompson, hadst thou blown the horn,
> Thou hadst been the greatest man that ever was born.

A similar rhyme is used at Sewingshields. Other northern localities have similar stories; as with Welsh legend, the place-name was changed by each storyteller.

Cadbury in Somerset also claims to be Arthur's sleeping-place, although he has never been seen there. It was here that an incident related to Dean Robinson of Wells by a friend took place:

> When I was a student at Wells Theological College in the year 1902, the late Mr A. Clarke, an old artist and antiquarian who was then living in the Vicar's Close, told me that he had paid a visit with a party of antiquaries to Cadbury Camp, and while there, had been approached by an old man, a native of the place, with the question, *Have you come to take the king out?*[7]

[7] J. Armitage Robinson, *Two Glastonbury Legends* (Cambridge 1926) 53.

This tradition, however, goes back to a sixteenth-century identification of Cadbury with Camelot, first recorded by Leland:

At the very south ende of the chirch of South-Cadbyri standith Camallate, sumtyme a famose toun or castelle, apon a verry torre or hille, wunderfully enstrengtheid of nature.... In the upper parte of the coppe of the hille be 4 diches or trenches, and a balky waulle of yerth betwixt every one of them. In the very toppe of the hille above al the trenchis is *magna area* or *campus* of a 20. acres or more by estimation, wher yn dyverse places men may se fundations and *rudera* of walles. There was much dusky blew stone that people of the villages therby hath caryid away.... Much gold, sylver and coper of the Romaine coynes hath be found ther yn plouing; and lykewise in the rootes of this hille, with many other antique thinges, and especial by este. Ther was found *in hominum memoria* a horse shoe of sylver at Camallate.

The people can telle nothing ther but that they have hard say that Arture much resortid to Camalat.... Diverse villages there about bere the name Camalat by an addition, as Quene-Camallat, and other.[8]

Leland betrays the reason for the original association of Cadbury and Camelot: the fortuitous presence nearby of a village named Camel, from the early form Cantmael found as far back as the tenth century. 'Queen's' refers to Edward I's gift of it to his wife in 1284. And we have already seen how slight the possible archaeological links between Arthur and Cadbury camp are; this is no echo of an old tradition, but the chance identification of two similar names.

When a Welsh monarch came at last to rule the whole of Britain, the folklore of Arthur was turned to political ends. Within a few years of the completion of *Le Mort Darthur*, it seemed that a real King Arthur might soon rule in England. The accession of Henry VII, proud of his deeply-rooted Welsh ancestry, brought to the throne a dynasty whose promise of a better order of things combined with a vigorous nationalist policy was symbolised in their political propaganda by the revival of the idea of the 'return of Arthur'. The eldest son of Henry VII was christened Arthur, and was created prince of Wales in November 1489, an event duly celebrated by John Skelton and the Court poets. Despite Arthur's untimely death in 1502, the Arthurian theme continued to play a large part in the mythology of the Tudor dynasty. Manuscript genealogies from Elizabeth's reign trace her lineage back to Arthur, and that strange magus Dr John Dee reported in 1580 on 'Her Majesties Title Royall, to many forrain Countries, kingdomes and provinces by good testimony and sufficient proofs recorded', based on the Arthurian stories in the *History of the Kings of Britain*; Elizabeth received the document with approval, though Burghley, her rational and cautious minister, took a dim view of such imperial ambitions. Perhaps influenced by his acquaintance with Dee, Richard

[8] *The Itinerary of John Leland* ed. Lucy Toulmin Smith (London 1907) I, 151.

138

Hakluyt began his *Principal Navigations of the English Nation* with an account of Arthur's northern conquests.

Tudor royal pageants were often constructed around the theme of the Nine Worthies, a popular subject inherited from medieval writers. Three classical, three pagan and three Christian heroes made up the nine, Arthur being the first of three Christian worthies, followed by Charlemagne and Godfrey of Bouillon, King of Jerusalem. Arthur appears at pageants at Coventry in 1498; at the marriage of Margaret Tudor and James IV of

39 *Arthur as emperor, from a set of tapestries depicting the Nine Worthies, woven in Paris in about 1400: the composition is not unlike that used for God the Father in a contemporary missal. (Metropolitan Museum of Art, New York).*

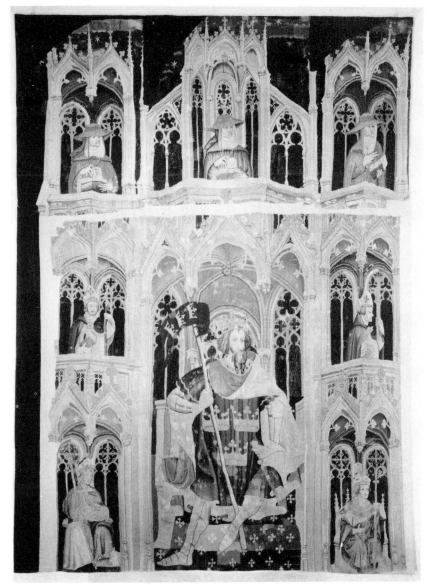

Scotland in 1503; at the Field of the Cloth of Gold in 1520; and in London processions of 1522 and 1554. At an entertainment for Elizabeth at Gray's Inn in 1587, a play modelled on Seneca, *The Misfortunes of Arthur* by Thomas Hughes, was the piece chosen, with subject matter from Geoffrey of Monmouth. The tradition was continued under the Stuarts: an anagram current early in James' reign, and quoted by Camden in his *Remaines Concerning Britain* reflected popular hopes under another new dynasty, identifying the Arthur whom Scottish historians had so reviled with the Scottish king:

> Charles Iames Steuart
> Claimes Arthures seat

Ben Jonson, writing masques for James' elder son, Prince Henry, introduced Arthurian themes. In *Prince Henry's Barriers* of 1612, devised as the framework for a tournament, Arthur appears in the guise of the star Arcturus to give his blessing to the proceedings; and *The Masque of Oberon*, in which Prince Henry played Oberon, pays homage to James as a second Arthur.

Meanwhile, Tudor antiquarians, encouraged to investigate Arthurian history by the royal use of the legend, were fighting out a bitter battle over his real character. Polydore Vergil, an Italian who spent some years in England on Papal business, was the first to attempt to question Geoffrey of Monmouth's wilder flights of fancy in his *Historia Anglica*, published at Basle in 1534. This was violently attacked by nationalist historians. John Leland, as King's Antiquary to Henry VIII, was almost duty bound to offer a defence to such passages as this in Polydore Vergil:

> As concerninge this noble prince, for the marvelus force of his boddie, and the invincible valiaunce of his minde, his posteritee hath allmoste vaunted and divulged such gestes, as in our memorie emonge the Italiens are commonlie noysed of Roland, the nephew of Charles the Great bie his sister, allbeit hee perished in the floure of his yowthe; for the common people is at this presence soe affectioned, that with wonderus admiration they extol Arthure unto the heavens, alleginge that hee daunted three capitans of the Saxons in plain feelde; that hee subdewed Scotlande with the Iles adjoyninge; that in the teritorie of the Parisiens he manfulie overthrew the Romaines, with there capitan Lucius; that hee did depopulat Fraunce; that finallie hee slewe giauntes, and appalled the hostes of sterne and warlike menne.... Not manie years since in the abbey of Galstonburie was extructed for Arthur a magnificent sepulchre, that the posteritee might gather how worthie he was of all monuments, wheras in the dayes of Arthure this abbaye was not builded.[9]

[9] Polydore Vergil, *Polydore Vergil's English History* ed. Sir H. Ellis (Camden Society Old Series XXXVI) London 1846, 121–2.

40 *The Renaissance vision of Arthur: the statue of King Arthur from the monument of Maximilian I, himself a great patron of chivalry, in the Hofkirche at Innsbruck. The design is by Dürer, and the statue was cast by Peter Vischer of Nuremburg: it is over life-size, and has been called 'the finest knightly figure of the German Renaissance'.*

Leland's riposte, the *Assertio Inclytissimi Arturii (Assertion of the Most Noble Arthur)* appeared in 1544, and depended on enthusiasm rather than any tangible evidence:

But here if ouer and besides this I should endeavour largely, to adorne Arthure with praise as the multitude of Authours do most truly write and agree upon him; sooner should copy of eloquence faile, then magnificencie of lightsome testimony howsoever. Be it sufficient then that we use at this present the most famouse commendations, though of fewe writers. I pray you, what is the cause that Trittemeus in his breefe Crounicle maketh so excellent mention of Arthure. Doubtlesse the cause is plaine enough. For by reason he learned the same of others in plaine trouth, therefore did he as thankfull commit it unto posteritie which thing doubtlesse he would never have done, had he doubted of the veritie of the cause....

What just occasion wish I here to be given me of Polidorus the Italian, that even by some memorable testimony of his, I might also advance Arthures countinance, and make him looke aloft? He handleth Arthures cause in deed, but by the way, he yet is so fainte harted, luke warme and so negligent that he makes me not onely to laugh, but also to be angry (as while he is contrary to truth, and filled with Italian bitternesse) I know not whether he smile or be angry....[10]

In the purely literary field, other romances than Malory's enjoyed a degree of popularity, the most important being Lord Berners' translation of a widely-read fifteenth-century French romance, *Arthur of Little Britain*, which appeared *c.*1530. The translation itself does not approach that by the same author of *Huon of Bordeux*, but it is the plot which is of most interest to us. It is a fairy tale pure and simple, the story of a lover who beholds his beloved in a dream and seeks her human counterpart. Of this ethereal theme Arthur is the hero: and all pretence of reality disappears. It was not surprising that the Protestant moralists should attack the romances as part of the corrupt old order, and Roger Ascham put the case forcefully in his *Scholemaster*:

In our forefather's tyme, whan Papistrie, as a standynge poole, covered and overflowed all England, fewe bookes were read in our tong, savyng certaine bookes of chevalrie, as they said, for pastime and pleasure; which, as some say, were made in monasteries by idle monkes or wanton canons. As one, for example, *Morte Arthure*, the whole pleasure of which booke standeth in two speciall poyntes, in open mans slaughter and bold bawdrye. In which booke those be counted the noblest knightes, that do kill most men without any quarrell, and commit foulest aduoulteres by subtlest shiftes, as Sir Launcelote with the wife of King Arthure his master: Syr Tristram with the wife of Kyng Marke his

[10] John Leland, tr. R. Robinson, *The Assertion of King Arthure*, in Christopher Middleton, *The Famous History of Chinon of England* ed. W. E. Mead (EETS OS 165) (London 1925) 51–53.
[11] Roger Ascham, *The Scholemaster* ed J. E. B. Mayor (London 1863) 81–2.
[12] Edmund Spenser, *The Faerie Queene* (Cambridge 1909) i.526–7.

uncle: Syr Lamerocke with the wife of King Lote, that was his own aunte. This is good stuffe for wise men to laughe at, or honest men to take pleasure at. Yet I know, when God's Bible was banished the court, and Morte Arthure received into the Princes chamber.[11]

After such onslaughts, it is hardly surprising that the successors of *Arthur of Little Britain* are cast at a more popular level, such as Thomas Munday's translations of similar romances at the end of the sixteenth century. Two or three original works of slight merit appeared in the early seventeenth century, among them Richard Johnson's *Romance of Tom a Lincolne, the Red Rose Knight* of about 1610. It was a genre which soon descended even further to the level of popular chapbooks; those on Merlin were ridiculed *en passant* by Swift and Pope, but it was Fielding who demolished the romantic Arthur in *Tragedy of Tragedies or the Life and Death of Tom Thumb the Great*, a burlesque in which the diminutive hero is eventually devoured by 'the expanded jaws of a red-cow'.

More serious projects had meanwhile come to fruition, though even these are far removed from the medieval material on Arthur. First and foremost is Edmund Spenser's *The Faerie Queene* (1590). Spenser's starting point was the epic by Ariosto on the story of Roland, *Orlando Furioso*, tempered by the more sober example of another Italian working in the same epic vein, Torquato Tasso. Tasso had recommended Arthur as a suitable epic subject, though he himself chose the Crusades and he had also echoed Aristotle's advice that the epic hero should embody one particular virtue. Spenser's choice, in view of the Italianate sympathies of the period, may well have been determined by this advice. Writing to Raleigh, he asserts:

> The generall end therefore of all the booke is to fashion a gentleman or noble person in vertuous and gentle discipline: which for that I conceived shoulde be most plausible and pleasing, being coloured with an historicall fiction, the which most part of men delight to read, rather for variety of matter, then for profite of the ensample: I chose the historye of king Arthure, as most fitte for the excellency of his person, being made famous by many men's former workes, and also furthest from the danger of envy, and suspition of the present time. I labour to pourtraict in Arthure, before he was king, the image of a brave knight, perfected in the twelve private morall vertues, as Aristotle hath devised.... So in the person of prince Arthure I sette forth magnificence in particular, which vertue for that (according to Aristotle and the rest) it is the perfection of all the rest, and conteineth in it them all, therefore in the whole course I mention the deedes of Arthure applyable to that vertue which I write of in that booke.[12]

41 King Arthur as one of the great English monarchs, from a set of windows in St Mary's Hall, Coventry, dating from about 1450.

But *The Faerie Queene* borrows only the person of Arthur and some few trappings from the world of romance. It is above all an allegory, whose plot is dictated by the working out of a greater meaning. The whole concept owes much to the cult centred on Elizabeth herself as Gloriana, whose knight Arthur is. The use of this or that detail from romances, whether Malory, *Libeaus Desconus* or *Arthur of Little Britain*, does not make it a piece of true Arthurian literature; rather, following the fashion for Arthurian references in pageantry, Spenser has borrowed the name Arthur for his character Magnificence. And when the poet begins work, Arthur remains a shadowy figure beside the more vivid portraits in the individual episodes. It is for these that *The Faerie Queene* is remembered as poetry rather than the grandiose and eventually uncompleted architecture by which they are framed. And besides, because Magnificence partakes of all twelve virtues, to each of which a separate knight is assigned, Arthur's function becomes that of a double, often superfluous, to the other heroes. Yet his splendid appearance at the outset remains memorable.

> His haughtie helmet, horrid all with gold,
> Both glorious brightnesse, and great terrour bred;
> For all the crest a Dragon did enfold
> With greedie pawes, and over all did spred
> His golden wings; his dreadfull hideous hed,
> Close couched on the bever, seem'd to throw
> From flaming mouth bright sparkles fierie red,
> That suddeine horror to faint harts did show,
> And scaly tayle was strecht adowne his backe full low.[13]

I.vii.31

Spenser's vision of Prince Arthur is in many ways highly artificial, like the chivalry practiced at the Elizabethan court, with its elaborate mottoes and long-winded symbolism. The whole of *The Faerie Queene* has a deliberately archaic feeling, looking back to a golden age – a theme common in the celebration of 'Gloriana' herself – and Arthur is present as the monarch who had once ruled over such a golden age. Spenser deliberately chooses to portray a period of Arthur's life which does not appear in the romances or histories, before he was king; the careful avoidance of any conflict with the traditional account of Arthur says much about Spenser's respectful attitude towards his literary predecessors. In the end, however, *The Faerie Queene* is a cul-de-sac in terms of Arthurian tradition: only one writer, a decade or two later, took up Spenser's themes and despite the greatness of Spenser's literary achievement, it did not bring about a revival in Arthur's popularity.

[13] *The Faerie Queene* Book I, canto vii, 31 (Cambridge edn. i.90).

For *The Faerie Queene* was the only Arthurian project by a major writer to come to fruition during the sixteenth to eighteenth centuries. Milton considered an Arthurian epic, and it played an important part in the process of arriving at his final theme, *Paradise Lost*. Though there are only two definite references to his intention of writing this work, in *To Manso* and *Epitaphium Damonis*, his interest seems to have been keen for some time. But it was certainly never more than a project, and he later grew sceptical of the legends. In his *British History*, he questions the very existence of Arthur, and pours scorn on the stories told about him, as though on closer examination he had found that the subject lacked a firm basis and was therefore not suited to his great work.

Another project not fulfilled in its original form was that mentioned by John Dryden in the preface to his translation of Juvenal. He states his intention of giving up his dramatic work in order to write an Arthurian epic. Financial circumstances forced him to continue to write plays, which were more profitable, but his idea eventually took shape as a dramatic opera in collaboration with Purcell, *King Arthur*. The first version had a political bias in support of Charles II, but since production was delayed until 1691, substantial alterations had to be made. In the process most of the central part of the work was cut out, and its final form is a very free version of Arthur's struggle against the Saxons, treated in the same fairy-tale manner as his adaptation of *The Tempest* four years later. Enchantments play a large part in the rather strained plot, which is entirely of Dryden's invention. It is Purcell's music which has given the work a continuing life.

The first half of the eighteenth century marks the low ebb of Arthur's literary fortunes: the prevailing taste for the classical in literature and the arts, and the beginnings of serious scholarly work on the Anglo-Saxon period conspired to banish both the romances and the historical Arthur from the scene. In the period 1700–1750 there is no work of any note whatsoever on the Arthurian legends.

Chapter 8

The Search for the Spiritual: King Arthur in the Nineteenth Century

The extraordinary flowering of Arthurian literature in the nineteenth century after the Arthurian stories had lain dormant for so long, is a remarkable phenomenon. Despite a number of recent books on the subject the revival has not yet been adequately explained. Such books have tended to concentrate on a chronological approach; but there is another way of approaching the Arthurian revival. Why did it come about in the first place? What were the attraction or usefulness of the Arthurian legend to the many writers, artists and composers who created works based on it? How much was the success of one poet, Tennyson, responsible for the flood of works on the subject?

The vision of the past at the end of the eighteenth century was coloured by two very different intellectual movements, one scholarly and the other poetic. In the world of scholarship, the latter part of the eighteenth century saw the culmination of the work of the scholars of the Enlightenment, the rationalist tradition which stemmed from the renaissance rediscovery of classical philosophy. This culmination took the form of a number of historical works of synthesis, general histories on the grand scale. These relied for their source material on the fruit of long years of research by the scholars of the seventeenth century, that golden age of scholarship which saw the work of the Maurist monks in France on monastic history, the beginnings of the Bollandists' study of saints' lives, and the printing in accurate editions by a group of English scholars based on Oxford of most of the major chronicles of the English middle ages. Editions of the most important state papers in the English public records were also printed. From these editions, and from the work of Continental and English scholars on classical history, stemmed the histories of David Hume and William Robertson, of Pierre

Rapin and, most famous of all, Edward Gibbon. *The Decline and Fall of the Roman Empire* is still read today; but Hume's and Rapin's histories of England, and Rollin's vast history of the pre-classical world were equally influential in their time. But their attitude towards history was not that of mere curiosity; history was a branch of philosophy, 'philosophy teaching by examples' in Bolingbroke's words. There was no interest in the past for its own sake.

Such an interest in the dramatic moments of history, emotional and idealising and very far from the cool scepticism of a Gibbon or a Hume, was provided by the romantic movement of the early nineteenth century. Romantic interest in things medieval was partly a simple reaction against the insistence that classical art-forms were the only possible media of artistic expression, and classical or Biblical subjects the only possible themes. Classicism had held sway in France in the seventeenth century, and had influenced the embryonic German literature of the period. When the reaction against this classical tyranny came, it spread in turn to England, partly because French and German writers admired Shakespeare as the exemplar of an author free from classical restraints, and partly because the medieval literature of England was itself being rediscovered and admired. However, it was not the romantic poets who reshaped English attitudes to things medieval; Wordsworth, for all his rhapsodising over Tintern Abbey, was an obscure and avant-garde poet, published only in Bristol, with dangerous ideas about the French revolution. The English public had learned to look at the past in a new way from a very different source, the work of English painters. From 1760 onwards, the annual exhibitions of the Society of Artists, which became the Royal Academy in 1768, were full of vast canvases depicting the heroic moments of British history in a highly unhistorical fashion, usually in quite inappropriate eighteenth-century or classical dress. By the beginning of the nineteenth century, a note of historical realism had crept in, and soon the artists were avidly researching the available sources for true contemporary portraits and dress. This visual representation of the past pre-dates the major nineteenth-century literary works inspired by similar historical events, and is a major and hitherto underestimated influence on such literary activity. Artistic antiquarianism relied heavily on the works of Joseph Strutt, whose impressive series of volumes published between 1773 and 1801 on the visual records of the past, particularly manuscript illuminations, was the foundation of the scientific study of the history of costume. To take a single example of the effect of Strutt's work, the famous picture of *The Pilgrimage to Canterbury* by Thomas Stothard, painted in 1806–7 and now in the Tate Gallery, London, relies very heavily on Strutt's engravings for the

42 The discovery of Prince Arthur's tomb *by John Mortimer. This drawing of c.1767 is the only instance (to my knowledge) of one of the 'history-painters' attempting an Arthurian subject. It antedates Thomas Warton's poem* The Grave of Arthur *by ten years. (National Gallery of Scotland).*

correct dress for the two dozen characters portrayed, and several of the figures derive almost directly from the medieval illuminations in manuscripts of *The Canterbury Tales*.[1]

It is against this background that we need to look at the literary scholarship of the period, remembering that such pictures were made widely available to the public by engravings, and hence had a much wider influence than we might at first suppose. Major historical texts had been a legitimate subject for scholarship since the Renaissance, but in the literary field, only classical texts had been accorded the full attention of scholars. There were occasional exceptions, but by and large the printing of literature was a commercial operation, and the energy expended on obtaining a correct text was much less for a play or a poem than for a chronicle. Towards the end of the eighteenth century, this attitude began to change radically. Bishop Percy's *Reliques of Old English Poetry*, the work of La Curne de Sainte Palaye in France, and the editions produced by Thomas Warton and the eccentric, quarrelsome but often very accurate Joseph Ritson, all

[1] For the use of research by the history painters see Roy Strong, *And when did you last see your Father? The Victorian Painter and British History* (London 1978) 13–76.

combined to bring literary scholarship to bear for the first time on the masterpieces of the middle ages, using the principles outlined by the great classical editors of the eighteenth century and by Dr Johnson in relation to Shakespeare. Such an interest was encouraged by the new fashion for things Gothic, again part of the reaction against classicism; Hurd's *Letters on Chivalry and Romance* and the patronage of Horace Walpole at Strawberry Hill all helped to bring medieval literature out of the dusty cupboards where it had lain for so long and onto the library tables of scholars and antiquarians.

But the process of popularising such literature, in the way that the work of the history painters had been popularised through engravings, was to prove a slow one. Although Percy's *Reliques* included six Arthurian ballads, and Thomas Warton wrote a poem on the discovery of Arthur's body at Glastonbury, the first edition of a complete Arthurian romance in England did not appear until 1802, when Joseph Ritson printed three such medieval English romances. George Ellis included modernised versions of two more in his *Specimens of Early English Poetry* of 1805. Walter Scott edited the middle English version of the legend of Tristram and Iseult, a poem of no great merit, in 1804; but by association with his later success as a novelist, this edition was reprinted five times in the next four decades. In 1816–17, three editions of Malory's *Morte Darthur* appeared, and this was, at least for a time, the most popular and accessible version of the Arthurian tales. I say for a time, because a proper study of Malory reprints and editions in the nineteenth century is badly needed. It seems that there was no new edition of Malory between 1817 and 1858, and it is not clear whether the 1816–17 editions were reprinted frequently, or indeed reprinted at all, during that period. There was no edition of Malory in a popular series like Bohn's Antiquarian Library in the 1840s; instead, the enquiring reader would have found Ellis's modernised versions from *Specimens of Early English Poetry* available in a modestly priced edition, along with a volume containing Geoffrey of Monmouth and *The History of the Britons* in translation. These, rather than Malory, must have been many readers' first introduction to matters Arthurian.[2]

Nor were the first great successes of the medieval revival based on Arthurian material. Sir Walter Scott, although he had written an Arthurian poem in 1813[3], made his name with a series of historical novels, beginning with *Waverley* in 1814. These are the literary equivalents of the history paintings; based on sound antiquarian research, they offer an apparently realistic and plausible view of a real past, but one in which the novelist can manipulate character and event to a limited degree without offending the historical purist. Scott and his followers, men such

[2] For detailed accounts of the works in this chapter, see Beverly Taylor and Elisabeth Brewer, *The Return of King Arthur: British and American Arthurian Literature since 1800* (Cambridge & Totowa N. J., 1983).

as G. P. R. James, worked in a genre which had implicit restrictions on invention and portrayal of character: the novelist could not depart radically from the accepted historical reality.

This limitation made historical material difficult to use in many literary forms. It is precisely in these areas that the more fluid material offered by the stories about Arthur was at an advantage. Most works using the legend are poetic; there are a few plays at the end of the century and there are two major satires. (It is noticeable that serious Arthurian novels are almost unknown in the nineteenth century). Of the poems, the majority are narrative, while only two poems or groups of poems approach the epic, and only a very few are lyrics. So the key for which we are looking is a shift in public demand and poetic taste towards the narrative poem, but a narrative poem which differs from the romantic narrative poems in that it concentrates on a heroic ideal or figure rather than on the person of the poet or his double. This change in public taste can be plausibly set at the beginning of Victoria's reign; and within the first two decades of her reign we find the two epics just mentioned. Epic is a notoriously difficult form, and disastrous Arthurian epics are not uncommon. Edward Bulwer-Lytton's *King Arthur* (1848) is a good example of what can go wrong. Lytton's learning was immense, and when applied to the novel, as in *The Last Days of Pompeii* the result could be masterly. In *King Arthur*, it is disastrous. The plot is as rambling as that of *Don Juan*, attempting to bring in all kinds of classical and Norse myth. Lytton also tries his hand at humour, making Gawain a faintly comic figure as in some of the medieval romances, but the effect is only to devalue his serious passages, because it is hard to tell when he means to amuse us and when he does so unintentionally. Yet there was a demand for such ambitious works, successful or not; Lytton's poem went through four substantial editions in thirty years.[4]

The other Arthurian epic of the nineteenth century is of course Tennyson's *Idylls of the King*[5]. But any analysis of these poems must start from the fact that they were not written as a single epic. The earliest of his Arthurian poems, *The Lady of Shalott*, is a lyric, published in 1832, as are two of the three poems published in 1842. It was these early poems that inspired the Pre-Raphaelites to their Arthurian enthusiasm; in 1854, Burne-Jones instructed a friend to learn Tennyson's *Sir Galahad* by heart before joining the chivalric order which he and William Morris were proposing to found.

Yet although Tennyson published Arthurian lyrics in 1832 and 1842, he had been thinking of an epic, as a sketch written in 1833 shows:

[3] *The Bridal of Triermain* (part published anonymously in *The Edinburgh Review*, 1809); Taylor & Brewer 44–9.
[4] Taylor & Brewer, 75–9.
[5] Taylor & Brewer, 68–75, 89–128. The documentation for the evolution of Tennyson's poems is printed in *The Poems of Tennyson*, ed. Christopher Ricks (London 1969). See also F. E. L. Priestley, 'Tennyson's Idylls', *University of Toronto Quarterly* XIX, 1949 35–49, rpd in *Tennyson's Poetry* ed. Robert W. Hill jr (New York & London 1971) 634–48.

On the latest limit of the West in the Land of Lyonesse, where, save the rocky Isles of Scilly, all is now wild sea, rose the sacred Mount of Camelot. It rose from the deeps with gardens and bowers and palaces, and at the top of the Mount was King Arthur's hall, and the holy Minster with the Cross of gold. Here dwelt the King in glory apart, while the Saxons whom he had overthrown in twelve battles ravaged the land, and ever came nearer and nearer.

The Mount was the most beautiful in the world, sometimes green and fresh in the beam of morning, sometimes all one splendour, folded in the golden mists of the West. But all underneath it was hollow, and the mountain trembled when the seas rushed bellowing through the porphyry caves; and there ran a prophecy that the mountain and the city on some wild morning would topple into the abyss and be no more.

It was night. The King sat in his Hall. Beside him sat the sumptuous Guinevere and about him were all his lords and knights of the Table Round. There they feasted, and when the feast was over, the bards sang to the King's glory.[6]

He returns to the idea of an epic in the framework written to explain the fragment *Morte d'Arthur*, published in 1842. Tennyson here presents a very ambivalent view of the epic form. He draws a picture of friends from University days reunited in later years round the fire one Christmas eve, talking of the decline of old customs. The conversation turns on the poetry of one of them, who has written an epic but has destroyed it because, as another of the company says

> 'He thought that nothing new was said, or else
> Something so said 'twas nothing – that a truth
> Looks freshest in the fashion of the day;
> God knows; he has a mint of reasons; ask.
> It pleased *me* well enough.' 'Nay, nay,' said Hall,
> 'Why take the style of those heroic times?
> For nature brings not back the mastodon,
> Nor we those times; and why should any man
> Remodel models?...'

But Tennyson half-answers his own objections at the end of the poem, when the narrator, under the spell of the poem, dreams of Arthur's return:

> There came a bark that, blowing forward, bore
> King Arthur, like a modern gentleman
> Of stateliest port; and all the people cried,
> 'Arthur is come again: he cannot die.'
> Then those that stood upon the hills behind
> Repeated – 'Come again, and thrice as fair;'
> And, further inland, voices echoed – 'Come
> With all good things, and war shall be no more.'

6 Ricks 1460–1.

These lines contain the germ of Tennyson's approach to the Arthurian material; he uses the ancient stories to portray characters who are indeed modern gentlemen, but he does so because he knows that to idealise a modern hero in the way that it is possible to idealise Arthur would be an unrewarding and self-defeating task. The lines also contain an echo of the dangers of such an attempt, for the image of King Arthur as a modern gentleman 'of stateliest port' borders on the comic. But the tensions between modernity and the ancient tales were already satisfactorily resolved in the actual poem which lay between prologue and epilogue, and which was to form the central section of *The Passing of Arthur* in the final version of the Idylls.

The idea of a large-scale, if not epic, work continued to haunt Tennyson, and various sketches more or less relevant to the final design survive from the 1840s and 1850s. A second memorandum gives an outline of the underlying symbolism, traces of which were to persist in the finished version. King Arthur himself was to represent religious faith, and he was to have two wives, the first of whom was to be banished before he married the second, but later recalled. They were both to be called Guinevere, echoing the theme of the true and false Guineveres found in Welsh legend; the first was to be the symbol of primitive Christianity, the second of Roman Catholicism. Mordred represented scepticism and Merlin science; Merlin's daughter was to wed Mordred. The Lady of the Lake, Nimue, stood for evil and corruption, a role which was little altered in the final version. Among the objects associated with Arthur, Excalibur stood for war, and the Round Table for 'liberal institutions'.

The next draft, some years later, is cast in a very different outward form, as a masque; but hints of the symbolism remain. Had Tennyson completed it, it would have been an original, though probably unsuccessful, contribution to Arthurian lore, with its own chronology and treatment of characters. The outline runs as follows:

FIRST ACT: Sir Mordred and his party. Mordred inveighs against the King and the Round Table. The knights, and the quest. Mordred scoffs at the Ladies of the Lake, doubts whether they are supernatural beings, etc. Mordred's cringing interview with Guinevere. Mordred and the Lady of the Lake. Arthur lands in Albyn.

SECOND ACT: Lancelot's embassy and Guinevere. The Lady of the Lake meets Arthur and endeavours to persuade him not to fight with Sir Mordred. Arthur will not be moved from his purpose. Lamentation of the Lady of the lake. Elaine. Marriage of Arthur.

THIRD ACT: Oak tomb of Merlin. The song of Nimue. Sir Mordred comes to consult Merlin. Coming away meets Arthur. Their fierce dialogue. Arthur consults Sir L. and Sir Bedivere. Arthur weeps over Merlin and is reproved by Nimue, who inveighs against Merlin. Arthur asks Merlin the issue of the battle. Merlin will not enlighten him. Nimue requests Arthur to question Merlin again. Merlin tells him he shall bear rule again, but that the Ladies of the Lake can return no more. Guinevere throws away the diamonds into the river. The Court and the dead Elaine.

FOURTH ACT: Discovery by Merlin and Nimue of Lancelot and Guinevere. Arthur and Guinevere's meeting and parting.

FIFTH ACT: The battle. Chorus of the Ladies of the Lake. The throwing away of Excalibur and departure of Arthur.[7]

It was in fact only from 1857 onwards that Tennyson really began to work on the Arthurian legend again, and he began with four poems which are really separate love-stories taken from Malory. It was another decade before he began to shape the framework of the cycle, with the writing of 'The Coming of Arthur', and the last poem was written in 1874–5. The final version of the cycle did not appear until 1885. So *The Idylls of the King* was a work which evolved over a period of forty years; its unity does not arise from an original blueprint, faithfully followed, but from continual reshaping. Tennyson's adoption of the plan which he seemed to regard so ambivalently in 1842 needs to be examined against the background of his changing achievements and of changing public demand. In the 1860s and 1870s, Victorian ambition and confidence in Britain's imperial mission was growing, and the tone of the literary critics towards Tennyson's work had changed. From the doubtful comments on the Arthurian poems in 1842, the Poet Laureate of the greatest power in the world was expected to provide the nation with a suitable epic. Such a demand was never precisely formulated, but it was implied in many of the reviewers' comments as work progressed. *The Idylls of the King*, perhaps more than any other Arthurian work, reflects the social concerns, the aspirations, ambitions and ideals of the period in which they were written. This explains why in the end both critics and public found a medieval epic acceptable; indeed its spectacular popularity was undoubtedly due to its consciousness of the mood of the times, down to the faint hints of parallels between Arthur and Prince Albert, to whom the work was finally dedicated. And the reason why Tennyson was able to reconcile the tension between 'remodelling models' and producing the great and original work that the *Idylls* undoubtedly is, was that only the Arthurian legends could offer him the range of material which he needed in

[7] Ricks 1461–2.

order to satisfy his poetic impulse. The unity of the *Idylls* cannot conceal the fact that Tennyson has by no means told the whole story. Had he chosen a historical theme for the long-awaited epic, he would have been much more circumscribed. With the Arthurian stories, he could vary his mood and range from poem to poem, while still remaining within the framework provided by his original. This freedom meant that he was still free to respond to inspiration, and was not forced to work within a pre-determined plot; he works by antithesis – 'The Coming of Arthur'/'The Passing of Arthur', the two poems of 1859, 'Elaine'

43 *The great Victorian photographer Julia Margaret Cameron published two volumes of illustrations to Tennyson's poems; the first was entirely devoted to the* Idylls of the King, *the second included pictures based on two other poems. She used friends as models; Arthur was portrayed by her husband. The results are a remarkable insight into how the Victorians saw the* Idylls: *the three reproduced here are: 'And reverently they bore her into hall' ('Lancelot and Elaine'); 'So like a shattered column lay the King' ('The Passing of Arthur'); and 'The Parting of Sir Launcelot and Queen Guinevere'.*

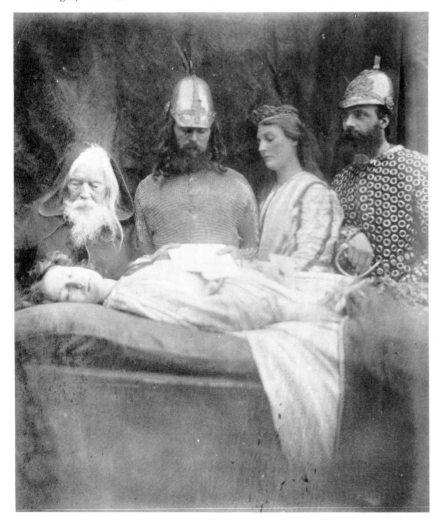

and 'Guinevere', published as *The True and the False* – rather than by deliberate linking of one poem to the next. Because of this relative freedom, he can create poetry like 'shot-silk, with many glancing colours. Every reader must find his own interpretation according to his ability.'

Despite Tennyson's warnings, it is not unreasonable to read a broad and general symbolism into the poems. The subject is that of man's Utopian dreams coming into contact with practical life and the warring elements of the flesh. The tragedy of Arthur stems from the ruin of high aspirations by a single sin. Arthur's birth is a mystery, as is his death: 'from the great deep to the great deep he goes.' Between the two lies life with its conflict of flesh and spirit. He attempts to realise himself in the sensual world, represented by Guinevere, and to control and elevate human passion and capacity by 'liberal institutions', represented here, as in the earlier draft, by the Round Table. Thus Sir

Galahad, who might at first seem to be the hero of the poems, is not in fact Tennyson's ideal: he is the figure of spiritual life divorced from this earth, who negates man's dual nature by withdrawing into purely spiritual realms. Merlin stands for the intellect, and his disastrous affair with Vivien is symbolic of the corruption of the intellectual by the sensual.

The keystone of Tennyson's cycle is therefore Arthur and the Round Table. Arthur himself appears as little short of perfect: warrior, statesman, the uniting force of the Round Table. The monk Ambrosius says of his knights:

> Good ye are and bad, and like to coins,
> Some true, some light, but every one of you
> Stamp'd with the image of the King;...
>
> (The Holy Grail 25–27)

To follow and obey Arthur is the foremost law of the Round Table; and the high demands he makes are learnt by Gareth before he rides out to seek Camelot and Arthur's company:

The King
Will bind thee by such vows, as is a shame
A man should not be bound by, yet the which
No man can keep...

(Gareth & Lynette 265–8)

The vows that the King demands are clear and restrained, lacking the fire which knightly ardour might well desire; they accord well with Guinevere's first assessment of him as 'cold, high, self-contain'd, and passionless', though the description of the founding of the Order shows how Arthur himself could breathe enthusiasm into his warriors. Tennyson's code is dutiful rather than inspiring:

To reverence the King, as if he were
Their conscience, and their conscience as their King,
To break the heathen and uphold the Christ,
To ride abroad redressing human wrongs,

44 *F.G.Stephens' painting* Morte D'Arthur *is unfinished, but all the more striking for that reason: it vividly conveys the sense of despair and isolation at the end of Arthur's tragedy. (Tate Gallery).*

To speak no slander, no, nor listen to it,
To honour his own word as if his God's,
To lead sweet lives in purest chastity,
To love one maiden only, cleave to her,
And worship her by years of noble deeds,
Until they won her.

(Guinevere 465–74)

It is in his match with Guinevere that Arthur fails. He misjudges Lancelot, misjudges Guinevere, failing to see the other side of the coin, the carnal passions which move him not at all. He chooses Guinevere partly because only the most beautiful bride can match his position and spiritual attainment, forgetting that earthly and heavenly beauty are not one and the same thing. And from the high hopes of the early poems, a steady progress towards the abyss of failure develops. Tennyson sums up Lancelot in paradoxes:

His honour rooted in dishonour stood
And faith unfaithful kept him falsely true

(Lancelot and Elaine 871–2)

The sin of Lancelot and Guinevere permeates the Court. Balin is unable to save himself because of the false ideals they have spread; Pelleas and Etarre imitate their sin; the Holy Grail is misunderstood and misused by the knights imbued with this worldly ideal, of whom Lancelot is the chief, and they approach it with superstition instead of reverence. *The Last Tournament* shows the final stage of the process, cynicism and sets the decay caused by the false ideal with the original truth. Lancelot the bold has become slothful, Tristram the courteous has forgotten his courtesy.

The cycle of poems is set at intervals throughout the natural year: *The Coming of Arthur* on New Year's Day, his wedding 'when the world is white with may', the appearance of the Grail at Camelot on a summer's night. *The Last Tournament* is in the dead time of the year, autumn, while the final battle in midwinter looks forward from present disaster to the hope of the future rebirth and spring, through Lancelot and Guinevere's repentance, and the forgiveness offered them by Arthur.

Tennyson handles his material with varying degrees of freedom. *The Coming of Arthur* is part of the allegorical scheme, and therefore at variance with earlier versions; Arthur's antecedents are stripped of their immoral medieval legend and shrouded in obscurity instead. *Gareth and Lynette, Balin and Balan* and *Merlin and Vivien* all depend on Malory, while the two Geraint poems go back to the *Mabinogion* romance also retold by Chrétien de Troyes in his *Erec et Enide*.

45 *The last meeting of Arthur and Guinevere, from Gustav Doré's illustrated* Guinevere. *Doré's large volumes, eventually issued as a collection, were among the most popular editions of Tennyson.*

In *The Holy Grail*, Tennyson treats Malory much as Malory had treated the French romances, extracting various incidents and welding them into a compact and unified narrative. He introduces *The Last Tournament* before the final catastrophe, to set the moral scene; and in *Guinevere*, the Queen's retirement is moved back to precede Arthur's last battle though the original plan had been for Arthur's speech at the end of the poem to round off the cycle (of which George Meredith said that Arthur lectured his Queen 'like a curate'). The adaptation of the *Morte*

D'Arthur from the 1842 collection was Tennyson's final solution, adding 169 lines at the beginning, describing Arthur's dream and the actual battle, and 29 lines at the end which hark back to the line in *The Coming of Arthur*, 'From the great deep to the great deep he goes'.

It is hard for us today to recapture Tennyson's original impact, so debased has his noble idiom become through imitation and too frequent quotation. He is dealing in ideal and allegory rather than character, and his protagonists are often unconvincing. If he seems on occasions to lack real feeling, there is an atmosphere of high purpose in the tone of the poetry. This nobility falls easy prey to modern cynicism, as he himself foreshadowed in *The Last Tournament*, and today we exalt passion and freedom over Tennyson's conservative chivalry and order. What we can admire is his craftsmanship as a poet, the many lovely descriptive passages – often in marked contrast to his moral attitude to the scene, as in Lancelot and Guinevere's first meeting in May – and the power with which he portrays the attraction of his ideals.

Tennyson's use of Malory as the basis for his narratives was imitated by a number of lesser poets, particularly in the latter part of the nineteenth century, when, as Poet Laureate, he was both successful and highly influential. But few of these imitations deserve re-reading today. We have already noted the effect of Tennyson's early poems on the young Pre-Raphaelites, and the Arthurian stories played an important part in their mature work. The Pre-Raphaelites were committed champions of all things medieval, as their name implies: they looked to the period before the Renaissance, and to the time before the work of the Italian painter Raphael, for their inspiration. William Morris read Malory at an early age, and admired the Arthurian lyrics in Tennyson's 1842 collection of poems. In art, the Pre-Raphaelites represented a reaction against the great set-pieces of the history-painters, and in literature it is therefore not surprising to find them preferring the lyric. Their poems are introspective, heirs to the Romantic tradition, but with a self-consciousness which the great Romantic poets lacked. The Rossettis and William Morris were the chief poets among them, and Morris wrote a handful of Arthurian lyrics, which were among the poems in the collection he published in 1858.[8] These deserve to stand beside Tennyson's lyrics; they are studies of mood and character in the manner of *The Lady of Shalott*, but with a feeling and poignancy that Tennyson's more detached manner rarely achieves. Morris presents us with characters in the throes of a crisis, as in the greatest of the poems, *The Defence of Guenevere*. He plunges straight into his subject, without any introduction:

[8] Taylor & Brewer 135–48.

But knowing that they would have her speak,
She threw her wet hair backward from her brow,
Her hand close to her mouth touching her cheek
(The Defence of Guinevere, 1–3)

Morris's technique is to reinforce his depiction of strong emotions with powerful visual images, a reminder that he was painter as well as poet. Guenevere's memories are almost all of vivid scenes, in which colour plays a large part. There is the strange episode of the angel with the 'choosing-cloths', the one 'blue, wavy and long', the other 'cut red and short', in which the usual colour symbolism is reversed, and blue stands for hell, not heaven. There is the queen at daily mass:

And every morn I scarce could pray at all,
For Launcelot's red-gold hair would play,
Instead of sunlight, on the painted wall,
Mingled with dreams of what the priest did say; ...
(The Defence of Guinevere)

Guenevere moves between past nostalgia and present defiance, affecting indifference to the outcome of the judgement, justifying her infidelity by Arthur's 'little love' for her, and rejecting Gawain's accusations out of hand.

God knows I speak truth, saying that you lie!
All I have said is truth, by Christ's dear tears.
(The Defence of Guinevere)

The sound of Lancelot's rescuing charger ends the poem amid joyous relief, but the picture that remains is one of tragedy and despair. This same sense of the dark side of the Arthurian world is to be found in *Sir Galahad*, where Sir Bors speaks of the knights coming home 'foil'd from the great quest, in vain;/ In vain they struggle for the vision fair'. And likewise in *The Chapel in Lyonesse*, Sir Ozana le Cure Hardy declares with his dying breath that 'my life went wrong'. Morris achieves in these short poems his objective of portraying 'the perception and experience of tragic truth, of subtle and noble, terrible and piteous things'.

Although Morris seems to have planned an Arthurian epic in his youth, it was to classical and Norse myth that he turned for his longer poems, perhaps because these were written at a time when Tennyson's *Idylls* were nearing completion, and he did not wish to compete. Furthermore, his political views – he was an ardent socialist – had led him away from the aristocratic world of the romances to a rougher and cruder view of the middle ages, and he preferred to write of the Germanic heroes or of the English peasants. He had by this time gone beyond the original

161

46 *Two paintings by D.G.Rossetti on the Grail theme:* Sir Galahad, Sir Galahad at the Ruined Chapel. *(Tate Gallery, City of Birmingham Art Gallery).*

beliefs of the Pre-Raphaelites, to pursue his own very individual vision.

The other Arthurian works by the Pre-Raphaelites are all paintings. In 1857–8, Dante Gabriel Rossetti and his friends undertook a major cycle of frescoes based on Arthurian themes for the Oxford Union, a commission which was attended by a great deal of publicity. The frescoes themselves were long thought to have decayed almost totally, but recent photography has shown that it is their placing – high under a dome, between windows – which has made them almost invisible.[9] The project was carried out hurriedly, before the building had dried out properly, and with little knowledge of the necessary technique; the Pre-Raphaelites were great believers in inspiration, and many of their paintings have an immediacy about them which at best is striking, but which can sometimes make them look like a hurried sketch. The ten episodes represented all come from Malory; seven belong to the original Pre-Raphaelite scheme, and three were supplied later because Rossetti and his friends had not completed their work. Interestingly, in view of Morris's penchant for the tragic side of the Arthurian stories, the most impressive of the paintings is Rossetti's *The Failure of Sir Launcelot to Achieve*

[9] John Christian, *The Oxford Union Murals* (Chicago & London 1981, with colour microfiche).

162

the Grail, in which Sir Launcelot lies outside the Grail chapel dreaming of Guinevere. Morris himself chose a similarly negative theme, *Sir Palomydes' Jealousy of Sir Tristram*.

There is a striking insistence on the tragic moment, the point at which tensions are highest; and the artist is attempting to convey deep psychological truths usually left to his literary peers. We do not look at an ideal medieval dream world, but one where emotions become even more overpowering by contrast with the idyllic settings. Dante Gabriel Rossetti's oil paintings and watercolours on Arthurian themes are also closely linked in mood to Morris's poetry, particularly *Arthur's Tomb: the Last Meeting of Launcelot and Guinevere* and *Galahad at the Ruined Chapel*.

Sir Edward Burne Jones, on the other hand, preferred the spiritual side of the romances, and returned again and again to the theme of the Holy Grail, though he ranged widely in his choice of subjects: at the Oxford Union, he chose to paint *Merlin and*

Nimue, a subject which he discussed with Tennyson in 1858. His most striking achievement was the remarkable series of tapestries on the Grail quest designed by him and manufactured by Morris and Co., where his sense of form and attention to detail result in works which would have graced any medieval palace. He also designed the sets for J. Comyns Carr's play *King Arthur* in 1895, to which we shall return.

Painters outside Rossetti's and Morris's immediate circle were also attracted by the Arthurian legend. Obviously this was in part due to Tennyson's poems, and many subjects derive directly from his work, notably William Holman Hunt's exotic *Lady of Shalott*, which overlays the simplicity of Tennyson's poem with a wild Eastern imagery of the artist's own invention. In similar vein are Arthur Sandys's *Morgan le Fay*, in which the enchantress is clad in a robe with strange hieroglyphics and primitive masks peer down from the wall and Arthur Hughes' turbulent *Sir Galahad*. Other works belong to the mainstream of Victorian art; James Archer's monumental *Death of King Arthur* is in the tradition of the history-painters, while G. F. Watts's *Sir Galahad*, painted for Eton College Chapel, is a highly individual character-sketch, owing something to the Pre-Raphaelites, but more to the artist's own distinctive style.

This necessarily brief survey of the Arthurian legend in nineteenth century art underlines its dependence on the literary scene. The paintings in question are all essentially illustrations, in that a knowledge of the literary text is needed if the picture is to be fully appreciated; but that was an entirely orthodox approach in the Victorian period, when artists like Holman Hunt would invent a story around which to create a painting and would then provide a 'programme note' to explain them. Narrative was the dominant form, and it is to the remaining major narrative poems on Arthurian themes that we now return.

Both these poems are on the legend of Tristram and Iseult, a legend which plays a relatively marginal role in Malory. The major versions of the legend were those of Beroul, Thomas and Gottfried von Strassburg; but these were not readily available to Victorian writers. Matthew Arnold in the 1840s was inspired to begin work on the story of Tristram by nothing more than a French prose summary of the legend in a scholarly article in the *Revue de Paris* of 1841; he supplemented this with a thorough reading of Southey's edition of Malory of 1817, which included some further material in the notes.[10] Arnold handles his material in an original way; the poem opens with Tristram on his deathbed, and the story unfolds in a series of flashbacks. It is difficult for us to recapture the original impact of the poem, for Arnold was telling a story relatively unfamiliar to his audience, whereas it is now one of the commonplaces of western literature.

[10] Taylor & Brewer, 79–85.

164

We learn of Tristram's prowess as a harpist and hunter, and watch him drink the love-potion with Iseult of Ireland, 'overhead the cloudless sky of May'; we follow him in banishment – and Arnold makes him join Arthur's great expedition to Rome after his marriage to Iseult of Brittany – unable to forget Iseult of Ireland; and we return to the present, where he lies in a fever, nursed by one Iseult but longing for the other. The first part ends with the arrival of Iseult of Ireland; the second deals with the lovers' last interview and their death in each other's arms. The final part departs entirely from the legend to portray Iseult of Brittany as a widow, alone with her children by Tristram, to whom she tells the story of Merlin and Vivien. Arnold seems to imply that this tale is both a warning to them of the dangers of love and an example of the power that had come between their father and mother; and the poem as a whole is perhaps best seen not so much as a character study – though the portrait of Iseult of Brittany is very striking – but as a meditation on the varying modes of love, passion, tenderness, and (in the tale of Merlin and Vivien) obsession. Arnold makes clear his ambivalent attitude towards love just before Iseult tells this tale:

> This, or some tyrannous single thought, some fit
> Of passion, which subdues our souls to it,
> Till for its sake alone we live and move –
> Call it ambition, or remorse, or love –
> This too can change us wholly, and make seem
> All which we did before, shadow and dream.
> And yet, I swear, it angers me to see
> How this fool passion gulls men potently;
> Being, in truth, but a diseased unrest,
> And an unnatural overheat at best.

The other great version of the legend of Tristram and Iseult in nineteenth century poetry is full of this 'diseased unrest' and 'unnatural overheat', and indeed positively revels in such moods. Algernon Swinburne was strongly influenced by Morris and the Pre-Raphaelites, and while still a student at Oxford published three lyrics very much in Morris's manner, using a similar ballad metre and with much emphasis on pictorial descriptions. Ten years later, he returned to the theme of Tristram, having by now broken away from the Pre-Raphaelites to evolve a highly individual approach of his own, with a verse-form constructed according to his own theories.[11] He read widely, and made much use of Sir Walter Scott's edition of the Middle English *Sir Tristrem*, but he did not have access to Gottfried von Strassburg; he claimed that Wagner's opera was a major influence, but it is unlikely that he could have seen more than the libretto, and heard it in a piano score version, at the time when he was writing. He

[11] Taylor & Brewer, 149–159: quotations from *Tristram of Lyonesse* (London 1917).

does not attempt to tell the story explicitly, but like Arnold, uses a series of set-pieces. But Swinburne's purpose is very different; whereas Arnold explores a range of different moods, particularly those of Iseult of Brittany, Swinburne concentrates on the essence of the story, the primal passion which Arnold regarded with such suspicion. He builds up through his set-pieces a picture of the development of the lovers' passion, rising to a climax and coming to a swift and tragic end when Iseult of Brittany deceives Tristram by telling him that Iseult of Ireland has not come. Mark and Iseult of Brittany are presented unfavourably; only the lovers matter to the poet, and the strength of their love is continually emphasised. Even if Wagner was not a direct influence, the mood of the poem is very close to that of the opera in its single-minded preoccupation with the lovers' feelings; and Swinburne, like Wagner, makes use of leit-motifs and recurrent themes, as for instance in his descriptions of the lovers' first and last kisses:

> Their heads neared, and their hands were drawn in one,
> And they saw dark, though still the unsunken sun
> Far through fine rain shot fire into the south;
> And their four lips became one burning mouth... (p. 38)
>   ... and her head
> Bowed, as to reach the spring that slakes all drouth;
> And their four lips became one silent mouth. (p. 148)

Likewise, the ship that bears Tristram on the first fateful voyage is named *Swallow*, while that which takes Iseult on her last journey is called *Swan*. One theme runs throughout the whole poem, pervading it and occasionally dominating the verse: the sea itself. Both for the unknown author of the *Prose Tristan* and for Malory, Tristram had been a knight of the greenwood, a hunter skilled in venery. But for the earliest romancers who had formed and shaped the heart of the legend, Tristram was essentially a man of the sea. Swinburne harks back to this, and the theme provides a powerful and closely connected background against which to set his poem. *Iseult at Tintagel*, which shows Iseult in separation thinking of her distant lover, is continually underlined by the mood of the sea:

> And all their past came wailing in the wind,
> And all their future thundered in the sea. (p. 82)

The sea sets off and heightens the great moments of the tragedy. The famous love-potion is drunk against a background of storm; Tristram and Iseult both look seawards for comfort when they are parted; the lovelessness of Tristram's marriage to Iseult of the White Hands is emphasised by the sea's absence, and the one calm moment of their tempestuous relationship, at Joyous Gard, is mirrored in the sea's mood:

Nor loved they life for death's sake less,
Nor feared they death for love's or life's sake more
And on the sounding soft funereal shore
They, watching till the day should wholly die,
Saw the far sky sweep to the long grey sea.
And night made one sweet mist of moor and lea,
And only far off shore the foam gave light.
And life in them sank silent as the night.   (p. 103)

Swinburne's poem is a reaction against Tennyson's upholding of the moral code; its erotic passages set out to be deliberately provocative, and it foreshadows the world of the 'decadents' and of the poets of the 1890s. In *The Last Tournament*, Tennyson had used the love of Tristram and Iseult as one of the symbols of the decline of the Arthurian world; Swinburne treats it as the most glorious episode of the stories, and eliminates almost all references to events which do not directly involve the lovers, another parallel with Wagner's treatment. Once again, we see how the sheer variety of the Arthurian legends is a crucial factor in their appeal to different generations: an episode scorned by one writer has become the keystone of his successor's work.

Arthurian drama is the last of the nineteenth century forms of the legend, and very much the least. Victorian theatre produced little that is really memorable today, and most of what survives is comedy or even farce, though the occasional melodrama is revived. Poetical plays such as Tennyson's *Becket* are largely forgotten, except as curiosities, and the one Arthurian play that enjoyed considerable success at the time would not shine very brightly if it were staged today. J. Comyns Carr's *King Arthur*[12] had all the great stars of the moment in its cast when it opened at the Lyceum Theatre in London in January 1895, under Henry Irving's management. Irving himself played Arthur, Ellen Terry was Guinevere, and Forbes Robertson was Lancelot; the sets were by Burne-Jones (his only excursion into the theatre) and Sir Arthur Sullivan composed the music. The result was a box-office success, but not a literary one: George Bernard Shaw described the contrast between the acting and the text in a typical outburst: '... all the time, while the voice, the gesture, the emotion expressed, are those of the hero-king, the talk is the talk of an angry and jealous costermonger, exalted by the abject submission of the other parties to a transport of magnanimity in refraining from reviling his wife and punching her lover's head'. But Carr started with the disadvantage pointed out by another critic, that the audience came to the theatre with their minds 'saturated with and steeped in the Tennysonian version of the legend', and the lines of an author who had never previously written poetry were unlikely to make a great impression.

12 Taylor & Brewer, 204–7.

47 *A late Victorian extravaganza on the theme of the battle of Camlann: the Ascot Jubilee Cup of 1887 (Julian Hartnoll).*

The resilience of the Arthurian legend is shown by the way in which two major writers were able to use the legend as a vehicle for satire. Thomas Love Peacock's *The Misfortunes of Elphin* is my favourite among Arthurian oddities, the work of a scholar with considerable knowledge of old Welsh poetry which he turns to surprising effect as a satire on contemporary morals with its own most distinctive flavour.[13] When Peacock was writing, the great political issue of the age was the reform of the parliamentary voting system, which had reached an absurd state of corruption and inefficiency; the boroughs into which the country was divided were based on medieval population levels, and took no account of the expansion of industrial England, while covert bribery of those qualified to vote – by no means everyone, as the franchise was limited to those with property worth £40 a year in rent – was the rule. Peacock portrays the defenders of the old system in the figure of Seithenyn, the drunken keeper of the embankment which preserves Elphin's kingdom from the inroads of the sea. In his cups, Seithenyn proclaims his belief that the crumbling works of which he is in charge are perfectly safe:

> 'Decay,' said Seithenyn, 'is one thing, and danger is another. Every thing that is old must decay. That the embankment is old, I am free to confess; that it is somewhat rotten in parts, I will not altogether deny; that it is any the worse for that, I do most sturdily gainsay. It does its business well; it works well; it keeps out the water from the land, and it lets in the wine upon the High Commission of Embankment. Cupbearer, fill. Our ancestors were wiser than we; they built it in their wisdom; and, if we should be so rash as to try to mend it, we should only mar it.'
> 'The stonework,' said Teithrin, 'is sapped and mined: the piles are rotten, broken and dislocated: the floodgates and sluices are leaky and creaky.'
> 'That is the beauty of it,' said Seithenyn. 'Some parts of it are rotten, and some parts of it are sound ... I say, the parts that are rotten given elasticity to those that are sound. If it were all sound, it would break by its own obstinate stiffness [when battered by the sea]; the soundness is checked by the rottenness, and the stiffness is balanced by the elasticity. It is well; it works well; let well alone. Cupbearer, fill. It was half rotten when I was born, and that is a conclusive reason why it should be three parts rotten when I die.'

Peacock's version of the history of Arthur is distinctly light-hearted, but he draws on his extensive knowledge of old Welsh literature; here are references to the lore of the Welsh poets, and translations of many of their poems, and the characters are exclusively drawn from Welsh legends. One of the central episodes is the abduction of Guenevere by King Melwas of Somerset, who takes her to Glastonbury, a story which is found

[13] Taylor & Brewer, 54–60.

in this form only in the Latin life of St Caradoc of Llancarfan, and which is one of the oldest surviving Arthurian tales. The result is an entirely original contribution to modern Arthurian literature; if Peacock draws on ancient precedents, he is not beholden to anyone for his wit and inventiveness.

The other writer to make satirical use of the Arthurian legend was of course Mark Twain, in *A Connecticut Yankee at King Arthur's Court*, the one major Arthurian work to appear in America in the nineteenth century.[14] It differs from Peacock's work in that it satirises the vogue for Arthuriana, as well as using the stories as a framework for wider satire, but then Peacock was writing in the 1820s when such a vogue was unknown, while Twain was in the midst of the enthusiasm for Tennyson and his imitators. His basis was entirely Malory as far as the groundwork was concerned, but there are a number of deliberate parodies of Tennyson. Twain seems to have been attracted to the theme by the simple comic possibilities, as an early notebook entry implies: 'Dream of being a knight errant in armor in the middle ages. Have the notions and habits of thought of the present day mixed with the necessities of that. No pockets in the armor. ... Can't scratch. Cold in the head – can't blow nose – can't get at handkerchief, can't use iron sleeve. Always getting struck by lightning. Fall down, can't get up ...' But in the end what emerges is not merely a lampoon on the modern Arthurian poets, but a savage indictment of modern society. Hank, his hero, changes from an amiable and slightly bemused youth into a resolute dictator, whose knowledge of modern science enables him to first create and then destroy a modern civilisation in the medieval setting. The final disaster of the Round Table is caused when Lancelot's manipulations of the Stock Exchange are uncovered; in revenge, the other knights tell Arthur of Guenevere's adultery, and the final tragedy is set in motion, played out by an army of knights who are electrocuted by Hank's specially constructed fence. Hank and his followers are hemmed in by bodies, and die of the plague caused as they putrefy. Hardly the expected ending for a light-hearted excursion into satire; but Twain's purpose seems to have deepened as he progressed, recognising that the story he was handling was in essence one of the world's great tragic tales, and that its serious substance could not be lightly dismissed, but had to be matched by an equally serious contribution from himself. In the end, Twain's book is as much about the need for ideals as Tennyson's finest poetry. The true value of the Arthurian legends to nineteenth century writers was that they found in them a perfect medium for the expression of their ideals, however varied and diverse they might be. They could at the same time respond to the power of the ancient stories and invest them with new meaning, and so present Arthur

14 Taylor & Brewer, 169–74.

and his knights, despite their medieval trappings, as heroes of a modern age.

For writers in France and Germany, the Arthurian legends, which had been truly international in the medieval period, were less attractive than to their English counterparts, because Arthur was regarded as a British national hero; and the nineteenth century was above all the era of nationalism.[15] There was considerable interest in the medieval legends, and from the mid-eighteenth century retellings are to be found both in France and Germany. The earliest of the retellings in either language seem to have been those of the Comte de la Vergne de Tressan in the *Bibliothèque des Romans* in the 1770s, revised and reprinted separately in 1788.[16] Tristan and Iseult appear in eighteenth century guise: as a sample of the author's presentation, take the moment when Tristan, having just been reunited with Iseult, introduces her to Lancelot:

> Lancelot leaps to the ground, unlaces his helm, runs to embrace Tristan, who leads him to his dear Iseult and introduces him to her. Lancelot goes down on one knee to kiss her hand; but Iseult quickly raises him up, and embraces him as Tristan's best friend, whose presence she has so long wished for.
>
> They walk together to the abbey. The author says that the supper was very gay; they told each other their adventures: they spoke much of charming Guinevere; and Lancelot, though alone, slept very peacefully.

Tressan's only other Arthurian retelling was the marginally Arthurian *Artus de Petite Bretagne*, concerning a knight named Arthur after the great king: not for him the tragic side of the legends or their higher implications. Subsequent French Arthurian works were chiefly editions or summaries of the medieval romances, the most notable being the series of volumes by Paulin Paris, the distinguished cataloguer of the romances in the Royal Library. In *Les romans de la table ronde* (*The romances of the Round Table*) (1865–8) he presented a modern French version of the whole cycle, which encouraged scholarly work on the legends, but had little influence on the creative literature of the period.

Before Paris's work appeared, a totally original legend had been created by Edgar Quinet in his *Merlin L'Enchanteur*, a long novel planned as early as 1830 but only written between 1853 and 1860. It is a kind of picaresque tour of the legendary world. Only the opening, telling how Satan fathers Merlin on a virgin, the nun Seraphina, as a conscious attempt to create Anti-Christ, belongs to the original story. Merlin only becomes a magician when he falls in love with Viviane: thereafter he acts as a kind of all-powerful director of human affairs for a time, establishing

[15] The only accounts of French and German nineteenth century works in English are M. W. MacCallum, *Tennyson's Idylls and Arthurian Story* (Glasgow 1894) 214–247, and entries in *The Arthurian Encyclopaedia* ed. Norris J. Lacy (New York 1985).

[16] *Oevres choisies du comte de Tressan*, t.7: *Corps d'extraits de romans de chevalerie* (Paris 1788), 137.

Helas ! ce flacon contenoit le boire amoureux ?

48 *Tristan transformed into eighteenth century guise: an illustration for Comte de la Vergne de Tressan's retelling of the story.*

Paris as the setting for Arthur's court and assembling all the heroes of northern, Christian and oriental love at the Round Table. But he loses touch with Viviane, and with her his magic powers depart: Arthur falls into an enchanted sleep, and, unable to wake him as the nations war around him, Merlin takes to the wilderness, where he cannot rest until Viviane returns, to enclose him with herself in a tomb. With her he at last finds peace, and his invisible voice brings comfort to mankind. In the final section Satan himself is converted, and destroys his own kingdom before kneeling in repentance, and the book ends with Merlin's triumph. *Merlin l'Enchanteur* is a strange work: it has deliberate echoes of Goethe's *Faust*: 'the legend of the human soul until death, and beyond death – that is my subject.'[17] Quinet invokes Milton, and declares that he has set out to retune 'the great lyre whose strings have been slackened and put out of key by time'; his aim is to recreate a great French national legend around the figure of Merlin. But the fatal weaknesses of his attempt are the deliberate lightness of tone which he adopts, which quickly becomes mere banter, and the overtones of political satire. His Satan is more of a comic figure than an awesome power, and he never convinces us of the heroic scale of his characters: Merlin and Viviane are romantic lovers who settle into a kind of domestic bliss. In the end the concept is not matched by the execution, and *Merlin L'Enchanteur* is amusing and curious rather than inspiring.

The most important French Arthurian work of the nineteenth century was in the field of opera. Ernest Chausson was a pupil of Franck and Massenet, and in 1882 wrote the symphonic poem *Viviane*, which tells the story of Merlin's love for Viviane and his enchantment by her. It is a delightful and unjustly neglected work, strikingly orchestrated and full of memorable passages. Even more unjustly neglected is his last work, *Le Roi Arthus*, left almost complete at his death in 1899.[18] It was first performed, to enthusiastic notices, in Brussels in 1903, but was unfairly branded as a mere shadow of Wagner, which is unquestionably not true: if there are occasional echoes of Wagner there are also moments that recall Berlioz and Massenet, but *Le Roi Arthus* is above all an original and generally successful work. Chausson wrote the libretto himself, which opens at the point of Arthur's triumph over the Saxons. At a great feast, Arthur acknowledges Lancelot as the true architect of his victory; but at the same time we learn of Lancelot's love for Guinevere, and hear Mordred's murmurings of discontent. A love scene between Lancelot and Guinevere follows: they are discovered by Mordred, who is wounded by Lancelot before the latter makes his escape. In the second act, Guinevere meets Lancelot in the countryside to tell him that Mordred is still alive, and that she is in mortal danger. Lancelot at first refuses to lie, saying he would rather be killed, but at last agrees to defend the queen. The scene changes to the court, where Arthur longs to see Merlin again: but when Merlin appears in a vision it is only to warn him that the Round Table is

[17] *Merlin L'Enchanteur*, introduction, p. vi.
[18] Tony Hunt, 'Ernest Chausson's "Le Roi Arthus"', *Arthurian Literature* IV, 127–54).

at an end: 'blind as we were, we trusted too much in men's virtue'. The last act opens with Guinevere alone as the final battle begins, overcome with guilt at the tragedy she has caused; and Lancelot appears, unable to fight against his king. She tries to urge him to fight for their love, but he stands firm and determines to try and stop the battle, which has already begun. He goes, and the noise of battle dies down: Guinevere, thinking that Lancelot is dead, strangles herself. The final scene is between the dying Lancelot and Arthur, also mortally wounded. Arthur refuses to avenge himself by killing Lancelot, and is borne away in a barge, while distant voices sing of his achievements and eventual return.

Chausson creates an impressive and sympathetic portrait of Arthur as a heroic king; Lancelot and Guinevere appear as victims of a love which can only be guilty and disastrous, in contrast to their essentially noble natures. His finest music is reserved for the ending, in which Arthur transcends his earthly tragedy, and accepts his departure from the world with calm resignation; but all the scenes contain accomplished and highly dramatic music. *Le Roi Arthus* is by far the best of modern attempts to produce a convincing theatrical version of the tragedy of Arthur.

In Germany, Merlin also attracted attention. Dorothea Schegel's *Geschichte des Zauberers Merlin* (*History of Merlin the magician*) (1804) and F. F. Hofstäter's version of the romances *Altdeutsche Gedichte aus den Zeiten der Tafelrunde* (1811) inspired two poets of some standing to look at Merlin's legend. Ludwig Uhland's ballads and romances include *Merlin the Wild*, written in 1829, portrays Merlin as an aging magician drawing new strength from nature: seized by the king's huntsmen, he answers the king's riddle with contemptuous ease, and departs, praising his life in the forest and implicitly condemning the ways of the court. It is a brief and clearly autobiographical poem addressed to a friend. Karl Immermann's play, *Merlin: Eine Mythe* is an altogether more ambitious work, shot through with gnostic philosophy and a highly individual view of the world. It is a philosophical drama to the extent that it belongs in the study rather than the theatre. Immermann's chief concern is the complex bond between God and Satan; he sees the latter, in Merlin's words, as 'demiurge, creator', an aspect of God, whose existence denies the unity of God but celebrates his multiplicity, 'a necessary development of God's being.' He is beyond good and evil, a lord of nature and of life and death: his activity contracts with the Christian contemplative life and self-denial. Merlin turns away from his father Satán and attempts the redemption of mankind: but his tragedy stems from the spiritual pride that this self-appointed task implies. His attempts to lead Arthur and his knights to the Grail result only in their death, while the wanderer Lohengrin finds the Grail without seeking it. For the Grail is a spiritual mystery, and Merlin cannot comprehend that God's laws may not be those of logic or nature. He himself succumbs to Niniana's charms and as token of his love (which is not mere wanton desire) tells her the secret word that alone can harm him. She innocently repeats it thinking she has not heard it rightly, and Merlin is at once locked in invisible chains of his own imagining. The epilogue tells first how Lohengrin, sent as the Grail's messenger into the world, finds Arthur and his knights dead, and Merlin mad: in a mood of deep pessimism, he sees that 'love, honour, courage are hunger-ravaged corpses' and 'the earth is only an empty, dismal treeless plain, strewn with bones, bare and barren, over which there waves the black pennon of destruction'. In the last scene Satan releases his son many years later, and demands his homage: but Merlin, citing the example of Job, declares that the more God punishes him for attempting to penetrate the hidden mysteries of the spirit, the more he will worship him, and dies whispering 'Hallowed be Thy Name.'

Immermann's *Merlin* is an ambitious, powerful and striking work, and at its best it echoes the greatest of German romantic dramas, Goethe's *Faust*. Yet it is ultimately a splendid failure rather than a masterpiece, for three reasons. Its theme is never stated with sufficient clarity and force: Merlin's longing for God does not convince in the way that we can believe in Faust's eternal striving. Merlin, the semi-diabolic hero turned to God, has none of the human appeal of Faust: he is too much the symbolic figure raised up by the religious poet of the early thirteenth century rather than a real character. And thirdly, Immermann is a good but rarely inspired poet. The ideas which he evokes are greater than the work which enshrines them.

Immermann later produced a rather tame version of Gottfried von Strassburg's *Tristan*, which had been edited three times by the 1840s, the first edition being as early as 1771. It was by far the most popular Arthurian theme in Germany: in addition to at least four nineteenth century versions, there were twenty plays on the theme between 1890 and 1930, as against eight on Parzival. But these undoubtedly owed their existence to the example of the greatest German Arthurian works of the nineteenth century, Richard Wagner's operas.

Wagner had read widely in medieval literature while he was living at Dresden, and had come across Kurtz's translation of Gottfried, which provided an ending to the unfinished original.[19] The earliest references to a projected opera on the subject imply that it was to be undertaken only on the completion of the *Ring of the Nibelungs*, which also owes its subject to medieval poetry. But Wagner again took up the subject when in difficulties over

[19] See H. F. Garten, *Wagner the Dramatist* (London 1977).

the composition of the *Ring* early in 1857, and *Tristan und Isolde* was completed in August 1859. Gottfried's poem, though simple enough in its powerful and tragic outline, required further simplification for dramatic purposes. Wagner reduces the action to the bare essentials: the first act deals with the love-potion, the second with the betrayal of the lovers, the third with their death. It is obviously impossible to discuss the opera in terms of its libretto only; as Ernest Newman wisely says, Wagner relies 'at least as much on music as on words to tell us who and what his characters are and what they feel at a given moment'. Indeed, Wagner wrote some of the music for *Tristan* before the libretto, which does not seem to have been the case with any of his other operas. But we must also remember Thomas Mann's comment that 'it seems to me absurd to doubt Wagner's power as poet', and in the resultant blend of words and music, the legend achieves an intensity which no modern poetry alone has matched. For Tristan and Isolde, even in the earliest versions of the legend, are conceived as being not quite of this world; they are bewitched, enchanted or possessed, and what they do is less important than what they feel. Hence music, with its direct appeal to the emotions, is arguably a more effective medium for an extended version of their story than poetry alone, which cannot sustain the lyrical mood of their love for more than a brief passage. Equally, the early versions of the legend can move us by their simplicity, a simplicity which rings false in the work of a modern writer. Where Wagner is on debatable ground is in his handling of the themes of day and night, life-wish and death-wish; but the literal death-wish which dominates some parts of the opera is also a longing for the annihilation of self in the ecstasy of love, a concept entirely apt to the ancient tragic tale. And there are brilliant dramatic inventions: when Isolde calls for the death potion, so that she can die rather than marry Mark, and take her enemy Tristan with her, Brangane substitutes the love potion. The real achievement of the opera, however, is to recreate the Tristan legend in the world of the German romantic poets and philosophers, a task which others had undertaken but in which only Wagner succeeded. *Tristan und Isolde* is faithful to the spirit of the medieval original and yet has created an entirely new image of the legend.

Wagner's treatment of the Grail legend was equally well based in medieval research. *Parsifal* was his last opera, completed in 1882. But the subject had attracted him for many years, and the first concrete mention of it is in an early sketch for *Tristan and Isolde* of 1854–5, where Parsifal was to appear as a pilgrim in the last act, as the archetype of a similar kind of eternal longing to that which haunted Tristan. Wagner had read both Simrock's and San Marte's versions of Wolfram in 1845; and the idea was to take many more years to mature. He found it difficult to achieve the simple outline and logical action which is a feature of all his later operas: just as the driving force in *Tristan* is passion, so the inconsequences of the *Conte del Graal* and Wolfram's *Parzival* had to be reduced to the theme of redemption. In 1857 the idea of the Good Friday scene had taken shape, and in 1859 he had found some of the answers: the mysterious spear of the Grail procession, cause of Amfortas' wound, became the spear with which Longinus had wounded our Lord at the Passion, an idea not to be found in Wolfram but borrowed from the French Vulgate Cycle. Here too he found the identification of the Grail as the cup used at the Last Supper. The crucial last step was the identification of Kundry the messenger with the temptress of the second act; in August 1860 Wagner wrote 'Since this has dawned upon me, almost all of this subject has become clear to me'.[20] The idea of the Grail brotherhood seems to have been derived from the Knights Templars; it is foreign to the medieval romances.

Parsifal is probably the most controversial of Wagner's operas; at worst it has been misread as a kind of Aryan brotherhood in embryo, or as the despairing repentance of an elderly lover of pleasure. In reality it is neither, nor is it specifically Christian. It is about redemption, certainly; but redemption is seen as a form of man's longing for the eternal, that same longing which in *Tristan und Isolde* was a desire to perpetuate love: both operas are deeply influenced by Schopenhauer's ideas.[21] The motivation of Parsifal's redemption is largely the composer's own creation. In Wolfram, Parzival's wisdom is gained through plumbing the depths of spiritual despair, the moment when he curses God for not rewarding his faithful service. Wagner, probably for dramatic reasons, but perhaps also from his own psychological motives, makes the experience of Kundry's kiss, sensual experience, the trigger of despair and eventual redemption, though compassion, *Mitleid*. Parsifal attains knowledge through his ability to feel for others: Amfortas had given way to passion, his own feelings, and can only be rescued by one who is proof against Kundry's temptation. This idea is drawn from the French Grail romances, though the final shaping of it is entirely Wagner's own. Indeed, the theme of redemption through love is central to *The Ring of the Nibelungs*: but there it brings destruction to the hero, whereas here it brings the highest blessings. As reshaped in *Parsifal*, the idea of redemption through compassion is as powerful an image as the reconciliation of man's spiritual and human physical nature in Wolfram. As to the question of its relationship to religion and to Christianity in particular, the best answer seems to me that given by Lucy Beckett:

[20] *Richard Wagner an Mathilde und Otto Wesendonk*, ed. Julius Kapp, (Leipzig 1915) 325–6.
[21] Lucy Beckett, *Richard Wagner: Parsifal* (Cambridge & New York 1981) is the best general account of the opera in English.

... *Parsifal* is, finally, created in the service of a greater truth. To the extent that the spiritual certainty to which it refers is thought to belong to the past, it will seem nostalgic, embarrassing, unhealthy, quaint, boring: and people will be driven to explain its beauty, if they find it beautiful, by separating the words from the music and ignoring the words. But to the extent that the spiritual certainty to which it refers is still thought, whether from within or from without, to have an incontrovertible experiential force, it will seem at once humbler, braver and more worthy of respect for the encouraging light it sheds upon the tormenting questions of real, human, life.[22]

Looking back at nineteenth century treatments of the Arthurian legends, they are characterised for the most part by this search for 'a greater truth'; whether it is Arthur himself, Tristan and Isolde or the Grail, the legends are accepted as heroic and spiritual symbols. There is no search for earthly reality, no questioning of their greatness; the stories are treated with reverence even if the conclusions which are drawn from them would have astonished their medieval creators. The twentieth century was to lay a very different emphasis on Arthur.

[22] Beckett, 147.

Chapter 9

Visions and Revisions

The twentieth century has seen more works on the Arthurian legend than any of its predecessors: yet the legends have not made as striking an impact as they did in nineteenth century England. If Tennyson bore witness to the power of the legends, twentieth century writers have confirmed their diversity: they have offered us everything from scholarly history to mystical poetry, from romantic novels to modern opera. A complete survey of all the facets of twentieth century Arthuriana would need a volume in itself: here we can only point to the most important developments in what has, not unaptly, been christened 'the Arthur industry' – of which this book itself is a minuscule part.

The most widespread form of Arthuriana up to the Second World War was drama, particularly poetic drama which often seemed intended for reading rather than performance. Our first example, Arthur Symons' *Tristan and Iseult* (1917) is a direct descendant of Wagner's opera on the same theme. Its restrained language and often acute psychological insights belong firmly in the world of the Georgian poets: even in the extremes of emotion, whether love, jealousy or hate, there is a curious reticence mixed with directness which creates a surprisingly powerful picture of the characters: Iseult young and resentful of her fate in marrying the elderly Mark, Tristan torn between his love for Iseult and his loyalty to the father-figure of his king, and Mark a statesman faced by a personal tragedy. The emphasis is not on high ecstasy, but on a slow—burning passion and the frustrations and anguish it arouses. As Iseult says after she has drunk the love-potion:

O what is love, and why is love so bitter
After the blundering sweetness of a moment?
I am afraid, I am afraid of love,
This is some death that has got hold of me.

The image of love as a destructive flame is invoked by Iseult as she contemplates Tristan in death:

This dust was a fire and burned the stars:
Now what little ashes holds the fire
That was blown out too early. There is nothing
Left in the world, and I am out of place.

Iseult is the dominating figure in this interesting and subtle play; Symons speaks with a distinctive voice which sets him apart from the imitators of Tennyson.

Laurence Binyon's *Arthur: A Tragedy*, first performed in London in 1923, must be classified as a piece firmly rooted in the late Victorian tradition, though it is greatly superior to Comyn Carr's spectacular version of 1895. The idiom seems uncertain, varying from archaic poetic diction at moments to a flat prose: isolated lines are often effective, but the speeches neither read well nor suggest that they would work on the stage. The strength of the play is in its skilful dramatic structure, but the actual execution of the plan is less compelling. Arthur is the hero of the play: but the relationship between Arthur and Guinevere remains the stumbling-block, diminishing Arthur's stature and preventing Binyon from creating a truly tragic figure.

Much more striking, but very strange, is Thomas Hardy's play, *The Famous Tragedy of the Queen of Cornwall* (1923). The structure of the play harks back to Greek tragedy with its use of male and female choruses to comment on the action. Hardy combines the tradition of Malory with that of the early writers, using the latter as background but the former for the action of the play itself. Mark it is who kills Tristram; Hardy adds his own sequel, Iseult's killing of Mark and suicide.

Hardy declared that he had 'tried to avoid turning the rude personages of, say, the fifth century into respectable Victorians, as was done by Tennyson, Swinburne, Arnold etc.' He chose an archaic vocabulary, and believed that by underplaying the dramatic side of the acting the play could achieve a 'curiously hypnotising' effect. On the page, it offers nothing more than a certain oddity: a conscious attempt at a medieval play every bit as anachronistic as the Victorian works he so decried. The characters have a rough–hewn quality but belong to Hardy's Wessex rather than a court in whatever age. It is a minor, curious work from a master's hand, with rare flashes of greater illumination.

Drama was also the favourite medium of German writers attracted by the Arthurian legends. The most ambitious project was the series of plays under the general title of 'The Grail' by Eduard Stucken, which enjoyed considerable popularity in the years before and after the First World War. *Gawain* (1908) the

49 *Two bronzes by George Frampton: Victorian sculpture of Arthur, apart from H.H. Armistead's rather insipid work in the House of Lords, is rare, but these portraits of* La Beale Isoude *and* Enid the Fair *are enchanting. (Phillips, Christopher Wood Gallery).*

50 The Edwardian view of Arthur: Charles Ernest Butler's King Arthur *(1903) (Christopher Wood Gallery).*

first play, went through at least seven impressions, and although the cycle was never completed five plays, variously entitled 'mysteries' and 'dramas', appeared. Stucken handles the legends fairly freely but effectively. In *Lancelot* (1909), for example, Elaine the daughter of King Pelles and Elaine the fair maid of Ascolat become one and the same person, daughter of the Grail king Anfortas: Lancelot's refusal to see her again after the night when Galahad is conceived is the direct cause of her death, and it is king Anfortas who sends her body down the river from the Grail castle to Camelot, in accordance with her last wishes. Stucken was widely read in mythology, and there are echoes of other heroic legends in his version of the stories: Lancelot, denied the sight of the Grail, expresses his anguish in words reminiscent of Tannhäuser, and just as Tannhäuser is cursed by the Pope, so Lancelot is cursed by Anfortas. The weakness of the plays is precisely this tendency to raise the emotional temperature: *Tristram and Iseult* (1916) ends in melodrama, as Tristram strangles Ysolt as he dies. In general, however, these are strong versions of the legends; the main characters are well drawn, and the poetic language is appropriately rich without being mannered. Stucken's plays were produced by the famous director Max Reinhardt at the Deutsches Theater, Berlin: Reinhardt's poetic and imaginative stagings, full of theatrical illusion, were in sharp contrast to the realist school which dominated other German theatre of the period.

Ernst Hardt's *Tantris der Narr* (*Tantris the Fool*) (1907) was a minor sensation in its day. Hardt's theme is the estrangement of Isolde from Tristan after the latter's marriage to Isolde of the White Hands. Tristan, despite Isolde's firm persuasion to the contrary, has not ceased to love her, and returns in disguise to Cornwall, even though the terms of his banishment were that if he was seen in Mark's realm again, both he and Iseult would be put to death. At his first return, he saves Iseult from the lepers to whom Mark has given her: the second time, he comes in the guise of a fool, and uses the jester's privilege to declare his love for and intimate knowledge of Iseult: but Iseult cannot believe that it is him until she throws him out and sets his hound Husdent on him, thinking that the dog will tear him to pieces. But Husdent recognises Tristan, and the two depart before Iseult can recall them, leaving her in despair. Tristan's love for Iseult has turned him, in society's eyes, into a leper and a fool: that point is well made by Hardt, but it is more difficult to understand why Iseult – and Mark, for that matter – fail to see through his altered appearance, though their persistent refusal to face the truth produces a fine dramatic tension.

A very different approach to problems of identity is that of Jean Cocteau in his *Les Chevaliers de la Table Ronde* (1937). Cocteau uses the theme of the false Guinevere and expands and extends it into a more general myth. The play is a kind of reaction to his obsession with the Greek myths, but it nonetheless

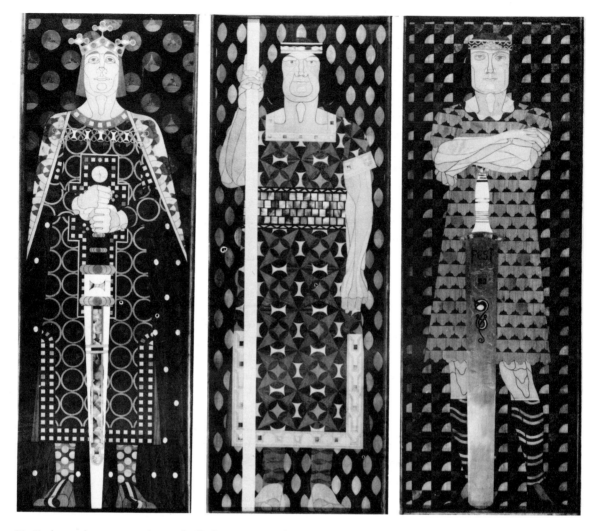

51 Perhaps the most curious of all the metamorphoses of Arthurian heroes: Arthur, Gawain and Lancelot portrayed in marquetry panels designed by Josef Engelhart in Vienna in 1904 (Österreichisches Museum für angewandte Kunst, inventory nos H 2253a–c).

deals in large symbols as well as the comedy derived from a reinterpretation of the story in unexpected ways. The crucial character, Ginifer, is a devil enslaved by Merlin, who impersonates Gawain, Guinevere and Galahad in turn. Merlin is an evil enchanter, who has laid Arthur's realm under a spell, so that it has become a Waste Land; and he produces a false Grail, which initiates the Grail quest. Only Galahad can resist him; he is so pure that he can lead others to the true Grail, truth itself, but cannot see it himself, for neither good nor evil affect him. He defeats Merlin's machinations, and releases the kingdom from its spell: but truth is bitter as well as beautiful, and Arthur kills Lancelot when he learns of his liaison with Guinevere. Guinevere dies of grief, and Arthur is left with his children, who prove to be the exact images of Lancelot and Guinevere. The message of his play seems to have disconcerted Cocteau, who wrote: 'It is pure theatrical chance if, in *Les Chevaliers*, what we usually call the good seems to triumph over what we call evil. These kinds of demonstrations seem to me to belong to the aesthetics of the moralist, the worst that I know.' For the play is above all a brilliant piece of theatre, in which one actress is called on to play Guinevere, Guinevere impersonated by Ginifer, and Guinevere reincarnated in her daughter Blandine: two actors have to play in similar fashion the false and real Gawain and the false and real Galahad. The deeper levels of the action – the search for happiness through self-knowledge, the ambiguity of good and evil are, as so often in Cocteau's work, veiled by the wit and sparkle of the dialogue. As a recent critic neatly puts it, 'his efforts to re–establish a moral issue are in contradiction to the very nature of his chosen frame of reference.'[1]

Cocteau's other foray into the Arthurian legend was in the realm of film, and deserves a brief mention. *L'Eternel Retour* (1944) was attacked by critics as supposedly Nazi: Patrice/ Tristan and Natalie/Isolde are modern, mindless 'beautiful people', as we would call them today, driving fast cars and drinking cocktails – one of which is the love potion. It is not one of Cocteau's masterpieces, and falls far short of *La belle et la bête*, but it has moments of real mythical power. As for the Nazi element, it amounts to little more than the fact that Patrice is 'blond, booted and bounding all over the place'.[2] But the problems of Arthurian films are another matter, to which we will briefly return in due course.

The finest work in the mass of twentieth-century Arthuriana undoubtedly belongs to the poets, from the Arthurian echoes in T. S. Eliot's *The Waste Land* to the private world of Charles Williams' Arthurian realms. *The Waste Land* is unusual in that part of its inspiration was a critical work on the legends, Jessie L. Weston's *From Ritual to Romance*; Eliot attributed not only the title, but the plan and a good deal of the incidental symbolism[3] to this work. The central thesis of Jessie Weston's book, that the lance and cup of the Grail procession are sexual symbols from the immemorial past, linked to the equally ancient lore contained in the Tarot pack, is little more than ingenious speculation: but out of it Eliot shapes a powerful vision of the spiritual desolation he felt in the modern world, where the Fisher King fishes hopelessly in the stagnant canal, and the abandoned chapel holds no hope of the vision of the Grail. Even the sea, in a line taken from Wagner's *Tristan und Isolde*, is 'öd' und leer', waste and empty. The myth survives, but the heroes have vanished: Eliot's work is a landmark in this respect, for he has

[1] Neal Oxenhandler, *Scandal & Parade: the theatre of Jean Cocteau* (New York 1957; London 1958) 177.
[2] Hannah Closs, 'Jean Cocteau's Tristan', *The Adelphi*, XXIII, 1946–7 79–81.
[3] T. S. Eliot, 'Notes on the Waste Land', *The Waste Land* (London 1922).

renewed the old themes in a new and totally non-chivalric setting.

Eliot's fellow-American, Edwin Arlington Robinson, was much more traditional in his approach to the legends. Robinson, born in 1870, belonged to an earlier generation, and his style is nearer to that of the English Georgian poets than to Eliot. But his three long Arthurian poems, written between 1917 and 1927, are outstanding, rising above any considerations of fashion or style. He was a highly respected and very popular poet, winning three Pulitzer prizes. On the surface, he might seem at the opposite pole to Eliot: yet they share much common ground. Both strip away the medieval trappings of the stories, and insist on the relevance of the central myths to the modern world. *Merlin*, published in 1917, deals with the theme of private fulfilment and public duty in a time of crisis. Robinson's poetry is striking in its range of expression: despite moments of Tennysonian pastiche (and these are rare) he uses a generally simple vocabulary to evoke the changing moods and feeling of his characters. He does not describe events, but evokes their emotional context instead, through powerful visual images, as in the passage where Vivian seduces Merlin for the first time:

> He stared a long time at the cup of gold
> Before him but he drank no more. There came
> Between him and the world a crumbling sky
> Of black and crimson, with a crimson cloud
> That held a far off town of many towers.
> All swayed and shaken, till at last they fell,
> And there was nothing but a crimson cloud
> That crumbled into nothing, like the sky
> That vanished with it, carrying away
> The world, the woman, and all memory of them,
> Until a slow light of another sky
> Made gray an open casement, showing him
> Faint shapes of an exotic furniture
> That glimmered with a dim magnificence,
> And letting in the sound of many birds
> That were, as he lay there remembering,
> The only occupation of his ears
> Until it seemed they shared a fainter sound,
> As if a sleeping child with a black head
> Beside him drew the breath of innocence.

Merlin has come willingly to Vivian, and lives with her in a kind of Eden for ten years: his 'grave' in Broceliande is a purely figurative one, for he has buried himself there of his own free will. Their love is idyllic, and Merlin, shorn of his wizard's hair and beard, lays aside his king-making powers to enjoy a youthfully passionate yet mature love affair. Robinson writes skilful dialogue, lively, witty, often matter of fact and yet never at odds with the greater themes of the poem: and through it he creates an entirely believable picture of their relationship. In the end, however, Merlin cannot resist answering Dagonet's urgent plea that he come to see Arthur: and in so doing, he finds that he is drawn back into the world. He returns to Vivian, but is restless, and sets out for Camelot just as the final tragedy breaks. Realising his impotence, he and Dagonet, the king's wizard and the king's fool, agree to keep each other company as they leave the doomed city to wander the world.

Lancelot, which Robinson began as soon as he had finished *Merlin*, looks at the same events from a different viewpoint. Robinson follows Malory's description of events, except in minor details: his chief interest is once more the psychology of his characters. He emphasises the change wrought in Lancelot by the Grail quest, and depicts him as anxious to leave the queen to continue his search for the 'Light'; but he is held back by the memory of their happiness together, and the tragedy unfolds. Once again, Robinson depends extensively on dialogue, even more so than in *Merlin*, and uses it to build up a direct image of the characters. The result can be very vivid, as in Lancelot's description of how he rode unwillingly to claim Guinevere as Arthur's bride, despite Merlin's warning:

> Then a great shout went up
> From shining men around me everywhere;
> And I remember more fair women's eyes
> Than there are stars in autumn, all of them
> Thrown on me for a glimpse of that high knight
> Sir Lancelot—Sir Lancelot of the Lake.
> I saw their faces and I saw not one
> To sever a tendril of my integrity;
> But I thought once again, to make myself
> Believe a silent lie, 'God save the King' …
> I saw your face, and there were no more kings.

Just as Robinson evokes echoes of Tristram and Iseult in Lancelot and Guinevere, so his poetry has more than a hint of Swinburne at moments, a poet who had been a great influence on him in his younger days, but whom he claimed to have rejected.[4] Yet the picture of Guinevere in Lancelot's arms after he has told her that she must return to Arthur has strong echoes of *Tristram of Lyonesse*:

> And there was no sound then of anything,
> Save the low moaning of a broken woman,
> And the cold rain roaring down of that long rain.

[4] Edwin S. Fussell, *Edwin Arlington Robinson: The Literary Background of a Traditional Poet* (Berkeley & Los Angeles 1964) 102.

The image of 'the Light' is contrasted with Guinevere's 'glory of white and gold'; Robinson seems to intend 'the Light' to stand for some kind of new order of human affairs, though its very lack of definition makes it appear more like Faust's 'immortal longings' than any tangible goal, and the end of the poem does little to define it, as Lancelot rides away from Guinevere. He has a momentary pang of desire for her: but he rides on, 'out of the world', seeing a vision of Galahad,

> … who had seen and died,
> And was alive, now in a mist of gold.
> He rode on into the dark, under the stars,
> And there were no more faces. There was nothing.
> But always in the darkness he rode on,
> Alone; and in the darkness came the Light.

Guinevere is perhaps Robinson's most interesting creation. Like Vivian, she represents the attractive side of love, individual happiness and fulfilment; but it is also she who, at their last meeting at Amesbury, sends Lancelot out to seek the light, having recognised that the time has come for stoicism and self-control.

Lancelot was not a popular success: Conrad Aiken called *Merlin* and *Lancelot* 'a Malory as Henry James might have rewritten and enlarged it, had Henry James been a poet', yet found *Lancelot* lacking in 'poetic energy' despite 'the nobility of theme, the austerity of treatment, and, of the latter half especially, the beauty.'[5] *Tristram*, which followed in 1927, was a best-seller, a Literary Guild choice which won him the Pulitzer prize. Again, there are echoes of Swinburne in the language and imagery, particularly in the use of the sea as a backcloth to the drama though Robinson constantly strove to avoid 'collisions' with the earlier work. It is more lyrical than either of the previous poems, as befits its subject. Some of the power of the writing may stem from Robinson's past: as a young man, he had fallen hopelessly in love with his elder brother's wife, and although the passion was not mutual, he nonetheless knew what love's triangle implied. He knew and loved Wagner's *Tristan* as well, and the outline had been sketched ten years earlier. Once again, Robinson's interest is in the psychology behind the story. He chooses three episodes set in castles beside the sea in Cornwall, England, and Brittany, and depicts Isolt's wedding night, the union of the lovers at Joyous Gard, and their death. His theme is the way in which love can transcend time: life is not to be measured in years, but in terms of love, and the lovers' brief summer at Joyous Gard is a whole lifetime in a brief timespan. This is the ground of the main plot: the subplots centre on Isolt of Brittany and on Mark, who cannot partake of real love, but instead come to that stoical self-knowledge which characterised

5 Conrad Aiken 'Three Reviews', in *Edwin Arlington Robinson: A collection of Critical Essays* ed. Francis Murphy (Englewood Cliffs 1970) 22.

Merlin and Lancelot. Isolt of Brittany, who has only known affection from Tristram, 'the pale wine of love that is not love', eventually comes to understand him and thus to achieve peace; Mark, who at last sees from Isolt of Ireland's 'white face' that he cannot break the lovers apart by force, reunites them for a last farewell, only to witness Tristram's death at the hands of his nephew Andret.

Robinson handles his subject with tenderness and clear sight, and produces moments of vivid imagery and a surging lyricism, as when he writes of Tristram and Isolt at Joyous Gard:

> He saw dark laughter sparkling
> Out of her eyes, but only until her face
> Found his, and on his mouth a moving fire
> Told him why there was death, and what lost song
> Ulysses heard, and would have given his hands
> And friends to follow and to die for.

Against this, he sets the quiet patience of Isolt of Brittany at the end of the story, when she knows Tristram is dead:

> ... Isolt of the white hands,
> Isolt with her grey eyes and her white face,
> Still gazed across the water for the north.
> But not now for a ship...
> ... Yet there she gazed
> Across the water, over the white waves,
> Upon a castle that she had never seen,
> And would not see, save as a phantom shape
> Against a phantom sky. He had been there,
> She thought, but not with her. He had died there,
> But not for her. He had not thought of her,
> Perhaps, and that was strange. He had been all,
> And would be always all there was for her,
> And he had not come back to her alive,
> Not even to go again.

John Masefield's *Midsummer Night and other tales in verse* (1927) presents us with a series of linked pictures and incidents that cover the main events of the life of Arthur, drawing on a wide range of sources, both classical and medieval, sometimes going back to early Welsh material, sometimes offering his own alternative version of the legend. '*The Begetting of Arthur*', at the opening of the cycle, has two such versions: one is a tragic love-story, in which Uther is slain by Ygerne's father, Merchyon, after one brief night of love as a result of which Arthur is born. The other, '*The Old Tale of the Begetting*', begins:

> The men of old that made the tale for us
> Declare that Uther begot Arthur thus

and continues with the story told by Geoffrey of Monmouth. The next two poems, on the birth of Mordred, rely on Malory, except that Morgause becomes Arthur's aunt instead of his half-sister. Arthur's hour of triumph is represented by '*Badon Hill*', in which he slaughters his Saxon enemies; and his connection with the mysteries of the other world is portrayed in '*The Sailing of Hell Race*', a new version of *The Spoils of Annwfn* in which Arthur visits the three kingdoms of hell, each with its allegorical rulers – Self and Mammon, War, Sloth and Pestilence.

The legends which follow set the tragedy in motion, which is brought about by Arthur's love for Guinevere and its consequences. In '*Arthur and his Ring*', Masefield borrows the classical story of the lover who slips his beloved's ring onto the finger of a statue of Venus, and has to beg it of the goddess herself before he can regain it. '*Midsummer Night*', echoing the tale of Arthur's survival in a cave in a sleep from which he awakens each Midsummer night, allows each of the characters involved to explain their part in the remorseless working of fate. The remaining poems tell the familiar story, save for the appearance of Mordred's wife Gwenivach as a protagonist of her husband's treachery. And by way of epilogue Masefield portrays Henry II at the grave of Arthur, setting against this vision of mortality and history another poem, '*On the Coming of Arthur*', in praise of his immortal spirit.

Masefield's work is in an unfashionable medium, a series of historical ballads, in ballad metre; and it is difficult to estimate their true worth. His handling of plot and character is strong, but the ballad form itself has a comfortable homeliness about it that ill consorts with the high romanticism of the story. For this is still an idealised treatment, for all its would-be realism. Masefield has a vivid way of lighting up a figure: Mordred's outburst of hatred – 'Thirty years anguish made by your idle lust' – strikes home, as does Arthur's helpless and equivocal relationship with his son and Guinevere looking at Lancelot in death: 'I had not thought of him as old.' And the cycle is well balanced, moving forward with the ease of the true story-teller, save for the digression of '*Arthur and his Ring*'. Masefield has not really come to terms with his theme, and the novelty of his use of different material to tell the same story, the dependence on Welsh sources or recent research, is no substitute for the inner spiritual power that the subject demands.

This spiritual power is achieved by a very different poet from Masefield, Charles Williams, in his two volumes *Taliessin through Logres* and *The Region of the Summer Stars*. In essence, though not in detail, it is an extension of Tennyson's vision of Arthur as ideal man, for in Williams' poems Arthur's kingdom of Logres is to be the perfect union between earth and heaven. The symbolism is involved to the point of being at moments laboured, and C. S. Lewis' exposition of it in *Arthurian Torso* is invaluable as an approach and guide. The poems are dominated by the concept of the Roman and Byzantine Empires seen most clearly in '*The Vision of the Empire*'. The image is that of a reclining female figure. The 'skull-stone' is the rocky outer edge of Britain/Logres, which stands as the Empire's soul and brain. The breasts are in Gaul, where the schools of Paris, famous in the Middle Ages, provide the nourishing milk of learning. On Rome the hands lie clasped: here the Pope says Mass with its 'heart-breaking manual acts'. Jerusalem is the womb, from which Adam, fallen man, came. Caucasia is the 'fool's shame', the bottom of the figure. Lastly there is Byzantium, the navel, in which all the 'dialects' arise and re-echo. These are the 'themes' of the Empire, which are related in the same way as the body.

There is an antithesis to the Empire, on the other side of the world, in P'o-lu, where the headless Emperor of the Antipodes walks. This is the consequence of the Fall: bodies become shameful instead of a glory of creation, and so here the 'feet of creation' walk backwards. For in P'o-Lu are the feet of the Empire, and they are feet of clay. It is from here that the failure of Arthur's mission springs.

At the opposite extreme, beyond Logres, lies the Wood of Broceliande – a sea-wood, Williams calls it – and beyond a certain part of it, Carbonek, the castle in which the Grail is kept. Beyond this and a stretch of open sea, is Sarras, the home of the Grail. It is towards this that Arthur's mission and the whole feeling of the poems tend, reflecting Williams' deep religious and mystical attitudes.

Through Broceliande lies the way from earth to heaven – as witness the Grail city and castle. But Williams insists that these last lie beyond only a certain part of it. If one goes far enough the Antipodes may be reached through these same regions. C. S. Lewis explains this apparent contradiction as follows:

> In a writer whose philosophy was Pantheistic or whose poetry was merely romantic, this formidable wood ... would undoubtedly figure as the Absolute itself ... All journeys away from the solid earth are equally, at the outset journeys into the abyss. Saint, sorcerer, lunatic and romantic lover, all alike are drawn to Broceliande, but Carbonek is beyond a certain part of it only. It is by no means the Absolute. It is rather what the Greeks called the Apeiron – the unlimited, the formless origin of forms.[6]

Such then is the geography, physical and spiritual, of Williams' world. Against this background Arthur, Taliessin and Merlin work out their mission. Nimue, lady of Broceliande, sends her children, Merlin and Brisen, to perform the great task of perfect

[6] C. S. Lewis *Arthurian Torso* (London & New York 1948) 100–101.

191

union. They meet Taliessin, still the pagan poet of Wales, as they go to create the kingdom of balanced humanity, an earthly kingdom parallel to the holy kingdom of Carbonek, in which the Empire and Broceliande, the physical, the intellectual and the spiritual shall meet. Arthur is to be their instrument; they depart for Logres, and Taliessin for Byzantium.

Taliessin's part in the mission is not immediately clear, but we learn that on his return from Byzantium he bears with him the vision of the Empire, standing for order, which he must impose on the as yet chaotic Logres; this must be accomplished before the Grail can come to dwell there. He is also the type of the poet, which is bound up in his personal task. The poet, in Williams' view, cannot inspire love for himself, yet can inspire others to it; this is illustrated in 'Taliessin's song of the unicorn', where the poet is likened to the legendary unicorn, attracted to a virgin; she will not love him, and her lover will come and kill the creature out of jealousy.

Taliessin's mission is a success, and the Golden Age of Logres ensues. The lyric pieces which describe this involve various philosophical concepts, but centre on the nature of love. The last of these is *The Coming of Palomides*; Palomides, learned in Arabic science, looks on Iseult and admires the geometrical beauty of her form. But at the end of the poem as he dreams of the first kind of love, physical consummation, the Questing Beast

> ... scratched itself in the blank between
> The Queen's substance and the Queen.

He must find the answer to the connection between the flesh and the spirit before he can find intellectual love.

But the plan as a whole is doomed to failure: the actual deeds which prevent Logres from becoming the kingdom of the Grail are Arthur's unwitting incest with Morgause, and Balin's equally unconscious slaying of his brother and giving of the Dolorous Blow. Both pairs act blindly; it is not their individual fault that these things are done, but the fault of human nature, of fallen man, operating deep below the surface of Logres.

Yet out of this failure springs a measure of success. The Grail cannot come to Logres; but the uncorrupted part of Logres may reach the Grail. It is again Taliessin's task to prepare the way. The company of his household are his instrument; at the base of their efforts lies salvation worked through poetry and the senses, Taliessin's own special task. It is Taliessin as head of this 'Company of the Redeemed' who greets the first of the future Grail band to arrive at court, Percivale and his sister Blanchefleur. By the machinations of Merlin and Brisen, Galahad is born, at the cost of the sanity of his father Lancelot, for which Galahad later atones. He is delivered into Blanchefleur's care, and the space of his youth is filled by one poem only: '*Palomides before his Christening*'. Palomides has failed in his quest; intellectual love is not for him. But through disillusionment comes his conversion to Christianity, if only as a belief in disbelief.

The coming of Galahad takes place in the evening of Palomides' christening, and we hear of it from Taliessin, Gareth and a slave as they discuss it afterwards. One of the more important images here is drawn from Book Five of Wordsworth's *The Prelude*. The stone and shell borne by the Arab in this poem are fitted in Galahad; the union which was to have been Logres has been fulfilled in one man only. None save three will succeed, and reach Carbonek; the rest will sink into Britain. The forces of Broceliande depart. Palomides finds the answer to his problem; what he had seen as ends in themselves, love, fame, irony, were only paths to a greater end, and, happy in this knowledge, he dies.

The climax and simultaneously the anti-climax are now reached. The Grail is achieved at the expense of the Round Table. So triumph on the one hand, in '*Percivale at Carbonek*' and '*The Last Voyage*' are balanced by the implied disaster of '*The Meditation of Mordred*' and '*The Prayers of the Pope*'. As the Grail is achieved, and withdrawn to Sarras, Logres sinks into the chaos out of which it had risen. Taliessin dissolves his company, but they gather for the last time, in flesh or in spirit, at the Mass performed by Lancelot. The mission has reached its end; all that could or can ever be achieved has been achieved. Lancelot's voice singing '*Ite; missa est*' is the signal for the irrevocable dispersal, and 'that which was once Taliessin' rides slowly away.

The poems are symbolic and sometimes obscure, but rich in concept; the poet in Williams struggles, sometimes unsuccessfully, with the philosopher. But the verse itself is brilliant in its incantation, and the words flow in a strange music. Here are two contrasting examples. Taliessin comes to Lancelot's Mass at the end of the cycle:

> I came to his altar when dew was bright on the grass:
> He – he was not sworn of the priesthood – began the Mass.
> The altar was an ancient stone laid upon stones;
> Carbonek's arch, Camelot's wall, frame of Bors' bones.
> In armour before the earthen footpace he stood;
> On his surcoat the lions of his house, dappled with blood,
> Rampant, regardant; but he wore no helm or sword,
> And his hands were bare as Lateran's to the work of our Lord.[7]

But this is less typical than the following passage, the climax of Merlin's and Brisen's incantations at the launching of the mission:

> The stars vanished; they gone, the illuminated dusk
> Under the spell darkened to the colour of porphyry

[7] Charles Williams, *Arthurian Poems* (Woodbridge 1982) 'Taliessin at Lancelot's Mass, 1–8.

The colour of the stair of Empire and the womb of women,
And the rich largesse of the Emperor; within was a point,
Deep beyond or deep within Logres,
As if it had swallowed all the summer stars.
And hollowed the porphyry night for its having and hiding –
Tiny, dark-rose, self-glowing,
As a firefly's egg or (beyond body and spirit,
Could the art of the king's poet in the court of Camelot,
After his journeys, find words for body and spirit)
The entire point of the thrice co-inherent Trinity
when every crown and every choir is vanished,
And all sight and hearing is nothing else.[8]

Williams has used the Arthurian legend as the mould for his individual and intensely Christian philosophy.. While the matter and events of the old tales are retained, characters and values are totally different. Yet this, in its mystical way, is one of the great works of Arthurian literature. It is a heightening of Tennyson's moral vision into mysticism, the spiritual application of Swinburne's intense study of physical love within the framework of the legend.

Another major poet who used the Arthurian stories was David Jones, whose dense and allusive works *In Parenthesis* (1937) and *The Anathemata* (1952) contain many references to Welsh Arthurian tradition and to Malory. His work depends on a deep knowledge of myth and legend, and is heavily annotated, following the style established by Eliot in *The Waste Land*. Although Jones believed that the reader would respond to myth even if he did not understand it, his use of the 'signs' from the living past is meaningful only to a handful of specialists or to a reader who is prepared to regard the text as some kind of intellectual puzzle, with clues to be solved before the meaning is revealed. Jones' poetry is deceptively simple in construction, and often striking: but it presumes too much on the reader's knowledge of the mysteries he is trying to expound. What is interesting is that a poet in his situation should nominate Arthur as the central myth of the British past.

At a very different level, undoubtedly the most successful retelling of the Arthurian legends in recent years is T. H. White's *The Once and Future King*, which engendered first the musical and then the film *Camelot*. Although the complete book only appeared in 1958, it was the result of a twenty-year exploration of Arthurian matters: White wrote the first part, *The Sword in the Stone* in the winter of 1937–8, and explained to a friend how he had come to write a 'preface to Malory':

Do you remember I once wrote a thesis on the Morte d'Arthur?
Naturally I did not read Malory when writing the thesis on him,

[8] *Ibid.* 'The Calling of Taliessin', 247–261.

52 David Jones as artist: one of his watercolour illustrations to Malory, this depicts the moment when the four queens find Lancelot asleep under the apple-tree and put a spell on him. They carry him to their castle, and threaten to imprison him for ever unless he will choose one of them as his mistress. (Tate Gallery).

195

but one night last autumn I got desperate among my books and picked him up in lack of anything else. Then I was thrilled and astonished to find (a) that the thing was a perfect tragedy, with a beginning, middle and an end implicit in the beginning and (b) that the characters were real people with recognizable reactions which could be forecast.[9]

He went on to say that *The Sword in the Stone* was 'more or less a kind of wish-fulfilment of the things I should like to have happened to me when I was a boy.' When he wrote it, he does not seem to have been planning a full treatment of the whole story of Arthur, as it stands very well by itself, ending with the transformation of Arthur from Wart – Sir Ector's adopted second son, very much junior to Kay – into the youthful king of England. Into this story of Arthur's upbringing, White put all his own enthusiasms: natural history is Merlyn's chosen means of teaching Arthur, and the author of *The Goshawk* displays his expertise in falconry. Merlyn is in many ways a self-portrait: White, the slightly eccentric schoolmaster, draws himself larger than life, with the same omnivorous mind ('The best thing for being sad is learning something!'); but Merlyn – a marvellous touch, this – lives backwards in time, and is therefore able to foretell the future because it is his own past. There is high comedy, too, in the duel of Merlyn and the wicked Madam Mim, and the whole book has a joyous, excited feeling. It was an immediate success.[10]

When White decided to continue with the story of Arthur, he found himself in deeper water. The first version of *The Witch in the Wood*, the second volume, was returned by the publishers for revision, and even when it appeared in print White began a second revision. He took a scholarly approach to his sources, and was insistent that it was Malory's story that he was telling, even if that brought him up against problems like Guinevere and the Holy Grail. *The Ill-Made Knight* appeared in 1940, but when White sent the last planned part, 'The Candle in the Wind' to his publishers, it was as a section of a book to be called *The Once and Future King*, with heavily revised versions of the first three books, and a new concluding book, 'The Book of Merlyn', which was to balance the 'prologue to Malory' and returned to the magical world of the opening, but this time in bitter and polemical mood. The publishers, alarmed by the length of the work in a time of paper rationing, and uneasy with the revisions and conclusion, refused to print it as it stood. It was only some seventeen years later, and after further revisions, that *The Once and Future King* finally appeared. Some of the high spirits had been taken out of *The Sword in the Stone*, and 'The Book of Merlyn', the diatribe against war, was withdrawn,[11] leaving a somewhat abrupt conclusion. Yet the overall result is a triumph:

[9] Sylvia Townsend Warner, *T. H. White: A Biography* (London 1971) p. 98.

[10] One of the unexpected by-products was Benjamin Britten's only Arthurian composition, incidental music for a radio serialisation of *The Sword in the Stone* in 1939.

[11] It was published separately in 1978: it is a disappointing conclusion. Written in the heat of the moment, its arguments are too direct, and the moral, that man is incurably vicious and inferior to other animals, is allowed to monopolise the narrative.

White's great strength is precisely a mixture of respect for the original, whose evocative power he uses skilfully, and the ability to conjure up a time and a place: Lancelot in the armoury, for instance:

> In the castle of Benwick, the French boy was looking at his face in the polished surface of a kettle hat. It flashed in the sunlight with the stubborn gleam of metal. It was practically the same as the steel helmet which soldiers still wear, and it did not make a good mirror, but it was the best he could get....[12]

This immediacy and the ease with which White imparts his vast knowledge of medieval detail make the tales much more real than any orthodox retelling would. To the main plot, White adds little: 'I have invented a love affair for King Pellinore – the only addition to Malory, except that he did not say that Lancelot was ugly.' But there is another, larger, change of emphasis: the tension between Gawain and his kin, including Mordred on one hand and Arthur and Lancelot on the other hand is highlighted because Gawain's clan are Celtic, and White carefully and elaborately underlines this 'racial background'. The former represent the Old People, wronged by Uther when he seized and married Ygerne; and Uther's deed, as much as Morgause's incest with Arthur (which hardly takes place in White's version), is the germ of the tragedy. He portrays Arthur and Lancelot and the relationship between them superbly, but narrowly misses with Guinevere: we never really feel that we know her as we know Arthur or Gawain and his brothers, though the moment when Lancelot falls in love with her is well done. She is clumsily helping him, because he is her husband's best friend, to train a new hawk; he sees her only as an obstacle to his relationship with Arthur, and her clumsiness angers him. He reproaches her angrily, and 'knew in this moment, that he had hurt a real person, of his own age ... She was pretty Jenny, who could think and feel.' But the relationship here acquires the same force as in Malory. White is uneasy, too, with the Holy Grail – 'exact Catholic dogma' he called Malory's version in a letter to Sydney Cockerell.[13] He comes into his own again in the closing book, and it is perhaps a pity that the planned fifth volume distracted him at the very end: the ending is good, but pales before the original. White tacitly and neatly acknowledges this: for Arthur's last action before the final conflict is to talk to a page, Thomas Malory, of the dreams and ideals of his Round Table, before sending him home from the battlefield so that he can keep those ideals alive. All in all, *The Once and Future King* is a warm, often funny, often heroic account of Arthur, and with more than a touch of the authentic magic.

[12] T. H. White, *The Once and Future King* (London 1957) 327.
[13] Townsend Warner, *T. H. White*, 153.

Arthurian historical novels have enjoyed an immense popularity in recent years, and the sheer volume of such works is too great for anything more than a brief survey here. They range from the merely bland reworkings of Malory through curiosities like John Steinbeck's *The Acts of King Arthur and his Noble Knights* (1976) where one great writer attempts, too respectfully, to retell another, to powerful evocations of an imagined historical reality. By and large, recent writers have tended to move away from the vision of Arthur as a chivalric king and have recast him as the heroic British leader holding out against the Saxons, an idea first adopted in John Cowper Powys' novel *Porius* (1951) in which Arthur makes a brief appearance. This has the great advantage that the traditional characters of the stories, and their traditional relationships, can be retained, but the chivalric context, which tends to have Victorian overtones today, can be set aside. Twentieth century poets had largely accomplished this transition after the First World War; without needing to reset the stories in another age, they merely played down or ignored the chivalric element, to concentrate on character rather than action, myth rather than story. It is only in the last three decades that novelists have arrived at their solution. Yet none of the resulting works have been outstanding, except perhaps in their popular success. There is much excellent workmanship in Rosemary Sutcliffe's *Sword at Sunset* or Mary Stewart's trilogy about Merlin, but they are in a lower key: it is after all the sheer magnificence of Arthur's achievement which makes his tragedy so overpowering in the traditional account, and only an exceptional writer can wring the same pathos from the tribal brawls of fifth-century Britain. Several writers have tried to assert their independence from the chivalric tradition by wallowing in realistic filth, underlining the squalor of life in a barbaric early medieval society, but they nonetheless trade on the romantic connotations of their characters' names to justify such a treatment, a kind of conscious iconoclasm against the legend which leaves only the feeling that 'each man kills the thing he loves.' A more interesting departure has been into the realms of fantasy and science fiction, though here again there have been no notable successes.

A similar tendency can be found in Arthurian films. *Camelot* (1967) was a disastrously lavish travesty of T. H. White, who was almost better served by Walt Disney's cute version of *The Sword in the Stone*. Far more interesting artistically is Robert Bresson's *Lancelot du Lac* (1974), where the discomforts and dangers of medieval life are emphasised: knights creak and groan as they move in their heavy armour, and Lancelot and Guinevere meet in the drab surroundings of back rooms or haylofts. The forests are bleak and hostile, and death looms at every turn. It is a black and unromantic film, but nonetheless memorable. John Boorman's *Excalibur* (1983) is much more in the mainstream tradition, with an interesting mystical and visionary Merlin, a skilful element of fantasy and some remarkable images, such as the gilded mask-armour in the form of a naked youth worn by Mordred.

Perhaps the most remarkable feature of the part that Arthurian legend has played in intellectual and artistic life in the last decades is the growth of the 'Arthur industry' in the academic world, and in that of popular archaeology and history. Today most people's interest in Arthur is not as a romantic hero, but as a historical figure, and Arthurian literature has become the province of much research and scholarship. When the first version of this book appeared in 1961, dealing only with Arthur in English literature, the International Arthurian Society had issued 12 volumes of its annual listing of scholarship on Arthur, including some 2500 items all told: today, there are another 22 volumes, listing about 11000 further books, articles and reviews. To the layman, these figures may be astonishing, but they must be seen in perspective: the comparable totals for major authors like Chaucer and Shakespeare would be substantially higher, even though there is a smaller volume of original material to study. In this mass of learned argument, there have been some real, if unspectacular, advances in knowledge: but it is on the fringes of the learned world that the most striking reappraisals of Arthur have taken place.

Such reappraisals often tell us more about their authors and about today's values than they contribute to serious scholarship. There are two main themes, parallel to those we have noted in fiction and the cinema: the identification of the 'real' Arthur, and the use of Arthurian stories to demonstrate the survival of some secret myth or tradition. The keenest proponents of the idea that Arthur can be positively identified have been Geoffrey Ashe and John Morris: for Ashe, he is either the last Caesar, Artorius Augustus, or, in his latest book, Riothamus, a Breton ruler who may have led British troops into Gaul in 469–70. John Morris built up a much more elaborate picture in *The Age of Arthur*, a picture which has been comprehensively demolished by his fellow-historians. Faced with the problems of fifth-century history, such writers as these cannot bear to admit that we do not know the answers, and probably never shall: they comb the surviving traditions for the clues which will solve the mystery of Arthur once and for all. Such historical detective work can be very worthwhile if used with due caution: Ashe's Riothamus could have been the germ of Geoffrey of Monmouth's tale of Arthur's campaigns in France, but this is only one of a myriad such contributions to the twelfth century picture of Arthur, and does not mean that Riothamus has anything to do with the 'historical' Arthur. At worst, unchecked historical fantasy gives us the notorious *The Holy Blood and the Holy Grail*, a work which proves nothing except a current fashion for alternative history. There has always been a healthy tendency among laymen to question the orthodox view of the great events of history, but 'alternative' history is a product of a desire for a simple, all-embracing key to the events of an increasingly complex world. It is the modern equivalent of the Victorian quack with his universal panacea, or the seventeenth century religious fanatic with his exclusive way to salvation: only believers will find the way to the truth.

Against this we can set the valuable and serious work done by the archaeologists and scholars during this century. Where progress has been made, it has been in the careful reappraisal of the nature of the sources for the historical Arthur, and in attempts — so far very tentative — to explore the archaeological record of the fifth century. But results will be slow to appear, and in many cases are likely only to emphasise the great areas of doubt and difficulty.

Arthur plays a complex role in today's literature and history as an elusive and challenging part of our culture. He lives on in our imagination as an historical enigma, an intriguing question-mark in our past. We may read the Arthurian romances because they give us an unrivalled insight into the medieval mind, or because they contain human situations familiar in our own age, or because they reflect the lost ideals of an age of faith. But there is one transcending and much simpler reason why the Arthurian legends will continue to be read, which Caxton gave five centuries ago: because in them we shall find 'many joyous and playsaunt hystoryes and noble and renomed acts of humanyté, gentylenesse and chyvalryes'. As long as poetry is written, Arthur will be remembered; he may yet have many vicissitudes to come, but the legends are so integral to our heritage that his figure will always emerge again, mysterious, heroic, and yet human.

Sources of Illustrations

The author and publishers are grateful to the following for providing photographs and for permission to reproduce illustrations:

Bayerische Stadtbibliothek, Munich 30, 31
BBC Radio Times Hulton Picture Library, 40, 43
Professor R. Allen Brown 13
Bibliothèque Nationale, Paris 17, 18, 20, 21, 23, 25, 26, 34, 36, XVI
Bibliothèque Royale Albert Ier, Brussels 7, XVII
Bodleian Library, Oxford XVII
British Library 11, 15, 22, 24
British Tourist Authority 10
Bürgerbibliothek, Bern 5
Cardiff Public Library 4
City Art Galleries, Manchester XXIV
City of Birmingham Art Gallery 46, XXVI–XXVII
Department of the Environment Photographic Library XIX
Douai, Bibliothèque Municipale 6
Germanisches Nationalmuseum, Nurenburg 33
Koninklijke Bibliotheek, The Hague 38
Lambeth Palace Library 8
Mansell Collection/Foto Alinari 14
Metropolitan Museum of Art, New York 39
Musée du Louvre 19, 27
National Gallery of Scotland 42
Österreichisches Museum für angewandte Kunst 51
Phillips 49
Pierpont Morgan Library, New York 1–XV
Professor Martin Puhvel 35
Soprintendenza dei Monumenti, Bolzano 29
Tate Gallery 44, 46, 52, XX, XXI, XXV, XXVIII
Vigo-Sternberg Galleries XXII–XXIII
Christopher Wood Gallery 49, 50

Index